Tour de France

THE COMPLETE HISTORY OF THE WORLD'S GREATEST CYCLE RACE

Right: French tricolour flags line the Champs-Elysées in Paris as the peloton surges past on the final stage of the 2012 race.

First published by Carlton Books Ltd 2003

This edition published in 2013 by Carlton Books Ltd,
20 Mortimer Street, London W1T 3JW

10 9 8 7 6 5 4 3 2 1

A CIP catalogue record for this book is available from the British Library.

ISBN 978-1-78097-290-9

Printed and bound in Dubai

Acknowledgements
The publishers would like to thank the following for their help in the production of this book: Anna Southgate for copy-editing; Mary Morton, Chris Hawkes and David Ballheimer for sub-editing; Angus Barclay for indexing and Paul Roberts and Lorcan Devine at Offside for picture research.

The publishers would like to thank the following sources for their kind permission to reproduce the pictures in this book.
All photographs in this book are courtesy of © **Offside Sports Photography/ L'Equipe** except:
p.158, 177b: **Doug Pensinger/Getty Images**
p.172t, 177t: **Robert Laberge/Getty Images**
p.175b: **AFP/Getty Images**
p.184–185: **A. Bibard/Press Association Images**
p.203b: **Lionel Bonaventure/AFP/Getty Images**
Every effort has been made to acknowledge correctly and contact the source and/or copyright holder of each picture and Carlton Books Limited apologises for any unintentional errors or omissions that will be corrected in future editions of this book.

Tour de France

THE COMPLETE HISTORY OF THE WORLD'S GREATEST CYCLE RACE

NINTH EDITION
TOUR DE FRANCE 100TH RACE

MARGUERITE LAZELL

CARLTON
BOOKS

Contents

Four riders form a breakaway group ahead of the peloton on stage 9 between Toulon and Nice, 1921.

Journey to the limits of human endurance

When the first 60 riders set out into the unknown from the Café au Reveil Matin, Paris in 1903, no one had any idea how big the Tour was to become.

Back in 2003, the Tour de France celebrated its centenary. Interrupted only by world wars, the race has evolved from its origins as a chaotic scramble around France to become the biggest annual sporting event in the world. But this is no tale of humble beginnings and triumph over the odds – at least not for the race founder, Henri Desgrange.

Desgrange conceived the Tour as a publicity stunt to promote his newspaper *L'Auto*. Circulation soared as fans followed reports of the race around the country; it was an immediate success. French fans took the Tour so close to their hearts that the second edition of the race almost came to a sticky end, due to their desire to see their favourites win at all costs, as they turned to sabotage and violence to hinder other competitors. It was frightening, and it was dangerous, but it wasn't going to stop the race.

Initially the race was a contest of pure endurance. Stages lasted upwards of 16 hours, and there was little scope for team work. Desgrange constantly tweaked the rules, introducing new features – high mountains, individual time trials, subsidiary races within the race – until the Tour matured into its modern format.

In its modern guise, cycle racing is unique in that, while it is a team competition, all the glory – along with the rewards – goes to the individual winner. And therein lies its fascination: of 200 men under-taking the hardest test of their lives, 90 per cent are doing it for the benefit of their team leader.

To win the Tour de France is to become a legend. Five men – Jacques Anquetil, Eddy Merckx, Bernard Hinault and Miguel Indurain – have each won five times. In 2003, Lance Armstrong joined this elite group, and went on to win two more in 2004 and 2005. But in 2012, the steady drip-drip of suspicion about the Texan turned into a torrent as a host of former team-mates and support staff gave testimony under oath to the US Anti-Doping Agency, laying bare the systematic doping which had enabled him to crush the opposition for so long.

The contest for the yellow jersey, the symbol of race leadership, makes the headlines, but the struggles of the individual riders make up the fabric of the Tour. Just to complete the event is a momentous achievement; to take a stage, to be the King of the Mountains or the points winner is something to dine out on for the rest of a rider's life.

While the Tour will always be quintessentially French, its appeal is universal. Team against team, man against man, against the mountains, against the elements, against physical and mental limitations: its characteristics are understood the world over. Among the chapters in this book are special pages dedicated to the riders who excelled in all these ways – the five-time winners, as well as Louison Bobet, Bernard Thévenet,

Read all about it: PR girl in a print dress in Montpellier, 1962.

Opposite: Stage 12 in 2012; the peloton rides in the wake of eventual stage winner David Millar.

Greg Lemond, Laurent Fignon and numerous other Tour legends. If this selection seems to be drawn heavily from more recent years, that is simply because the earlier format of the Tour did not allow such domination by individual riders.

There is blatant commercialism, inherent danger as riders plummet down mountain passes at 80kph in the rain, and doping scandals, which have reached the very top of the race. The Tour is no Corinthian dream: it is a very human competition that requires superhuman performances from its participants. I hope that this book goes some way to commemorating the glorious victories and heroic failures that have made the Tour the greatest race in the world.

Marguerite Lazell,
April 2013

Chapter 1: 1903–1914

How the Tour Began

The very first Tour de France was designed by Henri Desgrange as a publicity stunt to promote his French newspaper. Testing riders to the limits of endurance, the race captivated the nation immediately and, although it evolved rapidly from its original incarnation, the event was an institution from the start and destined to become the world's greatest cycle race.

1903

The Tour de France has long been the biggest bicycle race in the world, but it certainly was not the first. It was launched by the proprietors of *L'Auto* newspaper in response to the success of another cycling event – Paris-Brest-Paris or P-B-P – which was being used to promote a rival sports daily, *Le Petit Journal*. Pierre Giffard, the journalist behind the P-B-P, had created a monstrous event: competitors mounted their bicycles in the capital, rode to Brest – the furthest point they could reach without falling into the Atlantic – then turned round and raced back. It was a huge success, combining 1,200 kilometres of non-stop torture for competitors, priceless exposure for sponsors and an enormous increase in circulation for the newspaper. So *L'Auto* went one better.

Henri Desgrange and Géo Lefèvre were charged with organizing an event to rival the P-B-P. If Giffard were holding a race to one corner of the country and back, they would take things further by staging a race that took riders to every corner of France. That way all sections of the population would feel compelled to purchase *L'Auto* as the race came through their home town or village.

"Six Day" racing had been extremely popular at the turn of the 20th century – velodromes would be packed out as races went on non-stop. So it seemed reasonable to Lefèvre that the Tour de France should also be held in six segments. The organization of the event proved arduous. Entries were slow – athletes were reticent to sign up for such an unprecedented event, and not just because of its extreme nature; for many the financial cost of travelling around the country for three weeks put the Tour out of reach. As the date of the Grand Départ approached with a start sheet only a quarter full, Desgrange was obliged to cut the entry fee, increase the prize fund

Above: Father of the Tour, Henri Desgrange. Below: A drawing shows Maurice Garin in action in 1903. Previous page: Stage 4 of the 1903 Tour – Toulouse-Bordeaux.

to 20,000 old French francs, and promise to contribute toward the expenses of the competitors.

THE VERY FIRST STAGE

On 1 July, 1903, 60 men lined up at the start of the first-ever Tour de France. Sponsored athletes and independent amateurs alike, they were all unsure what to expect. Maurice Garin, one of the pre-race favourites, won the first road stage from Paris to Lyon, taking 17 hours, 45 minutes to complete the 467 kilometres. His main rival, Hippolyte Aucouturier, struck back on the next two stages, winning them both, and taking over the race lead, at that time symbolized by a green armband.

Aucouturier's race ended as his body succumbed to the strain of the event. Stomach troubles forced him to abandon, leaving Garin with a clear path to final overall victory at the Parc des Princes. After four stages only 24 men remained in the competition; Garin won the last two stages, beating Lucien Pothier by a massive 2 hours, 49 minutes. The last man to finish, Arsène Millocheau, in 21st place, finally arrived at the stadium two days, 16 hours, 47 minutes and 22 seconds after Garin had collected the winner's bouquet. Circulation of *L'Auto* doubled during the race – it had been an even bigger success than Desgrange had hoped for.

1904

From a near-perfect start the Tour fell into disrepute in its second year. Maurice Garin lined up as clear favourite, with his brother César and Lucien Pothier as his La Française team-mates. Hippolyte Aucouturier assumed leadership of the Peugeot team. The route was the same: the peloton would leave from Paris, with consecutive stages to Lyon, Marseille, Toulouse, Bordeaux, Nantes and back to Paris. It had worked so well the previous year, there was no reason to change it.

Garin was as strong as ever; he won the opening stage with ease,

Sections of the crowd prepare for the next batch of riders, 1904.

while Aucouturier lost two hours, thwarted by accidents and mechanical problems. Of the 88 riders who began the race, 35 did not make it as far as the second stage; those that did found themselves ambushed. The race was due to go past Saint-Etienne, home town of Antoine Faure. The riders were mobbed by Faure's fans in the early hours of the morning; Garin and other leading contenders were held hostage by the crowds until their man had made good his chance to escape up the road. When the trapped riders tried to break free they were hit with fists and stones. Livid with rage, Desgrange and Lefèvre pulled up in the official car, firing revolvers into the air to disperse the crowd, so that the race could continue. Shaken and bruised, the captives remounted and rode on. Faure was caught, and Aucouturier won the stage.

It wasn't just the fans who were unconcerned with matters of fair play; Ferdinand Payan, who had finished 12th in the previous year's Tour, was feeling the strain. Repeatedly caught drafting behind a car, he was disqualified from the race. Now it was his fans' turn to riot. When the race came to his home town, Alais, without him, riders found broken glass and nails scattered across the road. When the riders finally reached Nîmes, they were attacked by as many as 50 men, with many more looking on with morbid curiosity. Again organizers fired warning shots to break up the angry mob; Payan was not reinstated.

STUMBLING TO PARIS

Only 28 men made it back to Paris. Aucouturier won the sixth stage – his fourth win of the race —but it was not enough to make up for his huge losses on the first day. He remained in fourth place overall; Maurice Garin won, flanked on either side of the podium by his brother César and his team-mate Lucien Pothier.

The Tour had spiralled out of control. In just two *editions* it had evolved to become more than just a sporting contest. It was a social phenomenon that had enthralled the nation, and partisan spectators had been so desperate to see their personal heroes triumph that violence had almost ended the race. Henri Desgrange was so angry that he declared the Tour over for good, a victim of its own popularity. The technical commission of the Union Vélocipédique de France, (UVF), the French governing body of the sport, opened an investigation into the gamut of irregularities that had occurred during the 2,428 kilometre race and, on 30 November, gave its verdict. The first four finalists – both Garin brothers, Pothier and Aucouturier – were disqualified for violating race rules. Twenty-year-old Henri Cornet, who had arrived at the Parc des Princes three hours down on Maurice Garin, was belatedly named overall winner. He had punctured 35 kilometres from the stadium; with only himself to rely on, he had decided that to dismount, remove his wheel, replace the tube and carry on would take too much time. Instead he rode on with a flat tyre, totally unaware that he was on his way to becoming the youngest Tour winner in history.

1905

While Paris-Brest-Paris remained unchanged, the Tour de France grew organically. Desgrange soon realized that he had started something far too big to stop now, and began devising a new route that he hoped would continue to hold the imagination of the public. Like all good journalists, he knew that scandals did wonders for circulation. When the verdict of the UVF was announced at the end of 1904, he promptly announced his plans to hold the race again the following year. This time it would be over 11 stages, with a longer total distance – 3,000 kilometres – but in smaller steps. The overall winner would be decided not on his cumulative time for the whole course, but on a ranking system, with points awarded for each stage. For the first and last stages riders would be paced and, more importantly, mountains would now feature along the route, the most significant of which was the

1906

The Tour de France was getting bigger in every sense. The prize money for winning overall was now 5,000 old French francs – a reflection of the increased difficulty of the race.

The total distance had jumped up to an enormous 4,545 kilometres, divided into 13 stages over 26 days, and took in several more mountains. Henri Desgrange received 101 entries for this fourth Tour, of which 75 started the race.

Emile Georget won the first stage, outsprinting Georges Passerieu and Louis Trousselier at Lille. It was a relatively short stage by the standards of the day – only 273 kilometres – but it was enough to eliminate 26 of the slowest riders, with another four men abandoning before the next stage began.

The 400-kilometre ride to Nancy required an early start. With 13 stages over 26 days, the peloton – in theory at least – should have a full day's rest between each stage. Following a 10-hour stint on day one, riders did indeed get a day off, but were obliged to start day three at a quarter past midnight in order to finish the stage without encroaching on the next rest day.

Road surfaces in Douai, where the stage started, were so bad that the *commissaires* had to neutralize the race and guide the peloton for the first two kilometres until it was safe enough for them to start racing. As they began the stage in earnest they hit upon a familiar problem: nails all over the road. It was impossible to avoid puncturing. René Pottier used up all the spare tyres he had been carrying around his shoulders, and rode for 25 kilometres on the rim before he could find a replacement. By the time he had made his machine roadworthy he was 30 minutes behind the leaders, and there were still 200 kilometres to ride. But Pottier was not so easily beaten: as the sun rose he pushed on alone, finally catching the breakaways just kilometres from the finish. He rode with Lucien Mazan – or "Petit-Breton" as he was affectionately known – as far as the

Ballon d'Alsace, a 1,247-metre peak.

The new format may have improved the sporting aspects of the competition, but it did little to quell the unsporting activities of the waiting spectators. Nails were strewn across the path of oncoming riders and, on the first stage, every rider but one – Jean-Baptiste Dortignacq – punctured as a result. Louis Trousselier was quickest to repair the damage and went on to win the opening stage by three minutes, only to face the same hazard the next day.

A TOUR REBORN

Trousselier lost the lead to René Pottier on the second stage to Besançon. Pottier had dropped the field on the Ballon d'Alsace, and seemed destined to win the Tour. But no sooner had he taken over than he was forced to abandon, after colliding with an over-enthusiastic fan and spraining his ankle badly. Hippolyte Aucouturier became race leader by dint of his strong, consistent riding on the hilly stages.

He found the going harder on the flat, exposed roads between Toulon and Nîmes. He was dropped on the 192-kilometre stage and finished 10th, while early leader Trousselier outsprinted the rest of the group and reclaimed control of the race.

The Frenchman's ability to sprint stood him in good stead for a race decided on points – he was third the next day, distancing himself further from second-placed Aucouturier in the overall classification, and won stage seven.

Even a stage win for Aucouturier did little to improve his chances, and he was relegated to defending his second place from a resurgent Jean-Baptiste Dortignacq, who won the final two stages and almost beat him to the runner's-up spot. The new-style Tour had been so successful that the memories of the scandalous 1904 race were all but forgotten. Henri Desgrange knew which way to take his race now; he would make things even longer and more mountainous the next time.

Above: Lucien "Petit-Breton" Mazan and Jean-Baptiste Dortignacq prepare to start racing in 1905.

final hill, then attacked and won the stage. With a fourth and a first place in the two completed stages he took over the lead, with Georget second.

POTTIER VERSUS PASSERIEU

The newer, more mountainous route suited Pottier ideally. On the next stage he made a 220-kilometre solo break over the Ballon d'Alsace, arriving at Dijon 48 minutes before Georges Passerieu. He won the next two stages through the low Alps, taking every advantage of the terrain to extend his lead over his rivals. By the time the peloton got to Nice his position looked impregnable. Pottier had used his resources wisely; he was just able to hang on to the leaders on the road to Marseille, where Passerieu took his first-stage victory. The general classification remained unchanged at the top – Pottier and Passerieu held fast – while Trousselier deftly moved upward. He won five of the next six stages, and must have cursed the points' system after escaping with the Petit-Breton on stage nine – finishing an hour ahead of Pottier, but having nothing more to show for it than if he had sat in and won a bunch sprint.

Only 14 men made it to the start line of the final stage. But there was one other way that the fallen riders could taste the applause as the race completed its journey – Hippolyte Aucouturier and Marcel Cadolle, who had both retired from the event, volunteered as pacemakers for their fellow Alcyon riders on the final stage. Emile and Léon Georget were the primary beneficiaries, while Peugeot brought in a raft of men to set the pace for its men, Pottier, Passerieu and Trousselier, to ensure that they made a clean sweep of the podium. The fundamental elements of the modern Tour – one rider working at his own expense for the benefit of another, and the commercial interests of the sponsors impressing themselves on the race – were already taking shape. Tragically, so were the pressures on the winner: six months later, Pottier hanged himself in the shed of the bicycle factory that had sponsored his winning ride.

Above: René Pottier (right) does battle with Georges Passerieu on the run into Paris in 1906. Below: Lucien Petit-Breton receives the adulation of the crowd after winning in 1907.

1907

Even from its early days, there were races within races at the Tour. The favourites always came from the professional classes – almost exclusively sponsored by bicycle manufacturers – but there was a subsidiary group, which in fact made up most of the field, known as the *poinçonnées*. These men were obliged to ride on standard bicycles, issued by Henri Desgrange, and marked before the start of the race so that they could prove they had used the same machine for the duration of the race. Petit-Breton had caused a stir by not only finishing first *poinçonnée* in 1905, but by taking fourth place overall, only bettered by the Peugeot trio. This time round he wanted to do even better.

Petit-Breton led the *poinçonnées* home in eighth place on the first stage from Paris to Roubaix, and took third the next day. Louis Trousselier was first on both occasions and, in the absence of defending champion René Pottier, found himself and second-placed Emile Georget regarded as race favourites.

Georget came to the fore over the Ballon d'Alsace, taking over the general classification and thriving in his new role as race leader. He won four out of the next six stages, never managing to get clear of his rivals early on, but always finding some last reserves to propel him to victory in the sprint. Petit-Breton meanwhile was holding his own, contesting the sprints when he could, and guarding his third place well.

ALCYON WALK-OUT

As the race reached Toulouse the excitement rose – roads joining on to the final stretch of the course were closed, and organizers erected grand-stands and invited local dignitaries to watch the race finish from a prime spot. When the riders reassembled at three o'clock in the morning to begin the ninth stage they were greeted by a fête, organized by the Toulouse Cycling Club to send them on their way. Within 80 kilometres of the 480-kilometre stage Petit-Breton had made his bid for glory – he attacked alone, unaware that, while he rode solo to victory, a scandal was unfolding in his wake. Emile Georget was declassified from the stage for twice changing bikes; he was placed last on the stage, and thus handi-capped with 48 points – more than enough to push him out of contention for the overall competition. But his rivals were not satisfied: Trousselier and the rest of the Alcyon riders with-drew from the race when Desgrange refused to disqualify Georget completely. He remained in the race, but now in third place, behind Petit-Breton and Gustave Garrigou.

By the time the peloton reached

Paris, Petit-Breton and Georget had won another stage apiece. Without the penalty points, Georget would certainly have won the race overall, but Desgrange was a stickler for the rules and, most of all, for making sure everyone knew whose race it was. So Georget was left to ponder his misfortune as the strange young Petit-Breton won his first Tour de France, earning his place as star of road racing as well as on the track, where he had learned his craft.

1908

To date, no one in Tour history had been able to defend their title successfully. Maurice Garin had been hailed as a double winner for four months in 1904, before being excluded. Now Petit-Breton believed he could do it. Thanks to his track-racing background he could sprint brilliantly – absolutely vital for the Tour, given that the overall positions were still being calculated on a points, rather than time basis. But he had incredible stamina too – he had won 24-hour pursuit races, and had grown comfortable as a road rider at Paris-Roubaix, Paris-Tours and other tough, one-day races. Best of all – and this is what delighted Henri Desgrange – he was a character. Born in France, he had spent several years in Buenos Aires with his parents, and had earned his nickname – an essential for any sporting celebrity —whilst living there. In 1907 he had prepared specifically for the Tour, sacrificing possible wins at other, earlier season races in order to be in peak form for the three-week challenge.

Petit-Breton planned his campaign methodically: beating someone by five seconds would garner him no more points than if he were half an hour ahead of them on any given stage. In 14 stages he finished outside the first three only once, winning on five occasions and exercising an unprecedented form of control over the race. As he came closer to sealing his second victory the excitement infected every town that the race passed: fêtes greeted the

Above: Riders take a break during the 1908 Tour. Below: A sketch of Lucien Petit-Breton adorns the cover of a book commemorating his Tour successes.

peloton the length of their journey, with hundreds of people picnicking along the roadside as they waited for the famous Petit-Breton and his contemporaries to ride by.

PETIT-BRETON MAKES IT BIG

Despite leading the general classification from the second day, Petit-Breton did not have an easy time in the 1908 Tour. Luxembourg's François Faber won four stages and never allowed him to relax. As they rode over the Ballon d'Alsace, Georges Passerieu was the only competitor who managed to reach the summit without having to get off and push – a rare feat given the limited technology that meant riders had only two gears, one on either side of the rear wheel. Passerieu used brute strength to win races – a week later he took the penultimate stage, from Brest to Caen, more than 30 hours ahead of the last-placed rider, Alexandre Gilles.

All competitors were obliged to ride "sealed" machines in 1908 – identical bicycles, issued at the beginning of the Tour by the organizers, previously only ridden by the *poinçonnées*. If Henri Desgrange hoped this would lesssen the influence of the manufacturers on the race, he was sadly mistaken: all men must ride the same frames, and do their own repairs *en route*, but they could still chose some of their own components.

Aside from the main race, one of the sponsors, Wolber, devised another competition that would ensure that riders would use its products and give them plenty of publicity. An award of 3,500 old French francs was given to François Faber as the best-placed rider using Wolber tyres. The financial gains for his second overall and first in the "Prix Wolber" was more than Petit-Breton made from his history-making win but, fortunately for the winner, the rewards for being the first man to win two Tours de France were longer term: he wrote a book about his experiences, *Comment je cours sur route* (*How I race on the road*), thus ensuring his place in sporting history.

1909

The concept of all men riding the same machine arose from good intentions – to make the race a contest of human ability alone – but the Corinthian spirit of the Olympics had never been a driving force behind the Tour de France. Henri Desgrange reverted to the original format for the 1909 race, dividing the field into two sections: *coureurs groupés*, sponsored riders – most backed by bicycle manufacturers – and *coureurs isolés*, the self-sufficient individuals who made up the majority of the peloton.

Almost 200 men applied to ride in the seventh *edition* of the Tour, of which 150 were accepted. They set off from Paris at 5.30 a.m. and there was no gentle warm-up: a *prime* was on offer at the 100-kilometre mark, which subsequently went to Cyrille Van Hauwaert, one of the pre-race favourites. He was soon put in his place, however. François Faber won the next five stages with ease, using his phenomenal physical power to drop the field repeatedly over the flat roads. On the stage to Belfort he finished 33 minutes in advance of his nearest rival, after a 255-kilometre solo break, mostly through snow. On the road to Lyon, he broke his chain while leading the stage, but still

managed to run the final kilometre and win the stage by a clear 10 minutes, pushing the now-defunct bicycle as he went.

Faber was looking as strong as ever on stage seven, but two punctures in close succession left him trailing the leaders. In his haste to catch them up he rode straight past an obligatory checkpoint. When he was informed of his error he had no choice but to about-turn, ride back and sign the control sheet before rejoining the race. Sure enough he caught the front group, only to crash and finish the stage with the also-rans. His injuries were not serious, and his morale was undamaged – he went on to win the 10th stage to Bordeaux, putting himself totally out of reach in the general classification.

The *coureurs-isolés* category was won by Ernest Paul, better known as Ernest Faber, as he was in fact the foster brother of François. He was sixth overall. Meanwhile French champion Jean Alavoine claimed third place overall by winning the final race to the Parc des Princes stadium, while his brother Henri had an accident in the Parisian suburbs, and walked his bike the final 10 kilometres of the race. Just finishing the Tour – especially one that had been marred by such awful weather – was enough to make anyone a hero.

1909 – François Faber is forced to finish the stage to Lyon on foot after a mechanical failure, but still wins.

1910

The element that transformed the Tour de France into the greatest sporting contest in the world was the high mountains. Even Henri Desgrange initially recoiled at the idea of sending the peloton over the unmade 2,000-metre-high tracks through the Pyrenees – the Ballon d'Alsace seemed hard enough – but it would be a spectacle, and therefore be guaranteed to sell papers, so he revised the route extensively to scale the heights.

There was drama from the start: three men escaped on the first stage – Charles Crupelandt, Octave Lapize and Alphonse Charpiot – and were only separated when a cow wandered on to the road and felled Lapize. He was beaten again in the sprint on stage two, while François Faber took first place. Another stage win two days later put the defending champion in the lead, but Lapize was ready to make his move.

Crupelandt led over the first climb by four minutes, but punctured on the descent. Lapize cruised to victory on the stage, hardly able to believe his luck. It had been a hard ascent, but nothing compared to the mountains they were heading for. François Lafourcade attacked with Gustave Garrigou on the Aubisque, taking the honour of being the first man over the first high mountain of the Tour de France. By the time they reached the Tourmalet, Lapize had got ahead of them, but Garrigou – second to the top – was the only man to make it to the peak without putting a foot to the floor. He won a special *prime* of 100 old French francs for his efforts, but it cost him the stage – he was so exhausted that he could not respond as the chasers flooded past him on the descent. Lapize won the stage, and realized that he was now in a position to challenge Faber for the overall title. He moved even closer the next day, leading the peloton over every remaining peak – the col du Porte, the Portet d'Aspet, the Peyresourde, and the Aspin. Faber was a powerhouse on the flat stages, but had lost so

many places over the mountains that Lapize was now dangerously close.

Back on familiar, flat territory, Faber suffered further, crashing and losing the race lead to Lapize. The Luxembourg rider sought revenge next day, and looked to have found it, only to puncture while 15 minutes ahead of the bunch, thus losing his advantage. He was plagued by flat tyres – it seemed that every time he gained some time over Lapize he would lose it all kneeling on the roadside to repair damaged tyres.

The gap between them for the final four stages was never more than six points – every follower of the race was obliged to buy *L'Auto* each morning to find out who was out in front. Lapize held on to his slender lead to Paris, and the mountain stages were hailed a success by everyone but Faber. Meanwhile circulation of *L'Auto* hit 300,000 – twice the figure of 1908. There could be no arguing with that.

1911

The introduction of mountains into the Tour de France had not only altered the nature of the competition, but demanded new creativity on the part of the bicycle manufacturers whose reputations hinged on how well their rider performed over the climbs. In 1911 the high Alps were included in the route, making it even more important that riders were suitably equipped to tackle the steepest gradients.

Petit-Breton was among those with the latest technology – variable gears – but he never got to test them on the slopes for which they were intended. A drunken sailor stepped out into the path of the bunch on the first stage, and as a rider swerved to avoid him he collided with Petit-Breton. The two-time winner was taken to hospital and, although he was soon released, his race was over.

Gustave Garrigou, the hero of the Tourmalet in 1910, won the first stage. Having a climber win a flat stage was a worry to François Faber, who needed to build up his advantage before the Alps if he was to stand any chance of success. Two days later, while the race was neutralized, he flouted the rules and attacked. He was eventually caught by *commissaires* and made to stand at the side of the road for the length of time that he should have waited for previously, plus another 20 seconds for good measure. Despite this enforced delay the peloton had not reached him, so he set off again, alone, and won the stage.

As he had feared, Faber could not hold Garrigou in the first set of mountains. The Galibier proved his undoing – he could only finish 12th, and even a stage win at Nice could not mend the damage.

BROCCO MAKES TROUBLE

Two men – Paul Duboc and veteran Emile Georget – battled for stage victories in the Pyrenees. Garrigou finished third and fourth on the two stages, while Faber's challenge fell apart. He was struggling badly, and made a deal with *isolé* Maurice Brocco, offering him money to pace him. Brocco had been caught helping other riders several times already, deciding that, as he was not going to win any prize money on his own merit, he may as well earn it any way he could. He was dismissed for unsportsmanlike conduct, and Faber was left to finish the race alone.

But Brocco was not going to go away. He appealed to the UVF and, while the case was being considered, he was allowed to carry on racing. He was angry now, and it showed: on the next stage he caught the leaders on the Tourmalet, and even had breath to spar verbally with the *commissaires* in the official car.

He asked with heavy sarcasm if he would be permitted to ride with Garrigou, and was told that, if he had caught him so easily, why did he not go on alone? So he did, winning the stage by 34 minutes, only to be greeted by the news that his appeal had failed and that he was disqualified from the race.

He was not the only man to suffer a cruel fate that day – Duboc was found curled on the ground, gripped by sickness, 100 kilometres into the stage. Rumours that he had been poisoned could not be proved, but he lay on the ground for 90 minutes before being able to continue and complete the stage almost four hours after Brocco.

Anonymous letters cited Garrigou as the poisoner. Some of the letters made threats to the race leader, who – with the approval of the organizers – decided to ride the penultimate stage of the race without numbers pinned to his jersey, and with his frame repainted from bright blue to black, to make him more difficult to identify. He was escorted by two motorcars through Rouen, Duboc's home town. Duboc himself did not believe the stories, and to prove his good health he won the stage and finished second overall. He was fitter than everyone in the race bar Garrigou.

Above: François Faber signs on at a stage start during 1911. Below: A portrait of 1912 winner Odile Defraye. Facing Page: Lonely at the top – Octave Lapize during the 1910 tour.

1912

At first, it seemed that the 1912 Tour de France would be relatively uneventful. The Grand Départ was held on the Avenue de la Grande Armée, in front of the Luna Park, an immensely popular theme park in Paris. It was the first time the race had been held in such a venue, but it was well received – another example of astute planning from Henri Desgrange – ensuring maximum exposure for his race. Eighty years later the same logic would be used to send the Tour to Euro Disney, and to the Futuroscope Park.

Frenchman Charles Crupelandt won the first stage to Dunkirk, but it soon became clear that home riders were not going to have it all their own way. Belgium's Odile Defraye outsprinted Gustave Garrigou and Eugene Christophe to win stage two, and the next day, as a breakaway of 14 riders reached the foot of the Ballon d'Alsace, he attacked again.

Defraye reached the top of the nine-kilometre climb in 37-15, just ahead of Christophe and Garrigou. Christophe – an extremely accomplished climber – recovered well on

the descent, and easily outsprinted Defraye to the line. He went on to win the next two Alpine stages, but despite a heroic 315-kilometre solo ride to Grenoble, the Belgian kept his place at the top of the general classification. Defending champion Octave Lapize was in a strong position, but did not manage to win a stage until after the Alps. Defraye responded to the threat with another stage win of his own the next day, despite puncturing near the finish. Aside from the men riding the same bikes as him, he was being helped considerably by the patriotism of his fellow Belgians. Lapize, although French, and therefore a member of the dominant nation in the race, was not colluding with anyone apart from his legitimate team-mates. He refused to start on stage nine, fed up with the Belgians ganging up on him. Defraye was remorseless – he won the stage in Lapize's absence, and extended his race lead, holding it all the way to Paris.

TIME FOR A CHANGE
The 1912 race was the second time that Defraye had ridden the Tour and, although he competed in another five *editions*, it was the only time he ever completed the distance. The format of the race changed again over the winter, taking the peloton round France in an anti-clockwise direction, and reverting to total accumulated in

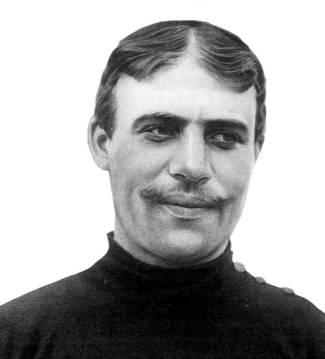

calculating the overall classification. Despite finishing in second place, Eugène Christophe had actually completed the 5,289 kilometres of the 1912 race at a higher average speed than Defraye.

Changes were also made to the team structure: squads would be of 10 rather than five men in the future. The larger French manufacturers, who all backed teams, had been acting in sponsorship as they did in business, using their smaller, subsidiary companies to sponsor separate teams, which would in fact be manipulated by the parent company. With fewer, larger teams, the organizers could now ensure that each sponsor was associated with only one squad. Within the team, pacemaking and real teamwork was, for the first time, actively encouraged.

In addition to this, organizers proposed to outlaw freewheeling, on the basis that it made the race too easy. Riders and fans protested, and the ongoing debate lasted as long, if not longer, than the discussion of the race itself.

1913

Of all the changes made before the start of the 1913 Tour, the decision to award the race lead to the man with the shortest total time, rather than best placings, was the most important. It was because of this ruling that the 10-strong teams were crucial – if anyone's team leader were to get into trouble, they would be expected to wait for him and pace him back to the group. Those who could not adapt would fall by the wayside.

The race did not begin well – the return of saboteurs throwing nails on the road ended the Tour for 29 men on the first stage to Le Havre. But worse, for one man at least, was to come: Eugène Christophe took over the race lead when Odile Defraye retired, and as the peloton rode over the Tourmalet he was in a strong position to win overall, but as he began the descent, his forks broke. He had no choice but to sling his bike across his shoulder and carry it for two hours to the nearest black-smith, in Sainte Marie de Campan. Under the new, stricter team regulations he was not allowed any outside assistance, so Christophe spent more than an hour inexpertly forging, welding and reassembling his bike. He had lost an inordinate amount of time, and the race, but that was of little interest to Henri Desgrange. He handed Christophe an additional three-minute time penalty for accepting help – he had let the blacksmith's apprentice pump the bellows for him while he worked.

BAD LUCK ALL ROUND

While Eugène Christophe lived through what would become one of the most famous incidents in Tour history, Philippe Thys took over the general classification. But another Belgian was waiting in the wings: Marcel Buysse attacked Thys on the Pyrenean stage to Perpignan, dropping him at Tarascon. The route passed over such high mountains that the road had been cut out of the snow to allow the riders to pass. Buysse was anxious to get out of the snow, and descended so fast – legs spinning wildly as he was not allowed to freewheel – that not even the official cars could keep up with him. He won the stage, and took over the lead from his compatriot.

Buysse's luck changed on stage eight – a bad fall left him only slightly injured, but with a mangled bike. He carried the frame for seven kilometres until he could repair it, counting the minutes all the way. After Christophe's escapade earlier in the race, Buysse did his mental arithmetic, and enlisted some help to mend his handlebars. He accepted 25 minutes' worth of time penalties as the price for the assistance he needed, and finished the stage in fifth overall.

On the stage to Geneva, both Buysse and Petit-Breton punctured almost immediately after the stage start. Their rivals took this opportunity to try and rule them out of the race entirely, but the two joined forces and caught the

Above: The 1913 Tour winner Philippe Thys completes his lap of honour. Below: Thys and fellow Belgian Jean Rossius climb off with relief after another long day in the saddle.

leading group. Buysse attacked on the Lauteret climb, rode solo over the Galibier, and won another stage.

There was only one mountain stage to go and, although Buysse won this one too, it was not enough to deprive Philippe Thys of the overall victory. Even though Buysse had to dismount to change gear (he had two speeds), he still caught and passed Petit-Breton, who was equipped with a Sturmey-Archer gear and could change while riding. Petit-Breton had the technology, Buysse had the legs, but Thys had all this plus the support of the Peugeot team, and good fortune – both essential ingredients for a Tour win.

1914

Philippe Thys was a Tour specialist. He had only won a single stage in the 1913 race, as he was more concerned with his overall position. He trained obsessively, paying attention to his diet and forfeiting other victories in order to be in the best form possible to contest the Tour in July. The organizers were being equally strict, and rules concerning outside assistance were being observed to the letter. In one instance a professional rider discarded a bag containing a half-eaten sandwich as he rode along. A few moments later, an *isolé* passed the spot, saw the food and ate it. The sponsored rider was penalized 30 minutes for inadvertently helping someone from another team.

By the end of the first week the 143-man field had been halved. But this was still too many for a sprint finish on the velodrome at the end of stage eight, so the riders all dismounted when they reached the finish town of Marseille, and contested the sprint in heats, semi-finals and a final for stage positions. In the early rounds Emile Engel – winner of stage three – collided with Maurice Brocco, the man who had been expelled from the 1912 race. Brocco was so vocal in his complaints that he was disqualified for repeatedly using foul language. The stage was eventually won by Octave Lapize, but not until he, too, had been verbally abused – this time by Oscar Egg – who escaped with a fine.

The mood of the organizers only served to encourage bad behaviour among the riders. On stage nine, the entire peloton jumped off its bikes and ran into the sea along the coast to Nice; only the approaching mountains could sober them.

Thys did not win a stage in the Alps, but still held the lead. Marcel Buysse retired from the race after crashing into a motorbike, but most of the pre-race favourites were living up to their reputations – there was no room for surprise challengers this time. Fortunately for Thys, the two men behind him in the overall classification were Peugeot team-mates Henri Pelissier and Jean Alavoine. On the penultimate stage he led by 32 minutes, and seemed certain of victory. But he fell after colliding with François Faber on the way to Dunkirk and, like any other professional rider, was left to choose between mending his own wheel, or suffering a time penalty if someone from outside the team helped.

He made his choice carefully: a 30-minute time penalty would slash his lead to just 1-50, but would mean he could finish the stage without losing time to his rivals. What had been a foregone conclusion became a race to the line on the final stage to Paris, but the gamble paid off and Thys won his second consecutive Tour. Nine days later the First World War broke out.

Tour Legends
Henri Desgrange

Henri Desgrange was a much better publicist and newspaperman than he was a cyclist. The highlight of his athletic career was to be a one-time holder of the Hour Record – but it was the race he created that brought him worldwide fame. Desgrange did not invent long-distance cycle racing, but he brought it into the 20th century. The initial structure of the race – to hold it in stages, mirroring the format of the celebrated Six Day races – was thought up by his colleague

> **"The ideal Tour would be one in which only one rider survived the ordeal."** Henri Desgrange

Géo Lefèvre, but it was Desgrange who breathed live into the Tour. He nurtured it and constantly altered it to keep it in tune with the sporting mood of the day as Europe changed, and also to make sure that everyone knew whose race it was.

From the comfort of the following car, Desgrange made sure that the Tour maintained its reputation as the toughest event on the calendar. Every technological innovation was frowned upon as another way to make the race easier, and no route was considered too difficult. Anyone who complained was given short shrift, and riders with egos to match Desgrange's – most famously Henri Pélissier – were expelled if they protested too loudly. No one was ever allowed to think that the Tour belonged to anyone other than Desgrange.

Le Grand Départ, 1938: Gino Bartali (left) poses alongside Henri Desgrange who had no need of bicycle clips.

Chapter 2: 1919–1939

The Years of Living Dangerously

In the 20 years between the two world wars, the Tour was beset with incidents that ranged from the tragic to the farcical. From those who survived the First World War to those who would go on to fight in the Second, there was a succession of heroes and fall guys who dedicated their lives to the race, and to its attractive new prize – the yellow jersey.

1919

France had barely started to recover from the First World War when the Tour began again. The roads were in no state to be raced over, and most of the riders were not fit to compete – they had hardly had time to train during the conflict, but Henri Desgrange insisted the race be reinstated as soon as possible. To add colour to proceedings, he introduced his new gimmick – the *maillot jaune* – a yellow jersey, to match the paper on which *L'Auto* was printed, which was to be worn by the leader of the race, beginning with the man who led after stage 10 to Grenoble.

If any man from the pre-war years deserved to come back to win the race it was Eugène Christophe. He did not win a stage, but nevertheless took over the race lead from Henri Pélissier on the fourth stage to Les Sables. After holding his lead through the Pyrenees, Christophe had no qualms about pulling on the *maillot jaune*, and he wore it with pride as he took a half-hour advantage across the Alps and on to Metz. There were only two stages remaining to Paris and, with only 11 of the 69 starters still there in the race, how could he possibly lose now?

Christophe's chances of winning

ended exactly the way they had in 1913; his forks broke and, by the time he had walked to the local bike factory in Valencienne, he had lost 70 minutes, along with the Tour. Firmin Lambot took the jersey to Paris, with Christophe in third place.

1920

The Tour has always been irresistible to the Belgians. For the first week of the 1920 Tour they were everywhere, with Louis Mottiat winning the opening stage, and his team leader Philippe Thys taking over the lead after his excellent stage win at Cherbourg. Only one man could drive a wedge into the Belgian team – Henri Pélissier.

Pélissier won stages three and four of the race, only to find himself penalized for discarding a tubular tyre *en route*. The regulations were clear – the professional-class riders must not take anything from outside sources during the race, nor could they leave their litter behind them. Pélissier stormed out of the race in disgust, criticized by Desgrange as a rider who "didn't know how to suffer, and would never win the Tour".

Thys paid no attention to Pélissier's tantrum. He won a further

three stages and built his lead to over an hour over second-placed Hector Heusghem, with yet another five Belgian riders crammed into the top seven behind them.

While Thys became the first-ever three-time winner with relative ease, the French team's race was saved only by the amazing heroics of Honoré Barthélémy, the best-placed home rider in eighth overall. After a series of crashes he finished the race with a dislocated shoulder and a broken wrist, and was carried in triumph to the Parc des Princes velodrome to accept the applause of 20,000 proud French fans.

1921

Much as it pained Henri Desgrange to admit it, the 1921 Tour was not as scintillating as it might have been. Louis Mottiat won the first stage, as he had done the year before. Honoré Barthélémy picked up his bad luck from where he had left it the previous year, puncturing no fewer than 11 times on that first race to Le Havre. Small joy for France as Romain Bellenger won the next day, only to see the jersey pass to another Belgian, Léon Scieur, 24 hours later. Nicknamed "The Locomotive",

Below: Firmin Lambot celebrates in Paris, 1919. Previous page: Philippe Thys leads his Belgian team-mates on stage 10, Nice–Grenoble, 1920.

Scieur was a late convert to cycling; he had not ridden competitively until he was 22 and now, 11 years later, was competing in his fifth Tour. He won the stage from Nice to Grenoble, stretching his lead at every opportunity while the French and Italian challengers looked on, seemingly paralysed by the Belgian's power. He rode to Paris without opposition, serenely topping the final general classification with another seven of his countrymen behind him in the top 10.

1922

It was a heart-warming sight to see Eugène Christophe pull the yellow jersey on at Sables d'Olonne. All of France wanted him to win the Tour, and at 37 he was unlikely to get a better chance in the future. Sporting a luxuriant moustache, he had matured from being "Le Gaulois" to "Le vieux Gaulois". But his age was telling and he lost the lead to another veteran, Jean Alavoine, in the Pyrenees.

Alavoine won three consecutive stages, to Bayonne, to Luchon and to Perpignan. Triple winner Philippe Thys repeated the feat to Toulon, to Nice and to Briançon, but the glory was all Alavoine's. As he followed Thys over the Izoard – the first time the mountain had been included in the Tour – he extended his lead by 22 minutes. Meanwhile Christophe's luck was about to run out yet again.

His forks broke once more and, as in 1913 and 1919, he had to shoulder his bike and walk down the mountain. The delay cost him any hope of winning the race. Then bad luck descended on another rider: Jean Alavoine.

Mechanical problems – and the freezing temperatures that made attending to them so difficult – thwarted Alavoine, and cost him the jersey. It landed on the shoulders of Hector Heusghem, who had finished runner-up the year before. But the Belgian was not destined to win the Tour; he crashed on the 13th stage to Metz and had to change bikes. The

Above: Brothers Francis and Henri Pélissier on stage 11, Briançon-Geneva, 1923. Henri beat Francis to the finish. Below: Eugène Christophe gets off and walks on stage 11, Briançon-Geneva, 1922.

swap was approved by a *commissaire*, but after the stage he was overruled and Heusghem was penalized by an hour. The final beneficiary of this series of disasters was Firmin Lambot. Just as he had done in 1919, he picked up the torn and tattered jersey from his crushed rivals and took it home to Paris.

1923

The French riders had had their fill of Belgians running away with their race. Henri Pélissier came back to the Tour in 1923 determined to bite his tongue and complete the race without any arguments. And he brought his brother Francis along for support.

Try as he might to suppress his temper, however, even wearing the yellow jersey on stage three did not lighten Pélissier's mood. He took the lead, but the next day he fell foul of Henri Desgrange's rules again, and was penalized for throwing away a damaged tyre. His sense of humour deserted him, and he trailed in 30 minutes after the stage winner Robert Jacquinot.

Jacquinot had ridden so brilliantly over the Tourmalet that he seemed a sure winner. But he had saved nothing to defend his lead; the next day, within sight of the summit of the Peyresourde, he cracked. He fell from his bike, so exhausted that he could do nothing but lie on the roadside and watch the rest ride by.

The race got more difficult for Pélissier, too, with the jersey going to his team-mate, Ottavio Bottecchia. Ignoring the protocol that a rider should not attack members of the same squad, he hatched a plan that would win him the race in the Alps.

On the lower slopes of the Izoard, Pélissier made his move, and won the stage alone. There was a six-minute gap to the next man, but Bottecchia was left more than half an hour behind, and ceded the jersey to Pélissier. Just to make sure of his lead, the Frenchman enlisted the help of his brother the following day, setting off on a two-man break that sealed his victory. Bottecchia recovered sufficiently to finish in second place; Pélissier acknowledged the Italian's talent, saying "Bottecchia will succeed me." But for 1923 at least, the Tour was his, and all arguments with Desgrange were forgotten. Circulation for *L'Auto* topped the one million mark the morning after Pélissier rode into Paris, a fact that Pélissier was all too quick to remind Desgrange of in the future.

1924

Henri Pélissier couldn't stay on his best behaviour for ever. He'd won the Tour now and, as far as he was concerned, he'd therefore won his argument with Henri Desgrange. From now on it was a free-for-all. He did not have a problem with Bottecchia winning the first stage – after all he'd singled him out as a future star – but he could not accept the rules Desgrange imposed.

Stages were long, and the riders had to start before sunrise in order to finish the following afternoon. Naturally the temperature would increase during the day's ride, but Desgrange ruled that every rider had to finish the stage with everything he took with him, be it spare tyres or clothes. To Pélissier this was ridiculous: he tossed aside a long-sleeved jersey as the sun rose on stage two, only to be warned at the finish that he would be penalized for breaking the regulations of the race.

The next day he rode alongside his brother Francis and, together with team-mate Maurice Ville, they abandoned the race in protest.

Unfortunately for Desgrange, there was an eager journalist waiting to hear their sorry tale. Albert Londres sat with them as they waited for the train back to Paris, and published their story in *Petit Parisien* under the headline *Les Forcats de la Route*, the convicts of the road.

With Pélissier's words from 1923 ringing in his ears, Bottecchia won both Pyrenean stages to cement his lead and fulfil his predecessor's prophecy. He became the first Italian to win the Tour, just two years after becoming a professional rider.

1925

Ottavio Bottecchia wasted no time in launching the defence of his Tour title. He won the first stage, as he had done the previous year, and pulled on the yellow jersey. He went on to win two more stages, and held on to the lead until stage eight – the first day in the mountains – when a young Belgian rider, Adelin Benoit, won the stage and took the jersey.

Nearer to home soil in the Alps, Bottecchia found his rhythm again.

Through miserable, soaking rain he was ably assisted by his team-mate Lucien Buysse, and was happy to let his lieutenant win stages 11 and 12 to move into second position, as he himself regained control overall. The Italian fans, the *tifosi*, were delirious, flooding across the border to watch their hero ride past in yellow. They got even more than they were hoping for: yet another Italian, Bartolomeo Aymo, was first over the Col de Vars and the Izoard, and won the stage to Briançon.

Bottecchia could hardly be described as a handsome man, but the allure of the *maillot jaune* transformed him. Young Italian women threw roses on to the road as he approached, and he was constantly trailed by a throng of supporters as he tried to relax on the rest day. The enthusiasm was contagious: extra police were enlisted to control the French crowds at Evian, and three trains were specially provided to carry all of Nicholas Frantz's fans from Luxembourg to see him finish in fourth place overall.

But the final honours went to Bottecchia – he broke away on the way back to Paris with four other men, and then outsprinted them all to win the final stage in the Parc des Princes.

Above: Waiting for a train – journaist Albert Londres takes notes from the Pélissiers and Maurice Ville in Brest, 1924. Below: Italy's sweetheart Ottavio Bottecchia in Dunkirk after completing the penultimate stage in 1925.

1926

After completing a Tour double successfully, Bottecchia was fully expected to win again in 1926. As was his custom, Bottecchia wanted to win the first stage. But this year the race was not starting in Paris; it departed from Evian and rose quickly into the mountains. The defending champion attacked on the first hill but, following a demoralizing succession of four punctures, it was his team-mate Jules Buysse (brother of Marcel, who had won six stages in the 1913 Tour) who rode into Mulhouse as victor. Spectators were so convinced that it would be the Italian who came home first that they were already cheering "Bravo, Bottecchia!" as the Belgian approached the line. Taking it as a compliment, Buysse allowed himself the smallest of smiles as they realized their mistake.

Buysse lost the jersey to Gustaaf van Slembroek on stage three. Van Slembroek held it for a week, but when he rolled away from the start of stage 11, in Bayonne, he knew full well that this would be his last day in yellow. The peloton rode the 320-kilometre stage in constant rain; Lucien Buysse broke away with three others on the Aubisque, reaching the summit alone. Like his brother on stage one, he was mistakenly cheered on as if he was Bottecchia – the crowds were still expecting to see his Italian team-mate leading the race. But Bottecchia was in no state to ride, let alone race. He was sick, and abandoned in tears on the Tourmalet, hardly able to comprehend that his Tour was over. It was a hard, hard day for everyone: Lucien Buysse won the stage by 25 minutes, but still finished two hours behind schedule, and the last men did not reach Luchon until midnight.

Buysse confirmed his dominance by winning the second Pyrenean stage, and led the field comfortably to Paris. But not everybody had much reason to celebrate. Ottavio Bottecchia was so devastated by his failure to complete the Tour that he announced his retirement from the sport altogether. In just four years as

Belgian Gustaaf Van Slembroek smokes a cigarette en route to Strasbourg, stage 20, 1927. Slembroek ran out of puff and finished third on the stage, pipped to the line by two of his team-mates.

a professional rider he had won the race twice, and taken nine stages. But his immense physical talents were tempered by an emotional fragility that prevented him from fulfilling his potential. Shortly after he had quit the professional ranks, he was killed while out on a training ride.

1927

In the hope of avoiding the long, drawn-out parade of the flat stages, organizers set each team off separately at the start of the 1927 Tour. This giant time-trial format enlivened the first week of the race, with the lead changing frequently as riders were forced out of the shadow of the bunch. Henri Desgrange was always happy to tweak the format of the race to add to the spectacle, and now there would be 24 stages, compared to 17 in 1926, with rest days only between the mountains. The first two men to lead the race – Francis Pélissier then Ferdinand Le Drogo – put so much effort into controlling the event that they eventually had to abandon, one after the other, from sheer exhaustion.

Hector Martin took over the lead as the race approached the mountains, but it was clear that

Nicholas Frantz – twice runner-up in the Tour – was the more likely winner. He won the hardest stage, from Bayonne to Luchon over the Aubisque and the Tourmalet, and took the jersey from Martin.

The first four in the general classification – Frantz, Maurice De Waele, Julien Vervaecke and André Leducq – held on to their positions through the Alps and towards Paris. The lack of time to recover between stages made the race so arduous that only 39 of the 142 starters reached the French capital – even Desgrange had to concede that the race was getting close to impossible now.

1928

The effect of using a staggered start on the flat stages of the race was enormous. For the first eight stages, as each team rode in furious isolation, without any idea of how they were faring against their rivals, the average speed was over 32 kph as they bowled toward the Pyrenees. Nicholas Frantz won the opening stage, carried to the line by the invincible Alcyon team. He remained untroubled until the Pyrenees, and the stage that had already achieved mythical status, to Luchon. He attacked with aplomb,

and was surprised to see that Italian Victor Fontan finally got clear on the Tourmalet, and held his slim margin to win the stage.

Australia's first-ever Tour competitor, Hubert Opperman, was still finding his way in the strange culture of European racing. Although he did well on the climbs, he simply could not understand how the riders descended so quickly. He rode to the top of the Aubisque not far behind the race leaders, only to lose more than 40 minutes on the way down.

With a healthy lead over his nearest rivals, Frantz took advantage of the strength of his Alcyon *domestiques* for the next few days to augment it further. But it was not until stage 19 that he was reminded just how vital their services were. Riding from Metz to Charleville, his forks broke; with 100 kilometres to ride, any delays could cost him the race. He borrowed a woman's bike from a well-wisher and, led by team-mates, lost only 28 minutes to became the first man to wear the yellow jersey from start to finish of the Tour.

1929

The Tour had been slipping away from the French since before the First World War. Only one home rider – Octave Lapize – had won the race since 1911 and, by 1929, the fans hoped for nothing more than stage wins from their heroes. André Leducq obliged, winning stage two, and four subsequent stages before the race was over.

Defending champion Nicholas Frantz didn't win a thing until day seven, when a well-timed move netted him his first stage of the race. But his aggregate time now equalled that of Victor Fontan and André Leducq – the organizers had no solution but to reward all three with a yellow jersey at the end of the stage.

Fontan broke away on the first mountain stage, finishing second to his team-mate Salvador Cardona and ousting Leducq and Frantz from the lead. His joy did not last long. Ten kilometres into the next stage his forks snapped, leaving him stranded on the roadside. On a bike borrowed from a benevolent spectator, Fontan rode with his broken machine balanced across his shoulders to the next village, where he was able to botch a repair. He rejoined the race, but his spirit was broken and he abandoned. Belgium's Maurice De Waele, who had been second overall after the first Pyrenean stage, became *maillot jaune* and Alcyon's protected rider.

That De Waele held on to his lead was a tribute to his selfless team. He fell ill in the Alps and was nursed over every climb — literally pushed up the slopes by his team-mates — to ensure he did not lose the jersey. Extreme temperatures made things worse; it was so hot that at times the *commissaires* were forced to neutralize the race at feed zones, so all riders had a chance to get water. De Waele did not win a stage — it was all he could do to crawl to Paris on the wheel of team-mate Marcel Bidot. Henri Desgrange described it as a "moribund victory", but under the rules Desgrange himself had drawn up it was a victory nonetheless.

1930

The Alcyon team's utter domination of the race provoked an about-turn from Henri Desgrange. He decided that his new format in fact allowed the strongest teams to open up gaps on the flat stages, and left the weaker men without any hope of winning a stage. So in 1930 the race reverted to mass starts, the first of which was won by Charles Pélissier, the youngest of the three brothers.

Desgrange was in the mood for change. He ruled that all competitors must go back to riding identical bikes in order to prevent commercial interests from interfering with race tactics. Trade teams were replaced with national ones, and Desgrange presented sponsors with an alternative way to advertise themselves — a stream of vehicles, bedecked in logos, drove along the route ahead of the race to provoke anticipation

amongst the crowds as they waited for the peloton.

Young Italian Laerco Guerra took advantage of a peloton unused to mass starts on the flat stages and escaped on stage two. While the bunch took time to organize a chase, he opened up a gap and won the stage by 90 seconds. It was enough to put him in yellow and keep him there as far as the mountains.

The first stage in the Pyrenees ended Guerra's spell as race leader. He was dropped, along with the rest of the field, by Benoit Faure, the famous *touriste-routier* – the name given to riders not competing among the ranks of professionals – on the Aubisque. He too paid for his efforts later, being caught by Alfredo Binda, André Leducq and Pierre Magne before the stage was finished. Leducq took over the lead.

Into the Alps, and Leducq led Guerra by 22 minutes. He looked to be safe, until the final kilometres of the stage to Nice, where two punctures in quick succession cost him five minutes of his advantage. But the French team was determined that its leader would not be touched. Led by Pélissier they escorted Leducq

Touriste-routier Benoit Faure on stage 9, Pau–Luchon, 1930.

to the foot of the Galibier so that he could face Guerra for a final showdown. Both men reached the top of the climb with the lead group, but as they descended Leducq took one risk too many.

He crashed, somersaulting twice and sliding into the verge. Regaining his composure, he sought out his bike, and began the chase. Shaken, disoriented and badly cut on one knee, he had lost all but three minutes of his lead to Guerra.

Fortunately his team was there to guide him round the hairpins, carrying him back toward the Italian. Guerra screamed to the other breakaways to help him stay away, but they had no strength left. They were caught before the finish in Evian, where the French team even managed to lead out Leducq to win the stage. They had ridden superbly, and in doing so brought four more of their number – brothers Antonin and Pierre Magne, Marcel Bidot and Charles Pélissier – into the top 10. Pélissier himself won eight of the 21 stages. The new, modernized Tour was declared a success, not least because the French riders had acquitted themselves so well.

1931

The 1930 drama, complete with its fairytale ending, brought the Tour new popularity, and 1931 marked the silver jubilee. Huge crowds gathered at the start and finish of every stage, anxious to get a glimpse of the French team. Home riders won two of the first five stages, while Austrian *touriste-routier* Max Bulla proved himself equal to the professionals with a victory at Dinan. The crowds were so noisy that, at the start of stage seven, half the riders could not hear the official start signal – the rest of the peloton were six kilometres up the road before organizers were able to stop them and restart the stage. From then on, the professional riders were set off 10 minutes ahead of the *touristes-routiers* so that both groups could ride safely down the over-crowded streets. They were not brought back together again until the Pyrenees.

André Leducq was not in the kind of form needed to win the Tour, and he gracefully ceded team leadership to Antonin Magne. Magne repaid his trust by winning the crucial stage over the Tourmalet, seizing the yellow jersey and uniting the French team behind him. The home riders earned their wages in the Alps. Magne, Leducq and Léon Le Calvez were brought down in a crash on the descent of the Col du Nice; fortunately all three were unscathed and were able to work together to cancel out the time that Magne had lost in the accident.

Magne could not be beaten in the mountains and, once he was in a strong enough position, the team could allow Charles Pélissier to take care of his own interests – stage wins at both Cannes and Grenoble were his rewards for hard work in the service of Magne. But as the race neared its conclusion he was once again called on to protect his leader. Belgium's Jef Demuysère, in second place overall, was not ready to capitulate. On the penultimate stage, a typical Flandrian ride across flat, exposed cobbles, he attacked. Magne jumped on to his wheel and refused

to budge. Demuysère had nothing to lose, so he rode and rode, towing Magne to the line. He'd opened up a 17-minute gap by the time he won the stage; if only Magne had been on the other side of it Demuysère might have won the Tour.

1932

After two years of basing the final result on cumulative time, Henri Desgrange could not resist another tweak of the rules. He decreed that time bonuses would be awarded along with stage wins – four minutes, two minutes and one minute, respectively, for the first three places. And, should the first man cross the line more than three minutes ahead of the rest, he would gain an additional three-minute bonus.

For the first three days, the jersey passed between the stage winners – Jean Aerts, then Kurt Stoepel – before coming to rest with André Leducq on the third stage to Bordeaux.

Leducq did not win any stages in the Pyrenees, but, mindful of the bonuses on offer, took two second places. On stage 10 the Frenchman succumbed to the weather, losing three minutes to the German.

**Above: Antonin Magne celebrates the stage win, Pau–Luchon, that gave him the yellow jersey in 1931.
Below: A magazine cover shows second-placed Kurt Stoepel (left) posing with winner André Leducq in Paris, 1932.**

Bad weather continued as the peloton battled with the mountains. Through fog, rain, even snowstorms, Leducq chased Francesco Camusso up to the summit of the Galibier. He led the group back to the Italian on the descent, and then outsprinted them all at Aix-les-Bains. Stoepel was not with them. Time bonuses were handed out, and Leducq increased his lead to 13 minutes.

Another stage win two days later furthered Leducq's cause. He was feted by the French public at every turn of his pedals and, being the crowd-pleaser that he was, he wanted to give them even more reason to cheer. The team were happy to help and, on stage 18, a little too eager. Leducq crossed the line first, only to be relegated after being pushed by his team-mate Albert Barthélémy. Undeterred, Leducq went on to win the last two stages, and the Tour itself, by 24 minutes and three seconds from Stoepel. Without time bonuses, Leducq would have been 31 minutes slower, Stoepel just seven and the difference therefore between them would have been only three seconds.

1933

In 1933, to balance the bonus system, which favoured the sprinters, Henri Desgrange introduced a new competition, the King of the Mountains. Points would be given for the first men across each summit, according to difficulty. But first there were the flat stages to be completed.

Maurice Archambaud of France scored a lone victory on the first stage, taking a five-minute time bonus and a clear lead in the overall competition. Made up of the best riders of its generation, the French team was ready to take the race apart.

Charles Pélissier was riding behind a Press car, waiting for an opportunity to overtake. The car braked as he accelerated, and he rode straight into the back of it. Despite deep cuts to right leg and left arm, he refused to quit. He rode in agony to Metz, only to finish outside the time cut and be excluded from the race.

Italian climber Learco Guerra won both mountain stages, and the time bonuses he took enabled him to move up into second place overall. Archambaud regained some of his advantage on the flatter stage to Gap, but he could not match the specialists on the hardest slopes. Over the Col du Vars he was left to climb in solitude, nine minutes behind the leaders. Guerra should have taken the jersey, but he punctured. Instead Archambaud's team-mate Georges Speicher won the stage, and Belgium's Georges Lemaire – who had not won a stage himself but had finished consistently well and taken several minor time bonuses – took the jersey from him.

Archambaud was not ready to work for Speicher just yet – he won the stage to Cannes, and, thanks to the time bonus, regained the lead. It was a short revival. The next day he punctured, and Speicher showed him little sympathy, riding flat out on the descents, winning the stage and taking the jersey back again. The only interruption in Speicher's ride to Paris was on stage 22, when so many men reached the Caen velodrome together, officials decided the only fair way to classify them was to hold an impromptu one-lap time trial. It was another Frenchman, René Le Greves, who was quickest over the 400 metres.

1934

If 1933 was a good year for the French team, 1934 was a great one. Defending champion Georges Speicher won the opening stage, and the team swept all before them: René Le Greves took stage two, Roger Lapébie stages three and four, and then Le Greves and Speicher tied for the fifth stage. Unable to separate them, the judges split the bonuses for first and second place – 90 and 45 seconds – between them, 67 seconds each. And ahead of all this, Antonin Magne had taken the jersey after coming second on stage two, and carried his lead to the foot of the

Above: René Vietto weeps after sacrificing his bike for event-ual winner Antonin Magne in 1934. Below: Vicente Trueba, the first-ever King of the Mountains in 1933.

mountains, at Aix-les-Bains.

Magne stuck close to his nearest rival, Giuseppe Martano, over the Galibier, but the Italian snatched 45 seconds back for finishing second to René Vietto, and moved a little closer to the jersey. The men competing for the King of the Mountains' competition were paying little heed to the pair: Vicente Trueba, the "Spanish Flea", who had won the inaugural title 12 months previously, was first over the Col du Laffrey, but Vietto led over the Cols de Vars and Allos, building up to a lone victory at Digne and bonuses that took him up to sixth overall.

Then, riding over the Portet d'Aspet on Martano's wheel, Magne crashed. He was not badly hurt, but his rear wheel folded beneath him. He watched helplessly as riders streamed past him, waiting for a team car to help him. His saviour came from the opposite direction – René Vietto, his 20-year-old team-mate, appeared like a vision, riding back up the mountain in the wrong direction, riding against the flow of riders now overtaking him as well as Magne. He pulled up by his team leader and gave him his bike, sacrificing his own

chances in the race to make sure that Magne kept the jersey on French shoulders. Then he sat and wept as he waited alone for a spare wheel from the support vehicle to complete the stage. Vietto's selfless act saved the Tour for Magne; his reward was the King of the Mountains' prize and a place for ever in the hearts of the French public.

1935

France's luck had to run out eventually. It started to trickle away in Lille, where Belgian Romain Maes won the first stage. Under revised rules, his bonuses put him more than three minutes clear in the overall classification. Charles Pélissier restored French pride by winning stage two, but Maes would not be budged; even on the split stage on day five, which included an individual time trial, he stubbornly remained in yellow.

René Vietto had won the first Alpine stage, while his leader, Antonin Magne, moved closer to the jersey. Riding over the Telegraphe the next day, Magne was hit by a car. The defending champion was carried away from the race in agony, but worse was to come. On the descent of the Galibier, Spain's Francesco Cepeda crashed, fracturing his skull. He died from his injuries – the Tour's first victim.

Maes had at least made it through the mountains unscathed. Back on flatter territory, he won the coastal stage to Cannes. Two more days of split stages brought him, still in yellow, to the foot of the Pyrenees, with Georges Speicher's time-trial skills putting him in second. Maes's namesake, Sylvère, took off into the mountains with Félicien Vervaecke. The Belgian pair reached Luchon an incredible 13 minutes ahead, knowing that as long as their team leader was with the main group they were free to help themselves to King of the Mountains' points and a stage win.

The final mountain stage, from Luchon to Pau, saw Italy's Ambrogio Morelli strike out a lone path to move into second overall. With less than three minutes separating him from the jersey, just one ill-timed puncture between Pau and Paris could have cost Maes the Tour. The Belgians could not afford to let him sit so close to their leader; some brilliant team work followed against Morelli, dropping him for 11 minutes and securing Maes's victory.

1936

The 30th Tour de France began in a thunderstorm. For 190 kilometres 90 riders splashed and aquaplaned to Lille, where Paul Elgi won the stage. He held the jersey for just a day, ceding it to Maurice Archambaud at Charleville. The Frenchman in turn lost it to Arsène Mersch, but promptly regained it by winning the stage to Belfort. The Belgians may have lost the lead, but they were dominating the race, clustered in second, third, fourth, fifth and sixth places behind Archambaud in the general classification.

Best positioned of these Belgian hopefuls was Sylvère Maes, winner of the Luchon stage in the 1935 Tour. Without the benefit of any

time bonuses – he had not come first or second on any of the opening eight stages – Maes took the jersey from Archambaud when he broke down on the stage to Briançon.

With a team-mate, Félicien Vervaecke, in second place, just ahead of Antonin Magne, he was in relative safety. Vervaecke went with him when he attacked on the Tourmalet, anxious to protect his leader and his own position. But if he harboured any secret hopes of taking over the jersey, he was soon disillusioned. He punctured and rather than mend the tyre he borrowed a three-speed touring bike to complete the stage. He got an 11-minute time penalty for his indiscretion, and was relegated to a fight with Magne to regain second place. The Tour was Maes's by almost half an hour.

Above: Ready for the off – Marcel Kint, Sylvère Maes, Félicien Vervaecke and Romain Maes, members of the Belgian team that won both team time trials in 1936.
Below: Roger Lapébie leads the peloton over a level crossing, 1937.

1937

With the political landscape of Europe overtaking sporting events, the Italians had missed the 1936 Tour. Their return marked a grand reunion, which was completed by the presence of Henri Desgrange, who had been forced to abandon the race in 1936 owing to ill health.

Reigning Tour of Italy champion Gino Bartali was riding his first Tour de France and was already touted as a potential winner. He won the stage over the Galibier and took the jersey. Riding toward Briançon, Bartali crashed on a high-speed descent, sliding straight off the road, hitting a parapet, bouncing over it and down into a ravine. Suddenly he was being swept away with the current, drowning. Seconds later, his team-mate Francesco Camusso rushed down to the river's edge and hoisted him out unhurt. As far as the soaking-wet Bartali could see, there was only one thing to do: he got back on his bike and completed the stage.

Next day Bartali lost the jersey to defending champion Sylvère Maes, and soon retired with a fever. Maes meanwhile rode through the Pyrenees untroubled and Roger Lapébie established himself as the main competition. On the stage to Luchon, Lapébie glanced under his handlebars and realized with horror they had been sawn almost through.

final time trial. On the final stage, André Leducq and Antonin Magne, both double-Tour winners and both riding for the last time, escaped and reached the Parc des Princes five minutes ahead of the bunch. As they approached the finish, they threw arms around each other's shoulders, and crossed the line together. The *commissaires* decided to judge the stage in the spirit in which it had been contested: Leducq and Magne were awarded joint first place, the perfect way to end their respective Tour careers.

1939

The threat of war hung heavy over Europe in the summer of 1939. Neither Germany nor Italy sent riders to compete and, to make up numbers in the race, Belgium was allowed to field two teams, with French regional teams accommodating the second-string riders who did not make it on to the national squad.

The regional riders were quick to justify their selection: Amédée Fournier won the first stage, losing the lead to Jean Fontenay, who in turn handed the jersey to René Vietto. The hero of the 1937 Tour had been relegated to a regional team, but when he took the lead he believed he was capable of victory.

The Belgian Sylvère Maes had the benefit of two teams to support him in his quest but Vietto held on to the jersey through the Pyrenees. Maes was adopting Bartali's tactics: over the Allos and Vars, he tested Vietto, and on the Izoard he destroyed him. He won the stage by 17 minutes. The next afternoon saw the Tour's first-ever mountain time trial. There was little doubt as to who would win. Maes beat Vietto by 10 minutes over the 65-kilometre stage.

Maes broke his own record, set in the 1936 race, for the highest average speed of the Tour. He had completed the 4,224 kilometres at close to 32 kph, and won both the overall and the climbing competition. By the following July, France was occupied and the Tour was a world away.

Fingers pointed to the French, but no culprit was found.

There was yet more drama in the final week of the Tour. So many riders had abandoned that organizers thought the team time trial would be unfair. Days later, Lapébie was penalized for taking a push, and the French team threatened to withdraw. The next day Maes punctured, and was towed back to the bunch by two Belgians who were riding as "*individuels*", not for the national team – he was penalized, too, and left only 25 seconds clear of Lapébie. The entire Belgian squad walked out in a fit of pique, leaving Lapébie to take the jersey, and the Tour. In a race of elimination, he was the last one standing in Paris.

1938

The arcane rule that allowed individual entrants to the Tour was finally abandoned in 1938. The team ethic had become central to the race, and there was no room for hopeful amateurs. Those men not making the selection for the national teams made up a B team, the "*cadets*", and other

Above: High fives – Gino Bartali on the podium in Paris, 1938. Below: Sylvère Maes in the final time trial, Dôle–Dijon, in 1939.

stragglers were grouped into squads.

Riding what would be his last Tour, André Leducq had no time to sit back. He took the *maillot jaune* on the sixth stage, knowing that Gino Bartali would not start his campaign until the Pyrenees. He lost the lead on the first day in the mountains, as he had feared, but to Félicien Vervaecke. It took just one stage for Bartali to crush the Belgian. Over the Cols d'Allos, de Vars and de l'Izoard he put more than 20 minutes into his rival, upturning the general classification and taking the King of the Mountains' prize to boot. Vervaecke consoled himself by winning the

Tour Legends
Henri Pélissier

"Desgrange will have us carrying weights next."

Pélissier after abandoning in 1924

HENRI PÉLISSIER (FRA)
b. 22/1/1889 Paris; d. 1/5/1935

EIGHT PARTICIPATIONS
ONE VICTORY
10 STAGE WINS

1912 DID NOT FINISH

1913 DID NOT FINISH
ONE STAGE WIN: stage 3,
Cherbourg–Brest

1914 SECOND OVERALL
THREE STAGE WINS: stage 10,
Nice–Grenoble; stage 12, Geneva–
Belfort; stage 15, Dunkirk–Paris

1919 DID NOT FINISH
ONE STAGE WIN: stage 2,
Le Havre–Cherbourg

1920 DID NOT FINISH
TWO STAGE WINS: stage 3,
Cherbourg–Brest; stage 4, Brest–Les
Sables

1923 FIRST OVERALL
THREE STAGE WINS: stage 3,
Cherbourg–Brest; stage 10, Nice–
Briançon; stage 11, Briançon–Geneva

1924 DID NOT FINISH

1925 DID NOT FINISH

An exhausted Pélissier approaches the finish line in the yellow jersey on stage 14, Metz–Dunkirk, 1923.

When the Italians Ruled the Tour

Emerging from the Second World War, France, more than any other country in Europe, needed a great, sporting victory. Jean Robic lifted the nation's spirits by winning the first post-war race, but the era belonged to Italy, as Gino Bartali and Fausto Coppi fought for the honour of being the "campionissimo" – the champion of champions.

1947

The war threw Europe into chaos. Germany had wanted the Tour to continue uninterrupted – to show that France was not suffering unduly under Occupation, but Jacques Goddet, who took charge of the race following the death of Henri Desgrange in 1940, had refused.

It was not until 1947 that France was ready to host the race again, and this time it was with a new purpose: to lift the spirit of a broken nation as well as to remind the world that there are heroic endeavours other than just those of war.

Many riders lost their best competitive years to the war, some their health, others their lives. Of those who started the 1947 race, only 10 had competed in 1939. The rest were young, hopeful men – a catalogue of unknown quantities, all willing to test themselves against the older men, their teenage heroes. The favourite was René Vietto. Second in the last edition of the race, the Frenchman was now almost 40 years old, and the public felt that he deserved victory this time round, if

only because of his symbolic role as one of the generation of men whose dreams of winning the Tour had all but been destroyed.

Vietto made a promising start, winning the jersey after a long, solo break that lasted over 100 kilometres. Although he did not hold the lead straight through the Alps, he was back in yellow as the race exited the Pyrenees. Meanwhile Jean Robic, riding for the regional west France team, was moving slowly up the general classification. The diminutive rider – just five feet tall and newly married – was among a new generation of riders, competing in his first Tour de France and having won three stages already. This time round the home advantage was more than just psychological; food was still rationed and, while organizers provided extra meat, sugar and bananas for the peloton, the local boys got even more as their fans rallied round. Butter and eggs may not be ideal race food, but in an event as demanding as this the sheer volume of calories needed each day is so great that quantity becomes more important than quality.

Above: One of the few riders to compete before and after the Second World War, René Vietto led the pace for much of the Tour in 1947. Below: Jean Robic meets his fans, 1947.
Previous page: Coppi and Bartali prepare for stage 11 in Pau, 1949.

ADVANTAGE ROBIC

Entering the final time trial, Vietto led Italy's Pierre Brambilla, himself leading the King of the Mountains competition by 90 seconds. From Vannes to St Brieuc, the mammoth 140-kilometre *contre-la-montre* took its toll on everyone. For Vietto, who had spent so much energy defending his lead and was accustomed to riding flanked by his team-mates, it was disastrous. He lost 15 minutes to stage winner Raymond Impanis, while Robic finished in second place and moved to third overall behind Brambilla, who had taken over at the top of the general classification. Now Robic was reaping the benefit of being the home rider – parcels and letters of good luck were arriving from friends and family, boosting his morale as Vietto's slumped.

On the final road stage to Paris a series of attacks broke up the peloton – Robic did not get to the front of the race, but moved up through the field sufficiently for Vietto to lose sight of him. Not only had Vietto lost the lead after being ahead for 15 stages but now, just when he thought he had a chance of winning it back, the race was going on without him. Robic and Brambilla battled on, and the elder Frenchman allowed Robic to win on the final stage. The leader of the French national team, Eduoard Fachleitner, winner of the stage from Nice to Marseille, also produced a last-gasp effort, moving up into second place, but still four minutes behind the young Breton.

Before the race started, Robic had kissed goodbye to his new wife,

saying as he left, "I don't have a dowry, but I will offer you first place in the Tour." He did not pull on his first yellow jersey until he stepped up to claim final, overall victory, but he had kept his promise, and the Tour had kept hers.

1948

Ten years after winning his first Tour, Gino Bartali came back in 1948 as the most talked-about participant in the race. His supporters remembered his pre-war glory, but others thought him too old – he was 34, and had just lost the Giro d'Italia to Fiorenzo Magni. The Italian race had many repercussions. Magni had been pushed uphill to keep his *maglia rosa*, the pink jersey worn by the leader of the race. Second-placed Fausto Coppi was not pleased – he had won two stages, and was poised to take over the race lead. Organizers handed Magni a two-minute time penalty, but Coppi and his team withdrew from the race in disgust.

Bartali was not only sparring with Magni – his relationship with Coppi was as cool as ever. Their personalities drove their approach to the sport: devoutly Catholic Bartali kept a statue of the Virgin Mary by his bedside and trained the old-fashioned way – miles, and many of them. Coppi employed more "progressive" techniques. He did interval training, took vitamin pills and relied on himself, rather than his religion, for spiritual and moral strength. As the start of the Tour drew closer, the tension between the two – amplified by the Press to the limits of reason – reached new levels. Having mutually accused each other of destroying one another's chances in previous Tours, Coppi refused to compete in the French race, leaving Bartali to shoulder the responsibility of being sole Italian favourite. He wasted no time in proving that he had been the right choice.

Bartali won the first stage and took the yellow jersey. He attacked again the next day; at one point the break was six minutes clear, only to

The Tour cavalcade follows Bobet and Bartali to Aix-les-Bains in 1948.

tumble to a halt as the front riders crashed. Bartali was not badly hurt, but was held up for so long that he finished the stage four minutes down on fellow countryman Vincenzo Rossello, while Belgium's Jean Engels took the jersey. The lead changed again on stage six, as young Frenchman Louison Bobet won the stage to Biarritz and took overall control of the race.

BARTALI WITHOUT QUESTION

The race entered the Pyrenees on stage seven and Bartali knew that this was to be his chance. He was more than 20 minutes behind Bobet in the general classification, but he had not forgotten how to climb. Besides, he had something else on his side that day. The stage finished in Lourdes, and he, a devout Catholic who did not even swear when he punctured, had his faith to rely on when his legs seemed too tired to carry him. He won the stage, and the next one, then trounced the entire field in the Alps, winning three stages back to back, his peerless descending and

equally magnificent climbing skills ensuring that he also took the King of the Mountains' prize.

The first set of mountains, and the long, hard haul to the next, were almost too much for Bobet – at 23 he was too emotionally fragile for a race like the Tour. On the verge of quitting after 11 days of racing, he swung to the other extreme 24 hours later, winning the stage to Cannes. Italian national coach Alfredo Binda watched as the hunched-up little man scurried across the mountains in pursuit of the man in the *maillot jaune*. "If I had been his director, he would have won the Tour," said Binda.

There was only one time trial in the 1948 Tour, lasting 160 kilometres from Mulhouse to Strasbourg. Bartoli extended his lead over France's Guy Lapébie by six minutes, although he himself finished 12 minutes down on stage-winner Roger Lambrecht. The final four stages saw Bartoli win a seventh stage, but lose a little of his overall advantage as Belgian team leader Brik Schotte, winner of the final stage to Paris in 1947, moved up into second place.

Bartali reached the Parc des Princes with more than 16 minutes over Schotte. He had ridden almost 5,000 kilometres, not just through France, but also into Italy, Luxembourg, Belgium and Switzerland, and he would have to wait until next year to take on his greatest rival, Fausto Coppi, on the French stage.

1949

In 1949 Alfredo Binda performed a feat of great diplomacy by getting both Gino Bartali and Fausto Coppi to the start line of the Tour de France as team-mates. As defending champion and Italian team leader, Bartali took precedence, while Coppi was obliged to make his Tour debut as a second to his rival.

After four stages the pair were inseparable in equal 18th place, a quarter of an hour behind early leader Jacques Marinelli, who was rapidly making a name for himself

after wresting the jersey from Belgium's Norbert Callens. When the 19-year-old Parisian got into a break with Coppi on stage five, the race exploded. The group of seven men were six minutes clear and, with a man like Coppi among them, it should have been the defining move of the race. If Marinelli could hold his place in the line – which he seemed to be doing admirably – he would be sure of keeping the *maillot jaune* and moving up to the inner circle of overall contenders.

But the fans on the roadside knew it, too, and were delirious at the prospect of seeing their hero ride past at the *tête de la course* with the great Coppi on his wheel. A spectator stepped out just as they approached, knocking Martinelli to the ground and leaving Coppi nothing to do but follow. The yellow jersey jumped up and rode away, but Coppi was left with a mangled bike, surrounded by horrified fans. When the bunch came by Bartali stopped and waited with him as he changed to a replacement bike from the second team car – he had refused the spare on top of the car that had been following the break – and the two set off in pursuit of the bunch.

Coppi had stood helpless for seven minutes, fuming that Binda,

Fausto Coppi dominated the Tour at his first attempt in 1949, taking control in the Pyrenees.

who had been driving the car with his spare bike, had stayed behind with Bartali, rather than behind him in the break. His rhythm deserted him, and finally Bartali – conscious that at least one Italian had to be in contention before the mountain stages – had to leave him behind as his speed dwindled. While the defending champion lost five minutes on the stage, Coppi lost 18, and found himself 36 minutes behind Marinelli. Binda's diplomatic skills were fully needed again to persuade Coppi to start the next day's stage.

A SMALL STEP FOR COPPI...

The first time trial of the race was a turning point for the Italian. He won the stage, reclaiming eight minutes. In any other circumstances it would have been a huge margin, but from where Coppi stood it was just the first step to recovery. He would have to produce a spectacular effort in the mountains if he were to stand any chance of winning the race.

Fortunately, Coppi was pretty adept at the spectacular. On stage 11, a 190-kilometre slog across the Aubisque, the Soulor, the Tourmalet, the Aspin and the Peyresourde, he broke away with 1947-winner Jean Robic and another Frenchman, Lucien Lazarides. He slashed his

deficit to 14 minutes, and would have won the stage had he not punctured twice.

Coppi felt that he was back on terms with the leaders now, and knew that he must wait until the Alps before attacking again. On the first Alpine stage he broke away with Bartali and led him over the revered Col d'Izoard. Bartali was clearly not as strong as his companion, but Coppi was so confident in his own abilities that he eased up for him.

Thanks to the earlier incident Bartali was, for the time being at least, better-placed than Coppi, and took the jersey that afternoon. It was his 35th birthday, and Coppi presented him not only with the race leadership, but also the stage victory. But the younger Italian knew there were greater rewards waiting ahead for him in Paris.

The two men went away again on stage 17, and this time Coppi was riding only for himself. He paid no heed when Bartali punctured, but rode on alone all the way to the finish in Aoste, Switzerland, taking the *maillot jaune*. There was one more day of first-category mountains, and Bartali was obliged to ride in support of the new race leader – taking a time bonus for being first over the summit of the Great St Bernard Pass was the furthest he was permitted to stray.

Most of the peloton was grateful for the let-up: Rik Van Steenbergen, Coppi's nemesis in the one-day Classics, but an also-ran in the mountains, broke his rear brake, burst his tyre and crashed on the descent of the Vue des Alpes.

Team-mate and world champion Brik Schotte helped him replace his tyre, tied his brake cable to the handle bars, and then led him down the mountain hairpins at 75 kph with blood seeping through his hair and only one brake working.

In the end though, Coppi won the final time trial by a clear seven minutes, while Van Steenbergen – now with a fully functioning bike – snuck through the field to win the sprint for the last stage victory of the race on the Parc des Princes track. It was a reversal of fortunes, a miniature version of Coppi's triumph. The Italian had become the first man in history to win the tours of Italy and France together in the same year, and was nicknamed "campionissimo", the champion of champions, by all his fans back home.

Bartali's second place confirmed Alfredo Binda's long-held belief that he had the best two riders in the world in his team.

1950

Fausto Coppi had finally won his first Tour de France aged 29. He had waited until then to ride the race, fearful of the impact that such an arduous event would have on his health if he attempted to compete under-prepared.

His lean limbs were powerful, but they were prone to damage. His bones broke easily, and a crash at the 1950 Giro left him with a fractured pelvis and no chance of defending his Tour de France title. Gino Bartali took full control of the Italian team, while the French were led by Louison Bobet and the Swiss by Ferdi Kubler and Tour of Italy winner Hugo Koblet.

Above: The peloton seeks relief from the pressures of the Tour during the stage from Toulon to Menton, 1950. Below: Orson Welles helps start the Tour in Paris.

KUBLER'S DOING FINE

The race was officially started by Orson Welles – as riders became celebrities in their own right, stars from other fields found the Tour to be an attractive proposition too. The peloton made its way without incident through northeast France, through the corner of Belgium and down to Dinard, the venue of the first time trial. The 80-kilometre *contre-la-montre* was won by Ferdi Kubler, who finished 17 seconds ahead of Italian Fiorenzo Magni, only to have 15 seconds of his advantage snatched back by officials incensed that he was not wearing a regulation wool jersey. In addition to the time penalty, he was fined 1,000 French francs for wearing a silk jersey that he had chosen to make his upper body as aerodynamic as possible for the stage. He got into more trouble the next day, turning up late for the start and being fined another 100 francs, and suffered a further fine for taking an unsolicited push on the first mountain stage.

Bartali meanwhile was some 17 minutes in arrears in the general classification, confident that he and the Italian team would soon make up the difference in the mountains. He

too was being penalized for various indiscretions – multiple fines for lateness, and 500 francs for not completing the final lap of the track on stage 10. But he had much more to worry about the following day.

ITALIAN WALK-OUT

The first Pyrenean stage took the riders over the Col d'Aspin. Everyone who wanted to be in the race stuck with Bartali as he and Jean Robic led the group toward the summit. Forty metres from the King of the Mountains' *prime*, a French photographer stepped out to capture an image of the two former winners climb side by side to the peak. As he did so, he blocked their path; the two men were already using all their strength to maintain their rhythm, and could not steer away from him. The three tumbled into a heap, and onlookers began to jeer at Bartali. One even hit him as he scrambled back to his feet. Angry and insulted he flew down the mountain, catching the group and, still in a blind rage, outsprinted all eight of his companions to win the stage. Fellow breakaway Fiorenzo Magni

took the yellow jersey, but he never got to wear it. Still hardly able to believe what had happened, Bartali and the two Italian teams withdrew from the race. It was hard on Magni – constantly overshadowed by Coppi and Bartali – but he said nothing and walked away with his team leader, abandoning just when his own chances were at their strongest.

There was a little light relief as the race made its way along the Mediterranean coast. The Italians' withdrawal had left the peloton uncomfortable and unwilling to race; as they soft-pedalled along the seaside someone suggested going for a dip. Before the organizers knew what was happening, the entire Tour de France had dropped its bikes and was wading into the water. They had barely got knee-deep before a fuming official ordered them back on to the road to get on with the job in hand.

Switzerland's Ferdi Kubler took the *maillot jaune* the day after Bartali left the race and, despite two punctures and a lead of only 49 seconds over Bobet, he held it to the foot of the Alps, even winning a flat stage and taking a useful time bonus

Louison Bobet toils uphill on his way to winning stage 18, Gap to Briançon, in 1950.

as Bobet fell back. Only three of his team-mates were left in the race, while the French had many men to support Robic and Bobet. But Kubler's lead was sufficient for his two French rivals to have to attack alone to deprive him of the yellow jersey. Only Belgium's Stan Ockers was close enough – two minutes back – to hold a little in reserve.

SMALL HOPE FOR BOBET

The trio played a waiting game on the first Alpine stage. Robic sprinted for the *prime* at the top of the Cayolle Pass, but immediately sat up. Kubler just watched – for a rider with a reputation for being emotional and hot-headed, he was playing it remarkably cool.

Bobet knew time was running out. He didn't waste his energy on showy little sprints, but attacked near the summit of the Col de Vars with the full intention of staying away. He had a 37-second lead at the peak, and a puncture on the descent did little to damage it. As he raced to the next *col*, the Izoard, a storm started. Thunder echoed in the valleys as Bobet began the longest of the day's climbs. He was only a minute ahead at the 2,700-metre summit, but Kubler knew by then that, even if Bobet won the stage, he could not make up his 11-minute deficit. So the Frenchman careered down the pass, through the torrent of rainwater and loose gravel, making up another three minutes before he reached the line at Briançon. He would have to do it all again if he were to come within touching distance of the *maillot jaune*.

The next day Apo Lazarides broke away with regional team rider Marcel Dussault in search of some glory before the mountains ended. The pair held their lead over the Lauteret, but as they climbed toward St Niziers the real racing started behind them. Bobet attacked, as he had to, and caught the two Frenchmen, knowing that they would be only too happy to aid him in his escape. The fans were ecstatic.

Lazarides started to weaken first. Bobet had no time to carry another rider, and left him to drift back to the chasers. Kubler's group paid little attention as he joined them briefly; their pace was even faster than Bobet's, and Lazarides was soon abandoned to his fate for a second time. Kubler would not tolerate any easing off. He moved to the front whenever he felt the speed dropping. With the help of Stan Ockers and his *domestique* Raymond Impanis he caught a shattered Bobet on the final climb. The Frenchman would be King of the Mountains, but he would not win the Tour. Bobet and Kubler rode to Paris together in their respective jerseys.

1951

There were two pairs of riders vying for the hearts of their nation's supporters in the late 1950s. Coppi versus Bartali was taken as read. Meanwhile Ferdi Kubler and Hugo Koblet were emerging with equally intriguing rivalry.

DOUBLING UP FOR THE TOUR

Much like the Italian duo, Kubler and Koblet were cast as opposites. Kubler was considered the dark, strong man of the Swiss soil with Koblet the manicured urbanite, always riding with a comb in his back pocket. They were both equally prone to moments of absolute brilliance on a bike. When Kubler did not defend his Tour title, Koblet took over the leadership of the Swiss team with gusto.

Koblet had won the 1950 tours of Italy and Switzerland and now he had his sights on the biggest prize in the sport. He opened his account at the first time trial, winning the stage, with Louison Bobet, Coppi and Fiorenzo Magni coming in behind him. The four were still several minutes behind the yellow jersey – currently residing with Roger Leveque – but, with the Massif Central and two mountain ranges to negotiate, they were rather reticent about showing themselves too near the head of the general classification. Their relative performances were all that mattered.

It was Raphaël Geminiani who moved first on the opening mountain stage. He finished a minute up on the main contenders. Koblet punctured twice but had no trouble getting back to the group. The next day was equally slow: Koblet, Magni and Bobet were waiting and watching as Coppi concerned himself with more human desires, persuading the organizers to bend the "men only" policy in the tour caravan so that he could see his wife.

When Koblet attacked, he did it as he did everything, with style. He rode alone at the head of the race for 140 kilometres, winning the stage and moving into second place overall. The next day a group escaped, and the yellow-jersey favourites thought so little of them that they were allowed to gain an incredible 18 minutes over rolling terrain. Barrel-chested Wim Van Est became the first Dutchman to wear the yellow jersey in the race's history, a tremendous achievement that kept his team celebrating late into the night. Near tragedy struck the next day.

HOISTED TO SAFETY

Of course Van Est would never keep the jersey – he knew that and so did the rest of the peloton. He crept his way up the Col d'Aubisque, already tired from the climb of the Tourmalet, then, on the first

Above: Wim Van Est is rescued from a near-fatal crash off the side of the road in 1951. Below: The ever-stylish Hugo Koblet gets ready for stage 16 of the 1951 Tour.

hairpin of the descent he slipped on a rock-strewn corner and fell over the side of the pass. He fell 20 metres, rolling down the slope until he hit a ledge. That was lucky for him: the drop was 200 metres.

The race leader lay dazed on the tiny outcrop, riders streaming by above him, not realizing that the yellow jersey was stuck down the mountainside. Spectators made a rope from inner tubes and lowered it down to him, hauling him back up to a waiting ambulance. Half the field did not even know what had happened until they got to Tarbes – they had assumed he was still out on the road.

It had been an entertaining and, at times, terrifying few days. But now it was time for the serious business to resume. Koblet and Coppi escaped together on the second Pyrenean stage; the Italian led over the Aspin and the Peyresourde, but was unable to lose his companion. Koblet jumped him for the stage win, finally taking the yellow jersey, while Coppi moved into fifth place.

COPPI ABANDONS

The flat stage between the two sets of mountains should have been a time for the leaders to reflect on the race so far, allowing someone else to take the limelight, if only for a day. Algerian Abdel Kader Zaaf, riding his third Tour, and still hoping to finish for the first time, escaped early on. While he posed no great threat in himself, the men who chased him down definitely did.

First Geminiani, then Lucien Lazarides, and eventually Koblet moved across. Coppi went to follow, but as he came to within 30 seconds of the group he suddenly slowed, gripped by violent illness and vomiting on the road side. Bartali and Magni caught up with him, and chaperoned him to the stage finish, losing half an hour while Koblet won another stage.

Bobet won the stage over the Mont Ventoux, leaving his Swiss rival to take a 90-second lead into the Alps. Second-placed Geminiani had the stronger team behind him

and Coppi was no longer a threat. The Italian's brother Serse had been killed in a road race just weeks before the Tour, and Coppi was in no fit state to be riding any race, let alone the hardest event on the calendar. Unable to express his turmoil, he did what he knew best and rode away from the peloton on the hardest stage of the race, cresting the Col de Vars and the Izoard alone.

He won the stage, while Koblet finished third. Coppi took deserved plaudits for his courage, Koblet another nine minutes from Geminiani.

Koblet won the final time trial by more than four minutes. Few riders have ever made the Tour look easier. This time, he had maintained his languid style throughout the three weeks, seeming to ride effortlessly up any gradient, a picture of elegance at all times.

Coppi, equally debonair but crushed by his brother's death and his own illness, just could not compete on equal terms. Despite the outward insouciance, Koblet had ridden the best race of his life and, even if Coppi had been at the peak of his powers, he would have been hard pushed to better him.

Not a hair out of place: Hugo Koblet is proud victor of the 1951 Tour.

1952

Fausto Coppi returned to the Tour in 1952 with a clear head. Gino Bartali was there too – at 38 years old he was determined to carry on racing, as if to make up for the years he had lost to the war. Coppi himself was no longer a young man, but at 33 he was in the form of his life; his pedalling was absolutely fluid, his long limbs more powerful than ever. The entire peloton would have to ride as one if they were to tackle the Italian team successfully.

Rik Van Steenbergen, Coppi's old foe, took the yellow jersey on the opening stage, easily outsprinting two other riders and gaining seven minutes on the main bunch. His winning move set the tone for the following stages: small groups would break away on the long, flat roads of northern France and into Belgium as the Italians sat back. It was not until the fifth day that Coppi even hinted at his intentions. He finished second on the stage to Jean Dierderich, moving up into fifth place overall as the field was strung out behind him and the Luxembourg rider on the road to Namur.

Another Italian took centre stage the next day: Fiorenzo Magni made a solo break that won him more than five minutes over the field, and put him into the yellow jersey by 12 seconds. He lost it back to Frenchman Nello Lauredi in the time trial as Coppi moved ominously closer, winning the *contre-la-montre*. Magni was ready to ride for Coppi only once he had exhausted all his own possibilities, and they were not yet finished. He attacked again, winning a further stage and regaining the jersey, again only for a single day, as it passed to team-mate Andrea Carrea 24 hours later. The Italians were having a great race, and Coppi hadn't even made a serious attack yet.

It was 12 years since Coppi had first won the tour of Italy; and he was well-versed in the methods of three-week racing. He may have only ridden the Tour twice before, but he knew exactly how to go about the business of winning. On the

first mountain stage in the Alps, a group stayed together until the foot of the final climb, Alpe d'Huez. As they approached the first hairpin, a rejuvenated Jean Robic attacked, taking only Coppi with him. The pair rode shoulder to shoulder for 10 kilometres before Coppi made his move. He accelerated inexorably, opening up a gap between himself and the Frenchman without breaking his rhythm. In the final eight kilometres of the climb he gained 80 seconds, taking the race lead, with his compatriots Carrea and Magni falling in behind, second and third, shutting down the race for anyone but the Italians.

ALL DOUBTS ELIMINATED

The three Italians were reduced to just one the next day. Over the Cols de la Croix de Fer, du Galibier, Mont Genèvre and then up to the Col du Sestriere, Coppi flew away to a seven-minute stage win, and a lead in the general classification of 20 minutes. He could easily afford a day off now, and as the race headed to the Monaco coast he was happy to let an unknown Dutchman, Jan Nolten, run away with the stage victory. It was Nolten's second-ever professional race – he had only renounced his amateur status partway through the season – and it proved a spectacular diversion to Coppi's crushing dominance.

Oppressive heat became the main factor in the race for the intermediate stages – when two riders escaped on stage 15, the peloton was so stultified by the temperatures that it left them to reach Perpignan 24 minutes in front; Coppi was in such a strong position that many of his would-be rivals were too discouraged to even think about taking him on.

Into the Pyrenees, and Coppi rode steadily, watching over Stan Ockers, the man closest to him. They were both quick to respond when Jean Dotto broke away, and led their select group past the Frenchman on the Peyresourde. Once the group – which also included Raphaël Geminiani, Jean Robic and Spain's Antonio Gelabert – were safely over the summit, Geminiani was allowed the freedom to attack on the descent. He had trailed Coppi over the peak, but now he dropped so fast that no one followed. Geminiani rode solo up the Col d'Aspin, weaving through a packed crowd of delighted French fans and finishing the stage a minute ahead of the group on the far side.

Stage 18 encapsulated the Tour of 1952. Fausto Coppi led over every peak, the Tourmalet, the Aubisque, and to the finish line in Pau. The time gaps between the *maillot jaune* and his hapless pursuers were never huge – he didn't need them to be – but it was clear that this was only because Coppi didn't want to spend the entire day alone, ahead of the field. After each perfectly executed climb he would slow and allow the rest to regroup around him. Having dropped everyone on the Tourmalet, Coppi was descending at such a leisurely pace that he had time for a sandwich, a banana and some coffee before Ockers caught up with him. He could not afford to be so laissez-faire on the final run in to Pau – visibility was down to 25 metres, and the wet, gravel-strewn roads claimed several victims. Coppi had almost a minute's lead halfway down the

descent, but he sat up again, waiting for Robic, Ockers, Gilbert Bauvin and Bernardo Ruiz to join him. Then, with 350 metres to go, he attacked again, winning the stage by three seconds and taking another time bonus.

BEST OF THE REST

There was no doubt as to who would win the Tour now. In an effort to generate some excitement in the final part of the race, the organizers increased the prizes for second and third place, hoping to stimulate Ockers, Ruiz, Bartali and Robic into action. With one more summit finish, at the Puy du Dome, and a time trial still to be ridden, there were at least the minor podium placings to be fought for. Geminiani, who had finished second to Koblet the year before, but was in no danger of getting near the top three this time round, attacked first. Bartali followed him – his team-mate's lead was so solid that he was freed from protective duties. A group of five men had a 90-second advantage as the final 15-kilometre climb came into view; Bartali was struggling to maintain contact as Geminiani forced the pace. Suddenly Coppi shot out of the second group, and

Above: Emotions spill over for Fausto Coppi after retaining the yellow jersey to Paris in 1952. Below: Coppi savouring his victory lap in Paris.

fairly sprinted past them, winning the stage by 10 seconds, taking another time bonus, and leaving Jean Robic scrambling for second place and few more seconds to take him closer to Stan Ockers.

Coppi cruised through the final time trial, finishing 14th on the stage. He reached Paris with more than 28 minutes over Ockers, the biggest race-winning margin of post-war history. He had settled his scores with Bartali for good now – the era of Italian domination ended with "Gino the Pious" accepting his role as supporter of the *campionissimo*. Coppi's career had been interrupted not only by the Second World War – he was taken as a prisoner of war in Tunisia by the British Army – but also by the death of his brother and many injuries to his own fragile bones. Spindly-legged and ungainly off the bike, in just three Tours he had shown himself to be one of the best riders of all time. A year later he left his wife for his lover, scandalizing Italy, and deepening the divide between himself and Bartali. He was a legend in his own lifetime, and his early death – at 40, from malaria caught while on a hunting trip in Africa – only served to heighten his mythical status.

Tour Legends
Fausto Coppi

"He climbs like artists paint water colours, without any apparent extra effort. It's a mystery because when all is said and done Coppi has only two legs, two lungs, one heart, just like all the other Tour contestants." André Leducq

Left: Celebrating at the finish in Paris, 1952. Main Picture: Artist on a bicycle: Coppi during stage 11, Pau–Luchon, 1949.

FAUSTO COPPI (ITA)
b. 15/9/19 Castellania; d. 2/1/60

THREE PARTICIPATIONS
TWO VICTORIES
NINE STAGE WINS

1949 FIRST OVERALL
THREE STAGE WINS: stage 7, Les Sables–La Rochelle (time trial); stage 17, Briançon–Aoste; stage 20, Colmar–Nancy (time trial)

1951 10TH OVERALL
ONE STAGE WIN: stage 20, Gap–Briançon

1952 FIRST OVERALL
KING OF THE MOUNTAINS
FIVE STAGE WINS: stage 7, Metz–Nancy (time trial); stage 10, Lausanne–L'Alpe d'Huez; stage 11, Bourg d'Oisans–Sestriere; stage 18, Bagnères-de-Bigorre–Pau; stage 21, Limoges–Puy-de-Dôme

Tour Legends
Gino Bartali

"From snowstorm, water, ice, Bartali rose majestically like an angel covered in mud, wearing under his soaked tunic the precious soul of a champion. It took this day of apocalypse to show his quality." Jacques Goddet, after a tough day's ride, 1948

Main Picture: On stage 14 Briançon–Aix-les-Bains, Bartali wins the stage, 5-53 ahead of nearest rival, Belgian Stan Ockers. Right: Stage 14 in 1938 and Bartali wins, 5-51 ahead of team-mate Mario Vicini.

GINO BARTALI (ITA)
b. 18/7/14 Ripoli; d. 6/6/2000

EIGHT PARTICIPATIONS
TWO VICTORIES
12 STAGE WINS

1937 DID NOT FINISH
ONE STAGE WIN: stage 7, Aix-les-Bains–Grenoble

1938 FIRST OVERALL
FIRST KING OF THE MOUNTAINS
TWO STAGE WINS: stage 11, Montpellier–Marseille; stage 14, Digne–Briançon

1948 FIRST OVERALL
FIRST KING OF THE MOUNTAINS
SEVEN STAGE WINS: stage 1, Paris–Trouville; stage 7, Biarritz–Lourdes; stage 8, Lourdes–Toulouse; stage 13, Cannes–Briançon; stage 14, Briançon–Aix-les-Bains; stage 15, Aix-les-Bains–Lausanne; stage 19, Metz–Liège

1949 SECOND OVERALL
ONE STAGE WIN: stage 16, Cannes–Briançon

1950 DID NOT FINISH
ONE STAGE WIN: stage 11, Pau–Saint-Gaudens

1951 FOURTH OVERALL

1952 FOURTH OVERALL

1953 11TH OVERALL

The Making of a New French Hero

By the 1950s, the French public were in need of a hero to call their own. It would be difficult to find a rider of Coppi's stature, but there had to be someone to reclaim the Tour. The man to come forward was Louison Bobet – a Breton who first became a Tour winner, then a Tour great and, finally, a Tour legend as the first man to win the event three times in succession.

1953

There was no Fausto Coppi in the 1953 Tour de France. The defending champion had clashed with his Italian team management, giving them an ultimatum: either I ride, or Bartali does, but not both. They eventually chose Bartali but, while team decisions might have been in their hands, the race was no longer theirs for the taking.

Victor in 1951, Hugo Koblet stepped up to take on the role of favourite, attacking 20 kilometres into the opening stage, but it didn't last. Having made such an early effort, he missed the stage-winning move and finished 11 minutes down with the main bunch, while fellow Swiss Fritz Schaer won the jersey. Schaer went on to take the second day's race too, and held his lead as the Tour traversed the cobbles of northwest France and into Belgium.

Having shown how intent he was on winning the race again, Koblet was given no freedom, particularly as there were plenty of other riders who thought this could be their chance to succeed Coppi as winner. As the race headed toward the mountains, it was the flatlanders, the Dutchmen, who took advantage of the terrain, infiltrating breaks, winning stages and working their way into the top of the general classification. They eventually wrested the *maillot jaune* from Schaer on stage five. The Swiss rider got it back four days later when the man who had taken it from him, Roger Hassenforder, fell sick and could not hold the pace. Schaer was back in the lead just in time to ride into the Pyrenees.

By then Koblet was 12 minutes down overall. It was a sufficiently large deficit to prevent him taking over the race lead that afternoon, but he should at least have been able to move up in the standings and see who was coming with him. But Koblet had lost the fluidity that he had displayed in discarding Fausto Coppi four years earlier. Jesus Lerono escaped on the Aubisque, forcing Koblet to his limit just to stay in touch with the chasing group. He was

physically and mentally exhausted and, just one mountain into the Tour, he lost his nerve. On his descent from the Aubisque he took his feet out of his toe clips, as if pre-empting a fall. Fighting his bike on the way down, it became inevitable that he would crash and, when he did, he broke three ribs and hit his head hard on the ground, ending his race lying on the roadside.

Above: Hugo Koblet struggles to keep Jesus Lorono within reach on the Aubisque, 1953. Below: Jean Robic looks a beaten man after crashing out. Previous page: Louison Bobet with his arm round Charly Gaul (left) in 1955.

SOMEONE TO LOOK UP TO

Now no one had any idea where to look for a likely winner, so the task of leading the way fell to a man who knew how to win the Tour —1947 victor Jean Robic, the last Frenchman to have won. A nail-biting solo effort saw him cross the Tourmalet, the Aspin and the Peyresourde with no more than two minutes in hand over the field. He eased up on the final 15 kilometres, his nerves unable to withstand the onslaught of another knife-edge descent. Louison Bobet caught up to within a minute of him, while Schaer, who had held on so bravely on the climbs, finished five minutes down. Schaer lost the jersey by just 18 seconds, while the Dutch team fell out of the picture entirely.

Robic was nothing if not experienced. He commanded François Mahe to patrol any early moves and to join in the breaks, but not to work. Mahe did exactly what he was told, joining a 26-man move the next day and sitting in patiently, waiting for the rest of the French team to reel them in. His unquestioning loyalty to his team leader was rewarded several hours later, when the break finished some 20 minutes ahead of the peloton, and he was given the yellow jersey as unsuspecting race leader.

Robic could hardly complain about the way in which he'd lost the jersey. His luck had simply run out. He crashed and lost 30 minutes the next day and, although he was fit enough to complete the stage, he was so disheartened that he retired from the race.

Another Frenchman, Jean Mallejac, riding for the West France regional team, took over the *maillot jaune* the day Robic crashed. He was as unlikely to win the Tour as previous jersey-wearer Schaer and, with the Alps yet to come, the race was still wide open.

Riders and managers spent the official rest day in Monaco plotting their Alpine campaigns. The French national squad took the most straightforward option: they would send their team captain, Bobet, to attack on the hardest stage of the entire race. If he could win there, the Tour would be his. A group of three hopeful riders made a break within the first kilometre of the stage; Bobet and the other real contenders waited until the Col de Vars. Bobet made his move on the steepest section of the climb, with the yellow jersey and the others in close pursuit. King of the Mountains, Lerono, went with him over the summit. Then, satisfied that he had collected some more climbing points, he let Bobet escape on the descent.

Bobet caught and passed the long-time breakaways at the foot of the Izoard, and crossed its peak almost nine minutes clear. Despite a puncture during the final minutes of the descent, his victory was secure; the stage, the jersey, and the race belonged to him. He rode – and won – the final time trial with the same wide grin that he had pulled when he had worn the yellow jersey for the first time.

While Bobet carried on to the Parc des Princes to complete his lap of honour, a very old man was pedalling his way gingerly around the finishing circuit. Eighty-three-year-old Maurice Garin, victor of the first ever Tour de France, led the parade of past winners as they welcomed the new hero home. After so many years without success, what better time for France to win the Tour than during the race's 50th anniversary?

1954

French riders made up more than half the field in the 1954 Tour de France. With Bobet leading the national team, and five other regional squads also competing, some believed that the defending champion's chances of retaining his title were mainly down to his numerical advantage over Switzerland's two contestants, Ferdi Kubler and Hugo Koblet. And there was no Italian team: after a controversial Tour of Italy – where Fausto Coppi and the favourites had been admonished for not racing but allowing the *domestiques* to take stage win after stage win unhindered – the Tour de France organizers simply refused to invite anyone from the peninsula to compete in their race. While the Tour started, Coppi went out training with his team. He was hit as a wheel flew off a passing truck, knocking him to the ground and fracturing his skull. He did not ride again that year.

At the Tour itself, Koblet seized the initiative as he had done the previous year. His attack – the first of the race – split the field, and resulted in little more than a dozen men finishing nine minutes ahead of the others. Koblet did not actually take the jersey, but found himself in a commanding position, pulling back breaks and controlling the pace of the bunch for the subsequent stages.

Koblet's and Kubler's squad won the 10-kilometre team time trial, but second place for France was enough to put Bobet into yellow. He held on to it for three days while the two Swiss riders, aided by their strong team, attacked him from every direction. Koblet moved up into second place, a tribute to manager Alex Burtin, who had convinced the two men that, for the beginning of the race at least, they must work together to beat Bobet and save their own rivalry until there were no external

Christiane Bobet steps out of the crowd to cheer on her husband during the final time trial in 1953.

threats. But when Bobet did lose the jersey, it was not to either Swiss —it was to Holland's Wout Wagtmans.

On the eve of the race's entry into the Pyrenees most riders were hoping that someone unknown would move to the front and make a bid for a stage win, which would enable the rest to complete the day's ride at a steady pace. But Koblet did not allow anyone to ride easy. He crashed early on, losing more than four minutes on the peloton.

There was no sympathy from the bunch – Bobet and Wagtmans jumped away, pulling a group of 20 clear. The Swiss team rode in pursuit of them for 50 kilometres and, when his prey finally came in sight, Koblet launched himself off the front of the chasing group, catching Bobet and saving his position in the general classification. It had been the hardest day of the race, and they had not yet reached the mountains.

BAHAMONTÈS TAKES WING

Still bruised and cut from his fall, Koblet's legs inevitably stiffened up the night after his crash. He lost four minutes to Federico Bahamontès as he raced over the summit of the Aubisque, with the overall leaders only a minute behind him. In his desperation to catch up with Bobet, Koblet crashed twice on the descent, but still managed to reduce his final deficit to a little under two minutes. He was riding on courage, however, and that alone would not be enough to get him through the Pyrenees.

Stage 12 took the peloton over the Tourmalet, the Aspin and the Peyresourde. Again, it was Bahamontès who crossed the first peak at the front, displaying climbing skills that would make his reputation. Bobet was third, but Koblet had lost almost 20 minutes on the first of the three climbs. Kubler, his team-mate, was faring better, three places down on the *maillot jaune*, but he too slipped back on the next mountain.

It appeared that by now Koblet had lost his taste for descending. Unwilling to risk yet another crash, he eased himself down the slopes of the Aspin. In contrast, a puncture cost Bobet a minute, but physically he was still strong. In the end, he finished fourth on the stage, losing the jersey to Gilbert Bauvin, while Kubler lost seven minutes, and Koblet almost 30.

Koblet wanted to continue the Tour, to help Kubler now that he could no longer threaten Bobet himself, but his body could not cope. He retired after struggling through 90 kilometres of the next stage, injured, fatigued and mentally exhausted.

Bobet reclaimed the jersey two days later, when Bauvin punctured. His team-mates from the Northeast France regional team waited to assist him, but they were not fast enough to bring him back to the bunch, and the local hero was forced to chase alone. He was no match for the peloton in full flight.

Then, after two weeks of hard-fought racing, the peloton decided to sit up *en masse*. They toured along at 30 kph for the entire stage, seeking relief from the destructively high pace that had been set for the best part of the race.

Enough damage was still to come in the Alps – and most of it from Federico Bahamontès.

The Spaniard went to work from the gun, going clear before the first, third-category climb, and leading his breakaway riders to the finish without ever being in danger of Bobet's group catching them.

The biggest loser was Bauvin – he trailed in 20 minutes down, and sank without trace from his second

Huge crowds on the Col du Tourmalet urge Federico Bahamontès upwards during his solo ascent and subsequent victory on stage 12, 1954.

1955

Baker-turned-national-hero Louison Bobet made a promising start to his campaign for a third consecutive Tour win. No rider in history had achieved such a feat, and there were countless men ready and willing to stand in his way.

But despite the best efforts of the Italians and the Dutch team – Wout Wagtmans had taken the race lead on day one – Bobet still won stage two. Over the fearsome cobbles from Roubaix to Namur he pressurized the bunch unrelentingly, forging a break and then shattering it as he accelerated at the slightest let-up. He outsprinted Wagtmans and the remaining riders, sending a clear signal that he was more ready than ever to defend his title.

Meanwhile an arch-rival from 1954, Switzerland's Ferdi Kubler, was after his own bit of glory. The oldest man in the race, he wanted to win the stage to Zurich. He orchestrated the break and kept its momentum all the way to the Swiss finish with an average speed of 43 kph. But his age told in the sprint. He was beaten by French champion André Darrigade. Bobet rolled in with the bunch six minutes later – he had much ground to make up in the first set of mountains.

With one magnificent ride in the Alps, a new rider established himself as a Tour contender. Charly Gaul escaped on the Col des Aravis and, before the peloton realized what was happening, he was at the top of the Telegraphe and five minutes clear. He dropped the only man who had gone with him, Jan Nolten, and made up another 10 minutes on the Galibier. A belated effort from the bunch, combined with a fairly understandable slowing by the Luxembourger as he dropped down to the finish in Briançon, cut his lead by two minutes, but his epic ride put him in third place overall, ahead of Bobet and Wagtmans.

If Gaul was unsure how he would fare in the overall classification, he was certain that he could win in the mountains. He was first to top the Col de Vars the next day, and even when Bobet made up lost ground after puncturing Gaul was not afraid to try again. He led over the Col de Cayolle, but crashed on the descent after taking too many risks on the rain-soaked hairpins. Meanwhile Raphaël Geminiani who, at 25 minutes down, had been all but lost on the first climb, had somehow recouped his position. In the second half of the 200-kilometre stage he reversed his fortunes, by catching the leaders and passing them on the final

place on the general classification.

So the defending champion had a lead of 10 minutes, but he had not won a stage and still looked beatable. There was a matter of honour to settle in these mountains.

Bobet rode close to Bahamontès over the steep Col de Laffrey as well as the Bayard, and reached the foot of the Izoard with only the Spaniard and Kubler, his remaining rival, for company.

Five kilometres from the summit, when all that Bobet needed in order to win the Tour was to defend, he made the decision to attack. Through dust clouds and blinding sunlight on the unmade roads 2,500 metres above sea level, he drove onward and managed to gain a little time – two minutes – a stage win, and a new sense of pride in being the Tour leader.

There were two relatively quiet days before the final time trial. Bobet had won the Tour, but to be regarded as a great, rather than just a good rider, there was one more thing for him to do. In the 72-kilometre *contre-la-montre* he distanced Kubler by a further two and a half minutes, winning the stage and a place in the French public's heart as the nation's greatest-ever post-war rider.

Above: Bobet on the way to victory on stage 18 to Briançon in 1954. Below: Charly Gaul crosses the line in Briançon to win stage 8 of the 1995 Tour and join the ranks of the Tour greats.

for a wheel change and lost a minute. Gaul won the stage but Bobet's ride was enough to earn him the yellow jersey that he'd coveted for 17 days.

Bobet and Gaul had the lead in the classifications they wanted now – the overall and the climbing competition respectively. They rode the final mountain stage at the front, along with Geminiani and Belgium's Brankart, who won the sprint finish. There were two days of processional riding as the peloton made its way back toward Paris. Brankart took another stage – the final time trial – to clinch second place and a tired, but exalted, Bobet rode into the history books as the first man to win the Tour three times in succession.

1956

Louison Bobet's three glorious years had rekindled France's love of the Tour, and there was nationwide dismay when he pulled out in 1956 because of an operation. This year the race was going to be different.

Both the Tourmalet and the Galibier, two of the greatest climbs, were missed out and, reluctant to close main thoroughfares for the race, the French Ministry of the Interior pressurized organizers into routing the Tour along secondary roads wherever possible. In the event, the ever-increasing publicity caravan struggled to get through the narrow roads without causing traffic jams, and riders were plagued by punctures on the poorly surfaced roads. Whatever else happened, a new face was guaranteed to top the podium at the end of the three weeks.

There was no shortage of men eager to take their chances early on, in the hope that any advantage gained before the mountains could then be defended in the Pyrenees. Organizers upped the ante by increasing the prize funds: a total of £45,000 was to be shared between the stage and overall victors. There was even £20 for the unluckiest rider each day, usually awarded to the person who suffered the worst-timed crash or puncture.

climb to win the stage by two minutes. After two days of heroic mountain escapades, Frenchman Antonin Rolland – who had taken the jersey having won stage two – still held the race lead, with Bobet in third, and Gaul close behind in fourth.

BOBET RIDES INTO HISTORY

One last mountain stage remained before the Tour headed for the Pyrenees – over the Ventoux to Avignon. Gaul had dominated the Alps and Bobet had to do something to prevent the Luxembourg rider from attempting the same trick in the second set of mountains.

He attacked on the Ventoux, gaining more than five minutes on the yellow jersey, and nearly six on Gaul. He crossed the line unable to lift head or hand to salute the crowd, but it had been worthwhile. He was now in second place, with nine minutes over his main rival.

Kubler did not start the next stage – his efforts to complete the Ventoux stage had used up the last of his reserves, and he knew he would be little able to finish within the time cut as the next set of mountains

loomed ahead. He had no taste for riding over the three long stages to the Pyrenees – either in a merciless bid for glory in the break or as an anonymous rider in the bunch. The Italians were not so troubled – the team won its first stage thanks to Alessandro Fantini, and another courtesy of Luciano Pezzi.

Gaul's mountain campaign entered its second phase over the Aspin and the Peyresourde. Persistent rain deterred any action for the first part of the stage but, with the big climbs to come later in the day, this made no difference to the Luxembourger. He made a break on the early part of the Aspin, riding over the climb alone while Bobet trailed in his wake. Then, on the Peyresourde, Bobet made his move, dropping his team-mate Geminiani and holding Gaul within less than two minutes over the second peak. The gap had dropped to 30 seconds when Bobet slow-punctured. Twice he used compressed air to re-inflate the tyre, hoping that he would be able to make it to St Gaudens without stopping for mechanical assistance, but he was forced to stop

Bobet and Gaul share water on stage 18, the last in the mountains, en route to Pau, 1955.

And the tactics worked: the jersey jumped from rider to rider following a succession of attacks. Swiss team captain Fritz Schaer retired after crashing his chest into his handlebars, the highest-profile victim of the manic start to the race.

Charly Gaul was half an hour down on the race leader André Darrigade after just six days' racing. He dismissed the gap as irrelevant, confident that the forthcoming mountains would enable him to come to the fore. In a day that was typical of the 1956 Tour, but that would have been a grave anomaly in any other edition of the race, a break gained 19 minutes over the bunch on stage seven.

The French national team seemed oblivious to the move; they were too busy watching Gaul, Stan Ockers (Belgium) and Pasquale Fornara (Italy) to realize that Roger Walkowiak, a lowly French regional team rider, was far enough ahead to claim the jersey. Walkowiak was a pretty unlikely looking stage racer; at

more than six feet tall and weighing in at 90 kilograms he had to wait at the finish line while officials searched desperately for a yellow jersey that would fit him.

Walkowiak had dropped to seventh place by the eve of the mountains, but Gaul was an hour adrift. Dutchman Gerrit Voorting hung on valiantly to the jersey as the first Pyrenean stage took its toll, but lost it to André Darrigade, the sprinter-turned-roadman who could hold his own in all but the steepest of mountains. And finally Gaul began to show himself, attacking early on stage 12, only for his Luxembourg team-mate Jan Adriaenssens to take over the race lead. On the third day in the mountains Gaul made further huge efforts, but to no avail. His lacklustre performance made for a sombre atmosphere as the teams sat down to eat that evening. "I'm sorry that Gaul is not doing better, because the whole team is sad that I can't make jokes during dinner," said Portugal's Antonio Barbosa.

Above: Surprise winner Roger Walkowiak poses with his wife on arrival in Paris, 1956. Below: Charly Gaul mounts a last-gasp challenge for the _maillot jaune_ on the Croix de la Fer, the final ascent of the Alps.

WALKOWIAK THE WINNER

Back onto the flatlands and the race resumed its breakneck speed. Holland's Wout Wagtmans found himself in yellow following another successful breakaway. He took it into the Alps, knowing that he would be tested severely as the climbers tried to steal it from him. Gaul, Ockers and Bahamontès envisaged a 10-minute winning margin as they set off on stage 16, but despite the Montgenèvre and the pass over Sestriere the persistence of the bunch spoiled their every attempt to break clear. Wagtmans kept the jersey, Walkowiak moved back up to second place, and Gaul was left with one more chance to win the Tour.

The final Alpine stage to Grenoble sealed the result. Bahamontès attacked on the Mont Cenis, with Gaul, Ockers and Walkowiak among those in his wake. The Spaniard descended timidly, and was rejoined by most of the peloton. The race split apart again on the Croix de la Fer, and regrouped on the descent, leaving Gaul one climb to race on. He crested the final summit two minutes clear of Stan Ockers, but the effort left him unable to increase his lead on the 30-kilometre descent to the finish. He moved up from 24th to 17th place, while Walkowiak reclaimed the lead.

A man deemed not good enough for the national team had outsmarted the fallen heroes of the Tour. Walkowiak was forced to defend the _maillot jaune_ all the way to Paris, with Gaul, Bahamontès and the rest hoping that the pressure would destroy him. He lost all but 85 seconds of his lead in the final time trial, and won the race by the smallest margin in history.

The Tour was changing: teams had used radios for the first time to listen as officials in the lead car announced which riders needed mechanical assistance, riders were ditching huge pre-race breakfasts in favour of smaller, more frequent feeds and vitamin tablets. The stages were shorter, faster, more exciting, and there were plenty of new and exciting riders to race on them.

Tour Legends
Louison Bobet

"**In Bobet's eyes, there were no little races or unimportant victories. Every race mattered and he wanted to give his all to his public. Bobet knew only one way to race, whatever the sacrifices.**"

Jacques Anquetil

Left: Bobet arrives in Paris, 1953. Main picture: Eyes on the prize – Bobet collects his musette on stage 13, Albi–Béziers, 1953.

LOUIS "LOUISON" BOBET (FRA)
b. 12/3/25 Saint-Méen-le-Grand;
d. 13/3/83

10 PARTICIPATIONS
THREE VICTORIES
11 STAGE WINS

1947 DID NOT FINISH

1948 FOURTH OVERALL
TWO STAGE WINS: stage 6,
Bordeaux–Biarritz; stage 12, San
Remo–Cannes

1949 DID NOT FINISH

1950 THIRD OVERALL
KING OF THE MOUNTAINS
ONE STAGE WIN: stage 18, Gap–
Briançon

1951 20TH OVERALL
ONE STAGE WIN: stage 17,
Montpellier–Avignon

1953 FIRST OVERALL
TWO STAGE WINS: stage 18,
Gap–Briançon; stage 20, Lyon–Saint-
Etienne (time trial)

1954 FIRST OVERALL
THREE STAGE WINS: stage 2,
Beveren–Lille; stage 18, Grenoble–
Briançon; stage 21 part 2, Epinal–
Nancy (time trial)

1955 FIRST OVERALL
TWO STAGE WINS: stage 3, Roubaix–
Namur; stage 11, Marseille–Avignon

1958 SEVENTH OVERALL

1959 DID NOT FINISH

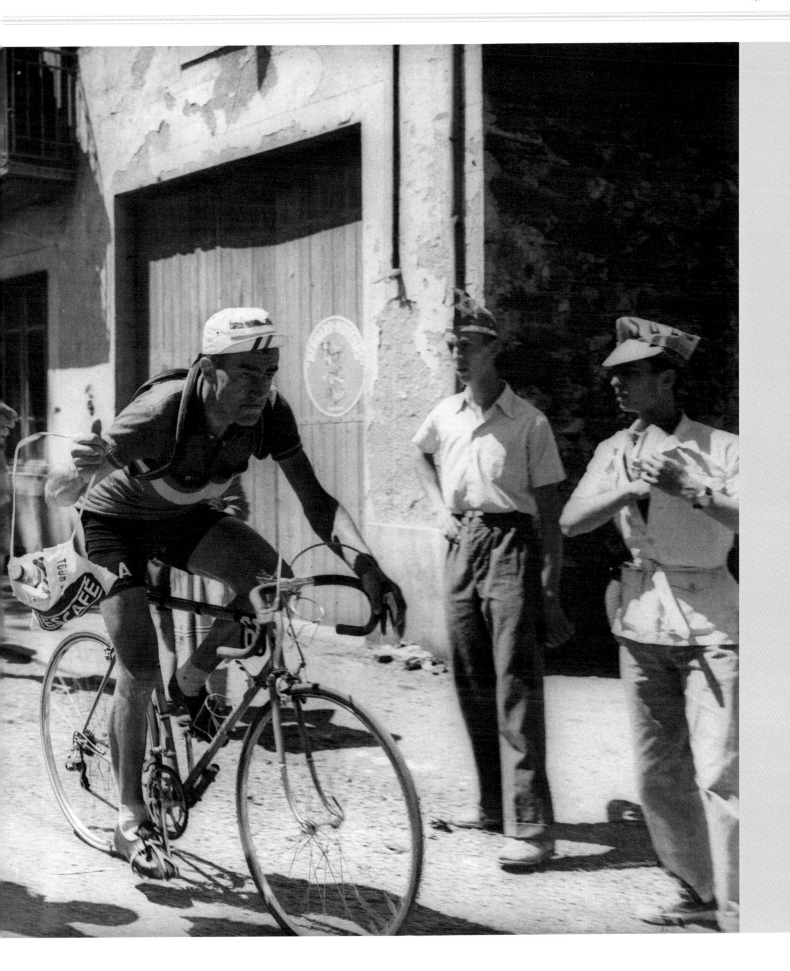

Tour Legends
Charly Gaul

"Gaul stood up on the pedals and, in the blink of an eye, he was 20 metres ahead. Then he disappeared round the next bend. The dark angel had passed; he fled in a cloud of dust."

Journalist Michel Claret in 1958

Main Picture: Charly Gaul on his way to winning stage 17 in 1955 – he finished 1-24 ahead of Bobet. Right: Gaul on stage 17, Luchon–Pau in 1961, which marked his eighth Tour participation.

CHARLY GAUL (LUX) b. 8/12/32 Pfaffenthal; d. 6/12/2005

10 PARTICIPATIONS
ONE VICTORY
10 STAGE WINS

1953 DID NOT FINISH

1954 DID NOT FINISH

1955 THIRD OVERALL
KING OF THE MOUNTAINS
TWO STAGE WINS: stage 8, Thonon–Briançon; stage 17, Toulouse–Saint-Gaudens

1956 13TH OVERALL
KING OF THE MOUNTAINS
TWO STAGE WINS: stage 3 part 2, Rouen Les Essarts (time trial); stage 18, Turin–Grenoble

1957 DID NOT FINISH

1958 FIRST OVERALL
FOUR STAGE WINS: stage 8, Châteaulin (time trial); stage 18, Mont Ventoux (time trial); stage 21, Briançon–Aix-les-Bains; stage 23, Besançon–Dijon (time trial)

1959 12TH OVERALL
ONE STAGE WIN: stage 17, Saint-Etienne–Grenoble

1961 THIRD OVERALL
ONE STAGE WIN: stage 9, Saint-Etienne–Grenoble

1962 NINTH OVERALL

1963 DID NOT FINISH

Anquetil: Master of the Peloton

Jacques Anquetil captured France's imagination from the moment he made his Tour debut. The first man to win the race five times, he did so with style, and without sacrificing the champagne lifestyle that came with being a Tour champion. As supercilious as he was brilliant, he claimed to train on cigarettes and beer but rode to win, and to win at all costs.

1957

Jacques Anquetil started his first Tour as a willing and able *domestique* in the service of defending champion Walkowiak. Recovering from illness, Walkowiak knew that he would need to use the opening week of the race to get up to speed, and with a strong French team to support him he was confident of his ability to do so. His chances were improved when Charly Gaul, one of his main adversaries, pulled out of the event after just two days. Within less than a week, a quarter of the 120 starters had abandoned – the intense heat had left some with such swollen mouths that they were unable to speak to ask for water. "This will be the Tour of the unknown, of the rank and file," said organizer Jacques Goddet.

Stage six saw a decisive break give five men a real advantage to take into the mountains. Anquetil was in the group, Walkowiak with the chasers, several minutes back. The gap remained stubbornly wide, despite numerous attempts to bridge across as it came down to less than two minutes. Then, after a week of debilitating heat, it started raining heavily. Seven kilometres from the finish Walkowiak fell, while his young team-mate took the yellow jersey. Going into the mountains the temperatures soared again, and more riders were forced to withdraw. Anquetil, inexperienced as he was, lost the lead to Nicolas Barone the day after he had won it, and finished in the main group nearly nine minutes down.

Federico Bahamontès was the next big name to retire; a boil on his left arm had left him unable to steer his bike, although some thought this move was a thinly disguised protest about being overlooked for team leadership ahead of Jesus Lorono. He had put in several attacks in the Alps, but could not maintain his aggressive rhythm with just one hand gripping the bars. Following the Spaniard's example, Anquetil took his turn to attack, taking the Belgian Joseph Planckaert with him. He won the stage in a group sprint, and regained all the time he had lost, which put him back in contention for the overall classification. His time-trial skills – borne out by his win on the split stage on day three – meant he was now a greater threat than ever.

ANQUETIL ASSERTS HIMSELF

There was no way of breaking up the bunch for the first part of the next stage. The road surfaces were so bad that the entire peloton was forced to carry its bikes across the pitted, flooded track, and could only race in earnest for the final 80 kilometres. Gastone Nencini led the attack when it did happen – on the Telegraphe – and kept his momentum over the Galibier as Janssen tried to go clear from the group. The Italian won the stage, while Anquetil produced a final flourish to recover all but a minute of the time he and the chasers had lost, and win back the jersey. He had reached the halfway point of the Tour in command of the peloton.

Landslides forced a short-notice rerouting of the next stage, eliminating the Col de Vars and allowing the French team to control the race. There were just 67 men left in the event and, of those, four of the top five were French – there was no way that anyone but a low-placed *domestique* would be allowed to ride away for a stage win. The addition of an extra time trial on what should have been a rest day only served to further Anquetil's purpose; he gained a few more seconds over his rivals and provided himself with an even bigger cushion for the mountains.

There were still plenty of heroics to be performed, even if the chances of winning the race were all but zero.

Below: Jacques Anquetil in yellow heads the peloton through an impromtu shower provided by local firemen, stage 6, Charleroi–Metz, 1957. Previous page: Anquetil is victorious in Paris, 1962.

Nencini crashed on stage 17, but went on to win the following day, riding one-handed, bandages and all. By now the head count was down to 60. The Frenchmen who had played such an important part supporting Anquetil found that they could not defend their own interests at the same time, and gradually slipped out of the top five. But they had done enough; Anquetil was in yellow, and with a time trial to extend his lead he reached Paris as a national hero, a brilliant time-triallist who had held his own in the mountains and who, the French hoped, would be able to fill the gap left by the greats of the previous generation.

1958

Defending champion Jacques Anquetil suffered an early upset when he returned to the Tour following his first victory. He crashed on stage one and, although he was unhurt, his rivals seized the opportunity to attack. It came to nothing, but the tone had been set – it was going to be a tough, aggressive race.

Louison Bobet was the first to make his attack count, forcing a decisive selection that cost Charly Gaul two minutes on the fifth stage. Two days later, Brian Robinson

**Above: Ladies' man Jacques Anquetil is among friends after winning the final time trial, Bordeaux–Libourne, 1957.
Below: Charly Gaul after winning the time trial at Châteaulin during the 1958 Tour.**

and Arigo Padovan had such an unseemly battle in the sprint that the Italian was relegated, giving Britain its first-ever Tour stage win.

The upsets were just starting; the next day a rolling, technical 46-kilometre time trial was won by climber Charly Gaul, while Anquetil, who excelled in the race against the watch, finished second. Suddenly the man from Luxembourg, twice King of the Mountains but only once on the podium, found himself bracketed with the potential winners – and not just those who were hoping for a stage win.

Sprinter André Darrigade was still in yellow, and his primary aim was to hold the jersey until the race reached his home town of Dax, not to keep it for the rest of the Tour. He got his wish. On the stage before the mountains the pace dropped dramatically as the peloton decided to give themselves an unofficial rest day – there were none on the race schedule – and Darrigade rode into Dax as leader of the race.

The first day in the mountains saw more hesitation as the peloton grew nervous. Fog and rain deterred the contenders from risking too much on the descents. It served as a chance to warm up the peloton's climbing muscles, so that when it started the next stage, the attacking began

before the riders had reached the first *col*. Federico Bahamontès, bidding for the King of the Mountains' prize, was quick to launch his move and was followed by Gaul, Bobet, Raphaël Geminiani and the other big names. The group eventually left Bahamontès to his own devices, and finished the stage together a good two minutes after the Spaniard.

THE VENTOUX TAKES ITS TOLL

Bahamontès made it his business to cross over every summit first, hoarding climbing points as if his life depended on it. Gaul pulled him back, anxious not only to maintain control of the race but also to ensure that his own reputation as a climber was not completely overshadowed. He knew that if he kept Bahamontès in check he could use the time trials to make up any lost time.

The fourth consecutive mountain stage forced the weaker riders to get off and push. They were already buckling at the prospect of the Mont Ventoux time trial, while Gaul was actually looking forward to it. This would be his chance to stake his claim for overall victory. A hundred thousand spectators lined the 21-kilometre route and watched him win the stage from Bahamontès by 31 seconds, moving into third place overall. With the Alps still to come, it seemed inevitable that he would surpass Raphaël Geminiani and Vito Favero within days.

All eyes were on Gaul as the 17th stage began. The peloton waited for him to attack, only to see that he was not even riding smoothly with the bunch, but was finding it hard to maintain the pace. Then he got into mechanical difficulty, struggling to change gear. It was the signal that the rest needed. They attacked him remorselessly, until half of his rivals – Anquetil, Geminiani and Favero – were clear. Paying for his efforts on the Ventoux, Gaul lost 10 minutes. He had ridden cautiously through the Pyrenees, preferring to save himself for the Alps, and now that he was here, he found nothing in his legs.

Gaul did nothing to answer his critics the next day. He knew that he must save himself for one do-or-die effort in the mountains, followed up by the final time trial. If that did not win him the Tour, then nothing would. So he attacked on the last day in the Alps, and he made it count. Geminiani lost 15 minutes, Anquetil 22. The Luxembourg rider made his move at the foot of the second *col* of the day, setting a pace that only Bahamontès could match. Even a mechanical problem, which forced him to ride 100 kilometres on an ill-fitting spare bike, could not stop him.

Victory was sealed in the time trial and, thanks to the organizers, Gaul had a long, long lap of honour. After 23 stages without rest, the peloton were sent on a 320-kilometre *randonée* to the finish of the Tour – Gaul had ample time to show off the yellow jersey that he had so convincingly taken from the French.

1959

Initially, it seemed that the French had regained the upper hand at the 1959 Tour. André Darrigade won the opening stage – for the fourth year in succession – and, when his team-mate Robert Cazala infiltrated a break on stage three, he ended up winning the stage, the time bonus that went with it and the jersey itself. His team leader and his roommate for the Tour, Louison Bobet, was delighted to see his young protégé in yellow – who better to keep it warm for him? The team would not waste too much energy defending Cazala's lead – they needed to keep the long-term goal of Bobet's overall win in mind – but he hung on for as long as he could. His only hope was that he could wear the jersey all the way to Bayonne, his home town, where his wife and three-year-old daughter – dressed in a bright-yellow sun-frock – would be waiting for him.

It was a 207-kilometre run to Bayonne, over hot, flat roads. The most likely outcome was a big sprint finish, exactly what Cazala wanted. But with 60 kilometres to go, the

Above: Charly Gaul and Federico Bahamontès during the 1959 Tour.
Below: André Darrigade wins stage 11, Bagnères de Bigorre–St Gaudens, 1959.

Belgian team started to get edgy. They attacked and, when the French team accelerated to go after them, Cazala fell back. Bobet had to make a choice: stay with his fading team-mate so that he might preserve the jersey for perhaps one more day, or look after his own, ultimately more realistic ambitions and bridge the gap to the escapees.

Bobet was fond of Cazala, but he was not blinded by affection. He chased down the breakaways, gaining vital time over those of his rivals left in the bunch. The thousands gathered in the Bayonne velodrome cheered as enthusiastically as they could when Cazala arrived, and

applauded politely as Eddie Pauwels mounted the podium to collect the jersey, but it was not what they had hoped for. After the ceremony Pauwels found Cazala's wife and gave her the winner's bouquet. Now Bobet had made his choice he would have to live up to it.

Into the Pyrenees, and the Spanish crowds came out to support Federico Bahamontès. He did not disappoint either, escaping with Charly Gaul on the Tourmalet. The Spaniard was considered to be a pure climber, no real threat to the overall classification, while Gaul, the defending champion, was obviously the most dangerous man in the race. If the Frenchmen were to upset him, they would have to do it before the Alps. The temperatures were still unbearably high – the sort of conditions that Gaul disliked. Now was Bobet's chance.

THE EAGLE FLIES

An early break was caught shortly after the feed zone, with Bahamontès and Anquetil both making it across to the front of the race. But neither Gaul, Bobet nor yellow jersey-wearer Michel Vermeulin went with them. Bobet tried to attack on the descent of a small, third-category climb, gaining a two-minute advantage over Gaul. It didn't last long; the Luxembourg rider rode straight past him on the Montsalvy, catching Roger Rivière with ease. Then he cracked. Rivière suddenly found himself re-passing Gaul and completely dropping him on the descent. At the foot of the hill Gaul climbed off to stick his head in the village water fountain; all he could think of at the time was to find some relief from the heat.

When Bahamontès won the mountain time trial to the Puy de Dôme, and moved to within four seconds of the *maillot jaune*, he had to be taken seriously. Going into the Alps he sensed that victory was within reach; Bobet was hardly able to pedal on the steepest climbs and, though Gaul had recovered from his Pyrenean disaster, he had an almost insurmountable time deficit. On the Col Romeyre, where he had audaciously stopped for an ice cream during the 1957 race, Bahamontès led Gaul by one minute. The two joined forces on the descent and, while Gaul won the stage, Bahamontès took the jersey.

For the first time, Bahamontès had to develop a defensive, rather than an aggressive strategy. He rode to the finish with a select group, 47 seconds after the stage winner Ercole Baldini. In second place now was Anglade – a Frenchman, but not a member of the national team. In the complicated world of French cycling, this made for a difficult situation. Neither Jacques Anquetil nor Rivière – the two strongest members of the French team – would attack. They would rather be beaten by a Spaniard than by a regional rider, who could then replace them in the hearts of their nation. The pair both put six minutes into Bahamontès in the final time trial; enough to show that they were capable of challenging, if they had wanted to. But by that stage it was too late – Bahamontès had proved himself to be not "just" a freakishly talented climber, but a consummate rider who could, and did, win the Tour.

Above: Gastone Nencini dons the yellow jersey in 1960. Below: Roger Rivière lies unconscious after crashing on the descent of the Col de Perjuret, 1960.

1960

After a succession of Tours dominated first by a Luxembourg rider, then a Spaniard, it became the turn of the Italians to deny France a home victory. Federico Bahamontès never had a chance to test his climbing legs, withdrawing after just two days, so sick that he was unable to eat, let alone race his bike. In the absence of Anquetil, Bobet and Gaul, Gastone Nencini took the yellow jersey, only to crash and lose it two days later to Frenchman Henry Anglade.

If the man in yellow thought he would be unchallenged until the mountain stages, he was soon disillusioned. Nencini, along with Roger Rivière, Jean Adriaenssens and Hans Junkermann, broke away on stage six, from St Malo to Lorient, and as the bunch struggled to organize the chase – with four nationalities in the break, few people had an incentive to ride at the front – they pulled away. Once it was clear they were not to be caught the peloton sat up, trailing in 13 minutes down, all but eliminating any other hopefuls.

Nencini retook the jersey on the first day in the Pyrenees, with Rivière holding on to second place after winning the stage. In the rush to better him over the next two stages, several strong riders crashed, including former race leader Anglade, who was involved in a multiple collision when a big group of riders came down in one of the tunnels on the mountain-side. But the real tragedy came on stage 14. Rivière, still second in the general classification, attacked on the Col de Perjuret, gaining a workable advantage by the summit. In a frenzy of adrenalin he tried too hard on the descent, and lost control of his bike. Unable to stop, he fell over the edge

of the ravine, tumbling down the slope and breaking two vertebrae. He did not race again that year.

NENCINI GOES FOR A RIDE

Anglade made three attempts to break Nencini on stage 15, but the Italian's team was too strong to let him get out of sight. Over the unmade roads and wooden bridges of stage 16 the contenders stayed together, shedding weaker men from the group, but unable to move away from the front.

The 20-kilometre descent to Briançon ensured that absolutely no one escaped, and the Italians had little to worry about – if Nencini were to falter, they had Graziano Battistini in third place to take on the responsibility of team leader, should he need to.

There was no need for Battistini to do anything other than keep an eye on the *maillot jaune*. Once he and Nencini had both finished safely in the front group on the stage to Aix-les-Bains, the danger had passed. The final day in the mountains was turned into a glory ride for a Spaniard, Fernando Manzaneque, who scaled the Col d'Aravis and Col de Colombière alone to win the stage by almost 13 minutes.

In contrast to the feared mountain time trials, the final stage against the watch this year went from Pontarlier to Besançon, dropping 560 metres' height in the course of 83 kilometres. Nencini had the Tour sewn up, which made riding the fast, technical course all the more exhilarating. He caught his three-minute man, Hans Junkermann, at the halfway point, and spent the next 40 kilometres trying to shake him off.

Junkermann simply stayed just far enough away to avoid being penalized for drafting, but used the Italian as a pacemaker, and as a marker to see how to take the dangerous corners. But what did Nencini care? He was three minutes faster than the German, had the yellow jersey on his back and had won the greatest race on earth. As far as he was concerned, it was time to sit back and enjoy the ride.

1961

Jacques Anquetil had failed to live up to his Tour debut of 1957. Winning the race at 22 years old had been an impossible success to follow, but after four years he felt that he now had the maturity to go with the innate talent that had singled him out as a potential Tour great. He believed he could win again, but only on his own terms. He demanded that he be designated sole leader of the French national team,

Above: Charly Gaul and Anquetil neck and neck in 1961.

and that he personally should oversee the selection of the men who would ride for him. Manager Marcel Bidot humoured his requests, confident that his faith would be repaid. Anquetil was incredibly confident. "I'll attack during the first half of the first stage," he told his rivals before the race had even started.

The very voicing of his plan seemed as ludicrous as the tactic itself – riders aiming for the general classification didn't waste their efforts attacking on the opening flat stages; they rode themselves in and then attacked in the mountains. Not Anquetil, however. He did exactly as he had said, finishing the first stage 4-48 ahead of all his rivals, in a small group that had been smart enough to stick with him when the break formed. Then he won the afternoon time trial to take the jersey. It seemed that the Tour was over before it had begun.

The French team should have had it easy defending the jersey – as well as the men in the national squad there were the regional teams whose natural alliance would be with Anquetil's men. But two of the French squad's most important *domestiques*, Roger Privat and François Mahe, did not make it past stage two. They crashed badly, with Privat immediately retiring, and Mahe struggling to the finish, only to miss the time cut. As the remaining nine men closed ranks to protect Anquetil they alienated the other Frenchmen in the race, chasing down every move that started. It was not until the sixth stage that the cracks began to show.

Charly Gaul was not going to attack properly until the mountains, but couldn't resist having a little dig on the second-category Ballon d'Alsace. He dropped Anquetil by 10 seconds in the last 500 metres of the climb, then sat up and waited for him, knowing for certain that he would be the better rider in the mountains.

WAITING FOR GAUL'S ATTACK

Anquetil's lead over Spain's Fernando Manzaneque was greater than four minutes when the race entered the Alps. He was more concerned about the eight minutes he had over Gaul —he was on the Luxembourg rider's territory now. As expected, Gaul attacked early on in the stage, leading by 1-30 over the Col de Granier, and by three minutes over the Cucheron. He could have pulled back five minutes on the stage, but crashed on the second descent, losing 45 seconds before he was able to remount. Determined not to waste the advantage he had gained, Gaul

Below: Anquetil on his way to winning the first time trial in 1961 at Versailles.

completed the final climb, the Col de Porte, without losing any more time, and salvaged just over two minutes of his lead. But the bruising to his hip, shoulder and knee left him unable to ride at full capacity for several days, and negated his climbing advantage for the remaining Alpine stages.

Both Anquetil and Gaul laid low for the rest of the second week. With the final individual time trial after the Pyrenees, Gaul would not only have to erase the Frenchman's lead, but he would have to reverse it if he were to have any chance of winning the race overall.

The stage to Superbagnères promised to be the big showdown of the Tour, with each of the two giants of the race battling to conquer the other, and the mountain itself. The spectators crowded on to the roadside, hoping that Gaul would choose their hairpin as the one on which to launch his move. The tension mounted as the group rode over the four *cols* – when would he attack? Anquetil fans calculated that he would need a 14-minute lead on the stage to hold the jersey until Paris – which was not the sort of time that could be made up with a late burst.

In the end though, nothing happened. Anquetil watched and waited until even the possibility of a challenge fizzled out. Gaul was sick, or had overeaten, or had not recovered from his earlier crash – for whatever reason he could not attack. Italian Imerio Massignan sprinted away for the stage win, but the rest of the peloton were left bemused and disappointed as Anquetil and Gaul ended the stage as they started it – side by side.

The time trial enabled Anquetil to stretch his lead to more than 10 minutes, and for Gaul to move into second place. In a final insult, Gaul lost his place to Guido Carlesi, who attacked in the final kilometre of the Tour to take back the four-second deficit he had to the Luxembourg rider. Anquetil had led the race from day one – the first person to do so in the post-war era. He had fulfilled his promise to his team manager, and his threat to the peloton.

1962

The character of the Tour changed in 1962, with national teams being replaced by professional, sponsored trade teams. For the first few days André Darrigade and Rudi Altig tussled for the yellow jersey, both anxious to have their sponsor's names – Louviet and Helyett-St Raphaël – emblazoned on the *maillot jaune* as it was photographed and printed all over Europe.

Initially Darrigade seemed to be winning the battle. Altig had been first to get his hands on the jersey before passing it to the Frenchman for a day after the team time trial.

He took it back with another stage win, but when other riders started to muscle in – forcing breaks and spoiling things for the sprinters – it was Darrigade who got into the winning move on stage seven, and then rode a strong enough time trial to take the jersey back as Anquetil won his first stage.

The jersey had gone to Willy Schroeders before the mountains and he defended it well on the first day of climbing. The biggest upset of the day was when a *commissaire's* bike crashed and brought down 30 riders. Overall contender Rik van Looy was forced to abandon, despite his best efforts to stay with the group after remounting. But this year the jersey was not destined to stay in any one place for long – Tom Simpson made history next day by becoming the first-ever Briton to lead the Tour and, with a strong ride to St Gaudens. Federico Bahamontès, the "Eagle of Toledo", controlled the stage, ensuring that he took the King of the Mountains' points, and furthered his cause the next day by winning the mountain time trial.

BOWING TO THE INEVITABLE

Joseph Planckaert was in yellow as the race headed into the plateau between the Pyrenees and the Alps, and, with the top five riders all within a span of two minutes, there was no one willing to attack him and risk burning out before the next set of mountain stages. The peloton was so reticent to make a move that, on the first day in the Alps, it took three hours to cover 75 kilometres.

The action finally erupted on the Col de Resteford, the highest point of the Tour. Bahamontès went first, taking maximum points at the summit before easing off on the descent. Others were not so cautious. Eddy Pauwels passed him, gaining more time as Bahamontès punctured twice, only to lose it as he crashed. Fortunately uninjured, he continued alone, and was finally caught on the Izoard by Bahamontès, then by a group including Charly Gaul, Planckaert, Simpson and Anquetil. After 241 kilometres the defending champion had moved into second place but little else changed. With a 67-kilometre time trial, Planckaert's 1-08 advantage was nowhere near enough to win him the Tour.

The two men were inseparable over the final mountain stage. Bahamontès engaged in a three-way battle with Charly Gaul and Imerio Massignan for the King of the Mountains' title, and as the trio rode away from the bunch in their own private race, it left the overall contenders unable to follow. Their elegant climbing stole the limelight from the rest of the pack.

Inevitably Anquetil overhauled Planckaert in the time trial, beating him by six minutes on the stage. The Belgian had no complaints – he had known from the outset that this stage would see Anquetil at his most dangerous. And when the Frenchman was at his most dangerous, there was nothing anyone could do about it.

1963

Sixty years after the race was founded, the Tour celebrated its 50th *edition*. It was unthinkable that the defending champion, Jacques Anquetil, might not even contest the race and blow his chance to become the first man ever to win four Tours. But it was not until 36 hours before the race started that he finally agreed to participate, after signing a two-year contract with his new sponsors, St Raphaël.

The wrangling had disrupted Anquetil – he had not had as good a build-up to the race as the previous year and his doctor had warned him not to start. To add to these disadvantages, he would be more marked than ever before. If he were to win this time round, he would have to ride into form in the first week, without losing any time to his rivals.

By the sixth day he had found his racing legs, winning the first time trial and slotting into the overall classification in a comfortable position, a few minutes behind new leader Gilbert Desmet. The next day, while the general classification hopefuls were preparing for their assault on the Pyrenees, a small group of men got away. It would have been an uneventful occurrence, had it not been for the fact that the man who won the stage was Pino Cerami, who took the only Tour win of his career at the age of 41, no fewer than 14 years after he had first competed in the race.

The opening *col* of the Tour, the Aubisque, took no time at all to end the dreams of many riders, including double stage-winner Rik van Looy. Then, on the Tourmalet, there was a second cull; Federico Bahamontès, Anquetil, Raymond Poulidor, José Perez-Frances and Esteban Martin were the five who got away.

Bahamontès could not drop the others over the climb, and instead satisfied himself with taking the maximum number of climbing points and then cruising across the line alongside the others.

Anquetil found a little something to win the sprint, thus winning his first-ever mountain stage in the Tour. It moved him up into second overall, and sent a shockwave through the peloton – if he could win in the time trials and in the mountains, how would anyone stop him taking the race?

Below: Tom Simpson poses as the English gentleman, 1962.

BAHAMONTÈS BEATEN BACK

Anquetil gained a little more time on Desmet on the next mountain stage, reeling him in to within three minutes. But it was not the Frenchman who dislodged Desmet; it was Bahamontès. His superb climb up the Col de Porte – on the day of his 35th birthday – combined with a minute's bonus for winning the stage, put him in second place and he was expected to produce a similar effort to take the jersey. But he didn't need to, and he simply wasn't able to – tired from his efforts he relied instead on Desmet being unable to follow the pace of the lead group. Riding through a road cut out through a corridor of snow and ice at the top of the Col d'Iseran, Bahamontès and Anquetil finished with a sizeable group, leaving them first and second overall, three seconds apart. As in 1962, the man leading the race was faced with the task of

opening up his advantage sufficiently before the final time trial to prevent Anquetil usurping him.

On each mountain of stage 17 the Spaniard attacked, only to sit up once he had collected the climbing points and then allow himself to be caught. Having used up valuable resources in this fashion, he found that when he attacked to get away he was unable to accelerate hard enough and Anquetil came with him. Over the Forclaz and the Col des Montes Anquetil followed Bahamontès, and then outsprinted him at the finish. He had taken his second mountain stage, the jersey and Bahamontès's thunder in one fell swoop.

Victory in the time trial sealed Anquetil's fourth Tour, and proved his completeness as a rider. With his outstanding performances in all areas he was now definitely seen not only as the best rider of his generation, but as the best Tour rider in history.

Above: Federico Bahamontès on stage 17, Val d'Isère–Chamonix, 1963. He lost the stage to Anquetil by one second.

1964

Jacques Anquetil's legendary status was due not only to his superlative riding, but to his forceful character. He did not seek out publicity – his *palmarès* were enough to ensure that he was always in the public eye – and he would not allow his sport to dictate every detail of his life. His dietary habits were famous – he ate red meat and fish in abundance, with or without vegetables, and liked to drink. "I drink a lot of alcohol, in fact far too much alcohol. I hardly ever drink water except if I am thirsty in a race. I used to drink about four or five pints of milk a day, but since my former trainer, Julien Schramm, told me that it was toxic I drink beer instead," he said.

So he started the 1964 Tour as favourite, having won the Giro with a record-breaking time trial. Only Fausto Coppi had won both the

tours of Italy and France in the same year. Following his earlier triumph, Anquetil announced that he would be taking things easy in the first week of the race.

Always a man of his word, there was little sign of the defending champion as the race rolled from Rennes all the way down to the Alps, with Germany's Rudi Altig, a team-mate of Anquetil's, taking the green points' jersey and then the yellow jersey as the Tour took a diversion into his home country. It was not until the Galibier that Anquetil's true state became apparent.

Anxious to show that he still had what it took to lead the peloton over the mountains, veteran climber Federico Bahamontès tried to take control. He attacked on the first Alpine stage, while Anquetil stood still. The Frenchman took huge gulps of ice-cold water as he struggled up the slopes, but was straining so hard that he could not even keep liquid down. He suffered more bad luck when a puncture on the final descent ended any chance he

Above: Jacques Anquetil and Raymond Poulidor do battle on the climb to Puy de Dôme, stage 20, 1964. Below: Anquetil relaxes with his wife Janine during a rest day barbecue at Andorra in 1964.

had of regaining the others. But he had more to worry about than Bahamontès – Raymond Poulidor, one of the few who could threaten him in the overall classification, had gone after the Spaniard, and although he could not keep up with him on the climb he was putting time into Anquetil, and took an additional time bonus for finishing second on the stage.

Fortunately for Anquetil, the exploits of the stage had exhausted the peloton and discouraged anyone from attacking early the next day. Bahamontès showed himself only to collect climbing points, and a group of 22 men were still together at the finish. With a supreme effort Anquetil was the first man on to the cinder track and held off Tom Simpson to win the stage. He comfortably won the next day's time trial, moving into second overall behind Georges Groussard – it was only then that he confessed how much he had suffered early on in the race, and how he had come close to abandoning. With his fifth Tour win in sight it

suddenly didn't seem quite so bad.

There was temporary relief from the suffering, but even though Anquetil led him in the overall standings Poulidor believed that he could make his rival suffer again. There were only 30 seconds between them – he was sure he could be the man to break Anquetil's hold on the race. But at the very moment that he could have streaked ahead he was stuck on the roadside with his mechanic trying to get his bike fixed. Anquetil had cracked on the Envalira, losing four minutes on the climb. He descended like a man possessed, catching the yellow-jersey group and limiting his losses.

NEAR MISS FOR POULIDOR
Both men had missed an opportunity to make a race-winning move, but although Poulidor had also lost time, he was now the stronger rider. He put in a devastating attack on the final *col* of the next stage, regaining the time he had lost and closing to within nine seconds of Anquetil. But they were not the only two men in

the race: Bahamontès sensed the tiredness in their legs, and his hopes of an overall win were rekindled. He attacked in his usual style, sweeping up all the mountains' points on offer, and winning the stage. By dint of Anquetil's very diligent chasing, the Spaniard's advantage was limited; he still moved into second overall, but by a margin that Anquetil could overcome in the time trial.

As Bahamontès had been the threat in the mountains, so Poulidor was now the danger in the *contre-la-montre*. At halfway Poulidor was only seven seconds down, but he punctured. His mechanic jumped out of the following car, but as he handed him a spare bike he slipped and fell, twisting the handlebars. Poulidor was left impotent as he waited for a machine to ride, losing another half-minute at least. Anquetil won the stage, and took a crucial 20-second time bonus. Both men were close to breaking point, and there were still two more stages that could alter the standings.

Stage 20 took the peloton to the top of the Puy de Dôme – time for Bahamontès again. Both he and Poulidor had sworn that this was where they would have their revenge on Anquetil; he had only worn the yellow jersey for two days, and they were convinced that he was not as strong as he had been in previous years. Bahamontès exploded out of the peloton, racing up the first slopes of the dormant volcano, bringing only Anquetil, Poulidor, Julio Jimenez and Vittorio Adorni with him. Within moments the two Spaniards were clear.

Adorni stuttered and dropped back, leaving the two Frenchmen – first and second in the general classification – less than a minute between them, to race man-on-man. The *maillot jaune* locked on to Poulidor's wheel – he was tired, but that was not for Poulidor to know. Anquetil held on and held on, until finally he cracked. In the 600 metres before the line he lost 42 seconds to Poulidor, cutting his lead to a barely tangible 14 seconds; it was either a very clever piece of riding, or a very lucky one.

The final time trial did not provide the upsets of the previous *contre-la-montre*; Anquetil won, giving Poulidor only a few moments to imagine that he might somehow have won as he waited for the yellow jersey to complete the course. But far from being disappointed, even after losing the Tour by a margin that could easily have been made up by one less puncture, Poulidor happily joined Anquetil on a lap of honour. "I know now that I can win the Tour," he said. It was the kind of optimism that would spur him on for a further 11 attempts.

1965

When Jacques Anquetil announced that he would not be contesting the 1965 Tour de France a whole crowd of riders jumped to the fore as potential winners. Poulidor stepped up to become the home favourite, first-year pro Felice Gimondi carried the hopes of Italy, while Federico

Spaniard José Perez-Frances leads the tour into Barcelona on stage 11, 1965.

Bahamontès assumed his normal role as animator in the mountains.

Rik van Looy struck first – he was no climber, and had no time to waste. He lost the *maillot jaune* to fellow Belgian Bernard van de Kerkhove soon after, happy to have felt the jersey against his skin. He knew that, however much his country wanted it, he was a Classics man and a sprinter, not a Tour contender.

Attention turned to Poulidor in the first time trial; in the absence of Anquetil he fulfilled expectations and won the stage. But seven seconds behind him was Gimondi, with a performance that exceeded his wildest expectations to win the yellow jersey. From winning the Tour de l'Avenir, the junior Tour de France, the previous year, he was now leading the real thing.

Gimondi lost the lead as promptly as he had won it. An alliance with the points' leader Guido Reybroeck limited the damage as a group of nine men rode away from the bunch. Now he would have to wait for the Pyrenees to see if he was a true Tour contender.

When the mountains came, they were more terrible than ever. Under searing heat and oppressive humidity the peloton faced a ride of seven hours. Bahamontès and Vittorio Adorni abandoned, sick with stomach cramps, unable to even think about racing in such conditions. Poulidor struggled, but his weakness remained unexposed as Gimondi punctured on the descent of the Tourmalet, allowing the Frenchman to regain contact, while Gimondi regained the jersey.

Van Looy was out of the running, but he wanted to show that he was not yet finished. He threw himself into action, attacking on the first climb while the others looked on bemused. His three companions wouldn't work. Arnauld Pamblianco was a team-mate of Gimondi; Reybroeck's team manager Driessens had fallen out with Van Looy and Auguste Verhaegen was being plain perverse. Undeterred, Van Looy rode on, only to be outsprinted by Reybroeck at the line.

Left: Felice Gimondi claims the yellow jersey after winning stage 3 in Rouen, 1965. Below: Overall winner Lucien Aimar poses with Jacques Anquetil, 1966.

POULIDOR SECOND AGAIN

The next day's hero was more fortunate. José Perez-Frances won the stage to Barcelona after a 220-kilometre solo break. But now it was time for Poulidor to show himself. Gimondi was wary of the Frenchman, and had not dared to test him since the time trial. Poulidor, on the other hand, stated loud and clear that he would win the stage to Mont Ventoux and, from that basis, launch his campaign to win the jersey.

He was as good as his word. Poulidor attacked with 10 kilometres of the climb remaining, gaining time and a bonus over Gimondi, to bring him to within 40 seconds of the race lead. Buoyed by the result, the Frenchman announced that his second strike would be on the final big climb of the Alps, the time trial to the Mont Revard, on stage 18.

His warning deadened the race. No one wanted to attack, knowing that Poulidor was planning his move for several days later. On the first day in the Alps, the highest mountain of the race, the Izoard, had been resurfaced – the gravel replaced by smooth tarmac, greatly easing the passage of the riders, but eliminating part of the danger, and therefore the excitement, of the climb. It was yet another reason for Gimondi to remain unruffled.

When stage 18 finally arrived Poulidor's plans were turned on their head. He rode as hard as he could, but Gimondi matched his efforts.

One of the Italian's sprockets broke, leaving him with a limited selection of gears, but the mechanical failure seemed only to spur him on.

He took 15 seconds out of Poulidor in the final kilometre, securing his lead on the very day that his rival had promised to take it away from him.

The forces that had prevented Poulidor from beating Anquetil were at work again when he challenged Felice Gimondi, and he was forced to make do with yet another second place as Gimondi won the Tour at his first attempt. "Frankly, I thought the Tour was going to eat me up and spit me out!" said Gimondi afterwards. "I thought it would be much harder than it was." A sentiment that Poulidor would be hard-pressed to agree with.

1966

At 32 years of age, Anquetil was beginning to suffer Tour fatigue. The immense pressure that had steadily accumulated over nine years was telling. He had already won the race not just once, but twice more than any other rider in history. He had worn yellow from day one until the finish in 1961; he had conclusively, and repeatedly, beaten Raymond Poulidor; and, when Felice Gimondi and Vittorio Adorni withdrew their entries from the 1966 Tour owing to illness, it seemed there was little left

for him to prove. But the lure of the *maillot jaune* was too great to resist.

The war between Anquetil and Poulidor broke out on stage two. Poulidor crashed and, with no time for ceremony, Anquetil attacked. Poulidor was strong enough to get back to the group, but he was furious. His antagonist dismissed him without mercy. "Cry-baby Poulidor," was how he described his rival to a radio interviewer. "He wants to learn how to stay upright on his bike. I don't see why I should wait for him when he can't. When I really do attack, he won't see me."

Arguments between the two men made the off-the-bike action more interesting than the race itself. The two Frenchmen were so intent on watching one another's progress that they paid little attention to anyone else. Until the Pyrenees, Anquetil was content to let anybody ride away, putting five, six, seven minutes into the bunch, just so long as

Poulidor didn't go with them. His mistake was to let the same thing happen again on the first day in the mountains.

Anquetil and Poulidor, along with Tom Simpson and Rudi Altig, lost more than nine minutes on the stage to Pau. The booing and catcalls at the end of the stage finally woke them from their stupor, and the next day they actually started to race. Both men got into the leading group, and Anquetil even sprinted away at the finish to beat Poulidor by two seconds. The fire of competition had been re-ignited.

The Vals les Bains time trial should have been the place for Anquetil to assert himself as the real leader of the race, no matter that he was not yet in the jersey. But on the short, twisting course he could not find his rhythm and Poulidor, who loved the circuit, beat him. They took their differences to the Alps, to settle them once and for all.

AIMAR TAKES THE YELLOW

Atrocious weather greeted the peloton on the first, lesser Alpine stage. With a long descent to the finish line, Anquetil thought that – provided he stayed with Poulidor as far as the last summit – there would be no aggravation on the final section of the stage. But while he had five Tours to his name and nothing to gain by risking his neck on the pockmarked road to Bourg d'Oisans, Poulidor needed to take risks.

He attacked over the top of the climb, taking his life in his hands as he tore down the mountain and gained a minute on his rival. Anquetil seemed strangely unmoved. "This is the moment he's waited for – he can smell a win. I'm certainly not going to kill myself in my last year on the Tour, so I'll take things easy. Poulidor needs the jersey more than I," he said.

But neither man had the jersey yet. The deficit they had allowed to build up in the first week still stood between them and the race lead. As they made their way through the Alps they realized the cost of their complacency.

Jan Janssen was in yellow, and when he lost it, it was to Lucien Aimar, one of Anquetil's *domestiques*, who had been near the head of the general classification since the first week. Poulidor led the defending champion by just over a minute, but he needed to make up four more if he was going to finally win the Tour at last.

Poulidor had only one chance left – the stage to Chamonix – before the race exited the Alps. He was burning with the adrenalin of a man who knows he might just win the Tour, but the occasion was so great, his nervousness so intense, that he waited too long. He attacked on the final climb, gaining 50 seconds on Aimar, who was helped by Anquetil. As the five-times winner had announced at the beginning of the race, if he wasn't going to win, then neither was Poulidor.

Anquetil retired from the race. The bad weather had brought back his bronchitis and, confident that

Suffering from bronchitis, Anquetil bows out of the Tour in 1966, safe in the knowledge that Poulidor will not win.

his great rival was beaten, there was nothing left for him to do. Aimar stated confidently that he would lose three minutes to Poulidor in the last time trial, and would therefore retain the jersey. In that final test, however, Poulidor not only failed to win the race, but failed even to win the stage. Whatever it is that ultimately makes a man a Tour winner, Poulidor did not, and never would, have it.

1967

Reverting to national, rather than trade teams in 1967, Tour organizers hoped that the first post-Anquetil race would signal the beginning of a new era. They could not have imagined how tragically the face of the Tour would be changed in those three weeks.

Tom Simpson, the 1965 world champion, had built his reputation as a future contender and was in full bloom, anxious to defy the bad luck that had plagued him throughout his Tour career. Instead, he lost his life to the race that he had lived for.

This was never going to be an uneventful race. Before a pedal had been turned, Felice Gimondi was in trouble with the organization – for agreeing to write exclusively for a Belgian paper during the race. Felice Levitan – anxious to keep the Tour in every paper and on every radio and television station in Europe – told the Italian that unless he annulled his

contract he would be thrown out of the race. Gimondi needed the Tour more than the Tour needed him, and he capitulated, returning his full efforts to racing.

For the first week of the race the stages were short – some little more than 150 kilometres – and run off at high speed. Late starts left the riders with time to relax in the morning and then to ride hard in the afternoon. Roger Pingeon, who had sworn he would never ride a bike again after abandoning the Paris-Nice stage race in disgust the previous year, completed his comeback by taking the yellow jersey on stage five, and this inspired him to ride better than ever.

Held up at a closed level crossing, he lost the lead to Ray Riotte two days later. But Pingeon had tasted the glory and on the first mountain stage of the race he claimed it back. 1966 winner Lucien Aimar won the stage, while Poulidor punctured, crashed and was written off again by the French Press.

VICTIM OF THE VENTOUX

Gimondi won the next mountain stage, while Simpson lost a little time and slipped to seventh place overall.

Then, as the race rolled toward the Ventoux, there were two days in which those who had lost time already had the chance for a stage win. The men in competition for the yellow jersey were preparing themselves for the mountain that might enable them to unseat Pingeon.

The slopes of the Ventoux were not lashed by the *mistral*, the prevailing wind in the South of France, on 13 July, 1967. Instead it was searingly hot and, as the already perspiring leaders came out from the shelter of the trees on to the moonscape of the giant of Provence, the heat was doubled as it reflected off the rock and into their faces. Poulidor and Jimenez had attacked in the forest, breaking up the peloton; anyone who wanted to be in the race had no choice but to follow.

Pingeon, Gimondi, Jan Janssen and Franco Balmanion gave chase, but Simpson was dropped. He held on to the second group, but as the sun beat down on him with its full glare he faltered.

Falling back from the group he weaved across the road, unable to accept that he would lose time to rivals. But he would not be beaten. Within a mile of the summit he fell

from his bike, wracked with heat exhaustion, barely able to communicate. British team mechanic Harry Hall rushed to his aid. Simpson tried to remount, but could not move the pedals, even as Hall pushed him on his way. He was lifted from his bike and flown by helicopter to Avignon. Oblivous to the drama, Janssen won the stage from Gimondi, while Pingeon retained his lead. Tom Simpson lost his life at 5.40 p.m.

Utterly dispirited, the Tour dragged itself to Paris with Simpson's shadow looming over every stage. Pingeon acquitted himself well, and Poulidor won the final time trial, but there was no spark left in the field.

Later, it transpired, amphetamines had been found in the pocket of Simpson's jersey, and alcohol in his bloodstream. In fact, the drugs had not killed him, but they had blocked out the pain as he rode – the pain that was trying to tell him to stop. The legend that his final words were "Put me back on my bike" remains a fitting epitaph to the rather eccentric English gentleman who had won the hearts of the peloton with his elegant manners, and who had given his life to the sport he loved.

Above: Heads bowed, the peloton pays tribute to Tom Simpson after his tragic death on the slopes of Mont Ventoux. Below: Simpson is unsuccessfully given the kiss of life by the roadside on Ventoux.

1968

After the death of Tom Simpson, the cold reality of drug use in the sport hit home. Organizers were anxious to bring in a new raft of stringent dope controls, but the riders were not so sure.

Led by the Italian team and former winner Roger Pingeon, now riding for the French A squad, the competitors and their managers protested. But the organizers would not budge; they offered the peloton a choice: either be tested by us, or be tested by the French police.

The French minister for sport had demanded that the anti-dope controls be as transparent as possible, to avoid the problems that had beset the Giro d'Italia earlier in the year and, if the organizers did not carry out the tests in a suitably rigorous fashion, he had threatened to step in, and thus make it a legal obligation for the riders. Unsurprisingly, the peloton decided to take the non-uniformed route and turned its attention to the race itself.

Having won the prologue at Paris-Nice and at the Giro d'Italia, few people were surprised to see French pursuit champion Charly Grosskost take the yellow jersey in the prologue. There was little more reaction when he sprinted to victory on the first road stage, and kept the lead for another 24 hours before ceding to the might of the Belgian A squad in the team time trial.

Herman van Springel was next keeper of the jersey, wearing it proudly as the race made its way from Brussels to Roubaix and on to Rouen. The race was now four days old, and none of the overall contenders had put themselves out to become early favourite. The jersey moved again, this time to Frenchman Jean-Pierre Genet after a successful breakaway foiled a hopelessly disorganized Belgian A squad. To make matters worse for them, one of the Belgian B riders, Georges Vandenberghe, was next in line for a turn in yellow.

At last the Tour reached the Pyrenees, and the general classification was knocked into some sort of shape. On stage 12, from Pau to St Gaudens, 14 riders abandoned and another four were disqualified for finishing outside the time limit.

But while the field totalled 71 men, only 29 were still in the running. The climb of the Tourmalet wreaked its inevitable havoc on the peloton, and the descent was just as devastating. Raymond Poulidor attacked on the way down, sweeping up the breakaways and forming a solid lead group that sorted out the genuine contenders. Vandenberghe courageously held on with the chasers to keep the jersey.

JANSSEN DEFIES THE ODDS

During the rest day, Roger Pingeon told French team manager Marcel Bidot that he was going to leave Poulidor to his own devices and that he, as rightful team leader, would

attack the next day. Spurred on by the Bastille Day crowd, he broke away on his own and, with the French riders blocking every chasing move, he established a lead of 13 minutes. The bunch only broke up when a motorbike swerved to avoid a spectator and, in doing so, ran straight into Poulidor. By the time he had wiped the blood from his eyes and got back on his bike the group chasing Pingeon was gone.

Pingeon's hopes of victory unravelled as he rode with Poulidor the next day, helping him to complete what would be his last day of the Tour. It was an unrelenting day's ride across the Massif Central, which finally deprived Vandenberghe of the jersey. As Poulidor travelled home to nurse his injuries, the new *maillot jaune* Franco Bitossi took over the King of the Mountains' lead after a day of constant effort, moving on to the head of a group still largely populated by men who were sure they could win the race.

Another epic ride by Pingeon, this time in the Alps, brought him

Above: Dutchman Jan Janssen offers a peace sign to the camera in Paris, 1968.
Below: Janssen on the final time trial into Paris, in which he beat Belgian Herman van Springel by 54 seconds to win the overall classification.

back into the top 10, all of whom were within three minutes of the leader Gregario San Miguel.

The Kas rider lost the jersey the next day to Van Springel, unable or unwilling to keep up with the others on a chaotic descent from the *col de la Colombière*. Now Jan Janssen, San Miguel and Bitossi were less than a minute behind Pingeon – if the Tour lacked any majestic patrons, it was not short of excitement. The Belgian riders had only one objective now: to stop Janssen winning any time bonuses.

They did it with ease, but Janssen was content to wait; he knew that they would be unable to foil his efforts in the final time trial. He shut out the temptation to ride too hard at the start, ignoring the intermediate time checks that put Van Springel ahead of him. He knew that the Belgian would pay for it in the final kilometres. In the end, he won the stage by a minute, and the Tour by 38 seconds – the narrowest margin in history and, with it, he became the first Dutchman ever to win the Tour.

Tour Legends
Jacques Anquetil

"He was total harmony, sublime, a phenomenon. He blended with his bicycle like a musician with his instrument."

Jacques Goddet on Anquetil

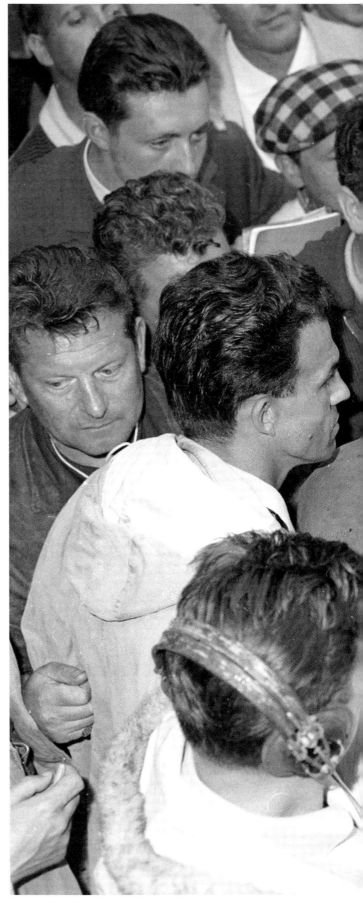

Left: Anquetil battles through the rain to win the stage 20 time trial, Bordeaux–Libourne, in 1957.
Main picture: Anquetil becomes the centre of attention after winning stage 19 in 1961.

JACQUES ANQUETIL (FRA)
b. 8/1/34 Mont-Saint-Aignan, Normandy; d. 18/11/87

EIGHT PARTICIPATIONS
FIVE VICTORIES
16 STAGE WINS

1957 FIRST OVERALL
FOUR STAGE WINS: stage 3 part 2, Caen–Rouen; stage 9, Besançon–Thonon; stage 15 part 2, Montjuich (time trial); stage 20, Bordeaux–Libourne (time-trial)

1958 DID NOT FINISH

1959 THIRD OVERALL

1961 FIRST OVERALL
TWO STAGE WINS: stage 1 part 2, Versailles (time trial); stage 19, Bergerac–Périgueux (time trial)

1962 FIRST OVERALL
TWO STAGE WINS: stage 8 part 2, Luçon–La Rochelle (time trial); stage 20, Bourgoin–Lyon (time trial)

1963 FIRST OVERALL
FOUR STAGE WINS: stage 6 part 2, Angers (time trial); stage 10, Pau–Bagnères-de-Bigorre; stage 17, Val d'Isère–Chamonix; stage 19, Arbois–Besançon (time trial)

1964 FIRST OVERALL
FOUR STAGE WINS: stage 9 Briançon–Monaco; stage 10 part 2, Hyères–Toulon (time trial); stage 17, Peyrehorade–Bayonne (time trial); stage 22 part 2, Versailles–Paris (time trial)

1965 DID NOT FINISH

Tour Legends
Raymond Poulidor

"If by some chance I don't win the Tour he won't win it either."

Jacques Anquetil on Poulidor in 1966, the year Lucien Aimar won

---

Main Picture: Always the bridesmaid, never the bride – Poulidor in 1966. Right: Next to Julio Jiminez on the slopes of Mont Ventoux, 1965. Poulidor crossed the line first.

RAYMOND POULIDOR (FRA)
b. 15/4/36 Masbaraud

14 PARTICIPATIONS
SEVEN STAGE WINS

1962 THIRD OVERALL
ONE STAGE WIN: stage 19,
Briançon–Aix-les-Bains

1963 EIGHTH OVERALL

1964 SECOND OVERALL
ONE STAGE WIN: stage 15,
Toulouse–Luchon

1965 SECOND OVERALL
TWO STAGE WINS: stage 5 part
2, Châteaulin (time trial); stage 14,
Montpellier–Mont Ventoux

1966 THIRD OVERALL
ONE STAGE WIN: stage 14 part 2,
Aubenas–Vals-les-Bains (time trial)

1967 NINTH OVERALL
ONE STAGE WIN: stage 22 part 2,
Versailles–Paris (time trial)

1968 DID NOT FINISH

1969 THIRD OVERALL

1970 SEVENTH OVERALL

1972 THIRD OVERALL

1973 DID NOT FINISH

1974 SECOND OVERALL
ONE STAGE WIN: stage 16, Seo de
Urgel–Saint-Lary-Soulan

1975 19TH OVERALL

1976 THIRD OVERALL

Chapter 6: 1969–1974

Merckx: The Belgian Cannibal

Everyone knew that when Eddy Merckx made his Tour debut it was going to be pretty spectacular, but no one could foresee that he would go from winning the race at his first attempt to totally dominating the race in every discipline, be it sprinting, time-trialling or climbing. Merckx ate up his opponents and swallowed them whole. He was the world's greatest-ever rider, competing in the world's greatest race – what more could anyone ask for?

1969

Eddy Merckx was famously known as the "Cannibal", not just because he ate up his opposition, but because, when he was feeling hungry, he swallowed them whole. He planned to make his Tour debut on 28 June, 1969, and he made no secret of his ambition to win it first time round.

Even at the age of 24 this kind of talk was more than just bravado – he was absolutely serious, and his rivals knew it. But a month before the race, while leading the Giro d'Italia, and looking unlikely to be threatened, he tested positive for amphetamines, and was expelled from the race.

Merckx was shattered by the news. He denied all wrongdoing vehemently, while his team, his doctor and his fans protested to anyone who would listen. After 18 days without competition – a vital part of a rider's Tour preparation – he was fully cleared by the International Federation of Professional Cycling, on the grounds that the test procedure had been flawed, and that it was far from conclusive. The fact that a mob of several hundred Belgian fans pressed against

the doors of the Belgian Cycling League's headquarters in Brussels, where the decision was being taken, made it difficult for them to come to any other conclusion. It was an inauspicious start to the Tour career of the world's greatest-ever cyclist.

With his name cleared, Merckx spent the final weeks leading up to the Tour hastily trying to regain his competitive edge. On the first road stage the race route would bring the peloton to within a few hundred metres of his home in Woluwe, a Brussels suburb, and he desperately wanted to give his nearest and dearest something to celebrate.

The drugs episode had unquestionably robbed Merckx of his peak form – he finished second in the opening prologue to Germany's Ruti Altig – but he had soon warmed up, and with the race heading toward Belgium he was more than ready to turn his fortunes round. The bunch knew exactly what was coming – Merckx chased down Barry Hoban as he made a bid for lone glory, and then did much of the work as the finish line loomed ever closer. Unable to contain himself, he opted

Above: Merckx stays close to rival Roger Pingeon in 1969. Below: Joachim Agostinho wins stage 5 at Mulhouse. Previous page: Merckx in 1969 when he attacked on the Tourmalet and doubled his lead to 16 minutes.

for an early sprint, but was overtaken in the final 50 metres – a brave move that won him the yellow jersey, if not the stage itself.

PLYING THEIR TRADE

Keen for the re-introduced trade teams to have a chance to show off their colours, organizers had included a second part to the first full day's racing. That afternoon there was a team time trial – the results would not count toward the individual classification save for the modest time bonuses awarded to the riders in the three fastest teams. Merckx's team – Faema – won by a comfortable margin, much to the delight of the crowds. Then the race disappeared into Holland, and the jersey was passed on to Julien Stevens who won the sprint. "It was a great moment for him to take over the yellow jersey," Merckx later said of his team-mate Stevens. "I was quite happy to give it up – temporarily. It is much too conspicuous."

The race started going uphill on stage five, and it was Frimatic's Joachim Agostinho who took the honours, rewarded for a long solo effort with Portugal's first-ever stage win at the Tour. Then the real racing started.

There was more than a little luck going Merckx's way on the stage to Belfort. First Gimondi punctured, and spent 15 kilometres chasing

the bunch, then Raymond Poulidor suffered from mechanical problems, leaving him to catch up on his own for 10 kilometres.

Before they had any chance of recovery Merckx was chasing down the early leaders, soon bridging the gap, and bringing Joaquin Galera and Roger De Vlaeminck with him. And he didn't stop when he reached the head of the race, but, with apparently no effort, he powered on. The stragglers clung to his wheel, unable to take a turn. De Vlaeminck fell and re-mounted, but no sooner had he got back to the group than Merckx had decimated it. The nine-kilometre climb to the Ballon d'Alsace saw Merckx ride unchallenged into the *maillot jaune* – the race was only six days old, and already he looked invincible.

The majority of the field were beginning to tire, and Merckx was only just getting going. The next time trial was a mere 8.8 kilometres – so short that it would be of little consequence to anyone other than those with their sights on a podium finish. Merckx won, pleased to better Altig, who had taken the opening prologue a week previously.

If Merckx needed to do anything more to prove his utter dominance of the 1969 Tour, he did it on stage nine. Having gone clear with France and Peugeot's Roger Pingeon over the Forclaz *hors-categorie* climb, the Belgian national champion wisely decided to ease the pain he was inflicting on the peloton by not trying too hard in the two-up sprint for the stage. Pingeon won the day, but Merckx succeeded in adding the King of the Mountains' and the points' jerseys to his collection.

The "gift" was subtle enough not to cause offence, and left the Frenchman as his closest rival for the overall classification.

MERCKX BUBBLES OVER

Over the Galibier and the Col de la Madeleine the race was battered by snow and rain – 14 riders abandoned the race before reaching Briançon. Merckx was content to let fellow Belgian Herman van Springel win

Merckx leaves rivals in his wake on the climb to the Ballon d'Alsace during stage 6, 1969.

the stage – Van Springel later said he had been fortified by a mouthful of champagne he had drunk when handed the bottle by some spectators on the Galibier – but he was not going to allow anyone else to pull off the same stunt. Pingeon tried to attack him the next day on the Col d'Allos, and his response was emphatic. He stomped on the pedals – Pingeon was unable to keep up for more than a few moments – and soon caught the pair of Spanish riders who had been away since the beginning of the stage. Point proved, he relaxed, and with 100 kilometres to go Pingeon and Gimondi had rejoined them. It was a technical descent to the finish, but Merckx was as good at going

down mountains as he was going up them, and brashly attacked in the final kilometres. Gimondi alone could hang on, but Merckx had had enough of letting other people win – and besides, he was going so fast that the Italian simply could not get past.

While any other man with such a safe lead would have used the next day's flat stage to recover his reserves, Merckx proved that he wanted not just to win the Tour overall, but also every stage he could *en route*. He attacked on stage 12 and, although Gimondi won the stage, it was from the move that Merckx had instigated. He won the next time trial and, with more than eight minutes in hand, he still wanted more. On the last Pyrenean stage he attacked again, on the Tourmalet, 140 kilometres from the finish. It was as brutal as it was unnecessary; and from anyone else it would have been tactical suicide. But Merckx wasn't anyone else. Over the Aubisque he doubled his lead to 16-18, and still had the energy to animate the race all the way to Paris. He rounded off his Tour with another time-trial win on the final stage – his sixth win in three weeks. Points' winner, King of the Mountains, winner of the Combine competition and the overall – Merckx had become the sport's greatest ever Tour rider on his debut.

1970

Merckx's dominance of the 1969 Tour had been so overwhelming that some of his rivals had spent the 12 months running up to the next season dreading what he would do to them next. He won the Giro in late spring – a fine riposte to those who had questioned him after the previous year's Italian Tour – and was at his absolute best for July.

Organizers tweaked the route in an effort to make it a more open competition, hoping that gentler mountain stages would give other riders the chance to outmanoeuvre the Belgian. A week into the race they were forced to acknowledge that the plan had not worked.

Merckx won the prologue, then lost the jersey to a Faemino team-mate, Italo Zilioli, two days later. Together they won the 10.7-kilometre team time trial by more than a minute. If Merckx were ever in need of help, which was doubtful, he had plenty of strong men ready to offer him a wheel.

Stage six took the peloton across Flanders, on the cobbled roads more familiar to riders of the Paris-Roubaix Classic, though covering only half the distance of the Classic's one-day event. With persistent rain, the jarring cobbles proved a treacherous surface – crashes, punctures and mechanical failures were inevitable.

Above: On the climb to Mont Ventoux in 1970, Merckx reaches for a drink as the heat takes its toll. Below: Joaquim Agostinho and Mogens Frey kiss and make up for the cameras at the end of stage 9 in Mulhouse.

Merckx suffered a flat tyre, and was left to chase alone for 20 kilometres – his team may have been strong, but they could make mistakes. Then, in the final kilometre, having worked hard to bring back the escapees, his back wheel collapsed.

No matter that he was instantly handed a spare bike; the leading group were perilously close to the finish, and could already smell the champagne that would go to whoever won the stage. Merckx had to produce a superhuman effort to bridge back to them before they entered the stadium at Valenciennes. He couldn't quite contest the stage victory, but thanks to his incredible 800-metre effort – and his early work that had broken up the peloton – he was back in the yellow jersey.

When Merckx won the first part of the split stage the next day, many assumed that he would cruise to victory in that afternoon's time trial to

make it a double. But he was beaten, on his home patch in Belgium, by Spain's José Gonzalez-Linares. It made no difference to the overall classification and, had it not been for his superb ride that morning, the insult would have been unbearable.

LOCKED IN COMBAT

The first hilly stage of the Tour is always dramatic, but on this occasion it proved more controversial than usual, with two Frimatic team-mates almost coming to blows after passing the line together. Denmark's Mogens Frey and Portugal's Joaquim Agostinho had ridden together for 30 kilometres, unable – because of the language barrier – to communicate with anything other than gestures. Agostinho did virtually all the work, the Dane sitting comfortably in his slipstream all the way to Mulhouse. Agostinho assumed that Frey would not challenge him in the sprint. So when Frey jumped for the line, Agostinho was so astonished that he threw out his arm to try and stop him coming past. The Portuguese rider finished first, but race *commissaires* reversed the two men's placings before the ceremony. Whatever language the unwritten code of cycling etiquette was written in, it certainly wasn't Danish.

Normality resumed the next day with Merckx winning the rolling stage, riding more aggressively than most would have done in an attempt to win a mountain stage. He wanted a victory for its own sake, and was not concerned about saving his strength for later. Merckx needed to win like he needed food and water.

Still not satisfied, the defending champion won the next time trial, and the first Alpine stage. It was Raymond Poulidor who summed up what everyone one was thinking: "I've got my eye on second place – Merckx is simply inaccessible at the moment." Inaccessible maybe, but there were some signs of human weakness, although it took the Ventoux to reveal them.

TOM SIMPSON'S MONUMENT

Wary of the extreme climate on the Giant of Provence, the stage to the Ventoux was scheduled to finish at 7 p.m., avoiding the worst of the heat. Merckx knew its reputation – it had claimed the life of his friend Tom Simpson just three years earlier – but he would not humble himself to man or mountain. When he attacked on the early slopes of the climb only Agostinho dared go with him.

Out on the arid mountainside, the Frimatic rider soon fell back. Merckx rode on alone, slowing only to acknowledge Simpson's memorial, where race director Jacques Goddet had laid a wreath when leading the race vehicles up to the summit. As in 1967, it was an extremely hot day and, even in the early evening, the exposed peak left Merckx nowhere to shelter. With 500 metres to go, his tremendous effort began to tell. Suddenly the pedals seemed to stick, his easy style replaced by a

grunting struggle and his hard-won lead beginning to peel away. Riding in among the lead cars in a cloud of fumes, he practically crept across the line and was rushed off to an ambulance for oxygen. A short while later he was back on his feet, while Martin Vandebossche (Molteni), whose own valiant ride had earned him second place on the stage, ahead of Lucien Van Impe, was driven away in a state of total exhaustion.

One of the few men who had harboured any real hope of beating Merckx in the Tour, Luis Ocana, had spent the first half of the race battling with bronchitis. A brilliant climber, the Spaniard had struggled to finish each stage without draining himself too much. With help from his team-mates he made it through to the final week, and gradually regained his form. He was so far down in the race for the jersey that Merckx was happy to see him win the stage to St Gaudens. He was not so happy the next day.

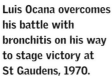

Luis Ocana overcomes his battle with bronchitis on his way to stage victory at St Gaudens, 1970.

The stage to La Mongie was short – 135.5 kilometres – but harsh. Merckx was naturally in the leading group, doing most of the work, but when it came to the final climb he cracked. Unable to get comfortable, the Belgian had already changed bikes several times and was finally dropped by the group, with Bernard Thévenet eventually winning the stage. Merckx's off day lost him 16 seconds, and he was still fourth on the stage – enough for him to regain the points' jersey to go with the leader's one. It was hardly a disaster.

In the event, Walter Godefroot (Salvarani) used the final, flat stages to wrestle the green jersey back from Merckx, while the man in yellow won the two remaining time trials. He confessed to being nervous on the final leg of the race, which was the 54-kilometre *contre-la-montre* from Versailles to Paris. "I can't help it, I'm scared of crashing," he said. "The race is never won until it is finished." Technically he was right,

but in reality, this race had been his for the taking from the very moment when he won the first time trial.

1971

As has always been the way for great sportsmen, Merckx found that, with two Tour wins to his name, the Press had decided it was time to stop building him up, and to start trying to knock him down. He had persuaded his new team, Molteni, that they should not compete in the Giro, and should instead concentrate on the defence of his Tour title, using French races as preparation. He had won the Dauphiné Libéré and the Midi Libre, while, he claimed, being far from peak fitness. But commentators suggested that he was growing vulnerable, and that Luis Ocana, who had been dogged by illness the previous year would be strong enough to test him this time around.

A change in sponsor did nothing to prevent Merckx and his *domestiques* winning the team time trial, this year run as the prologue. The next day was split into three short road stages, ensuring plenty of action and, after negotiations between the riders and organizers, a good deal of prize money being handed out.

On the first part-stage of the day, the peloton staged a go-slow until the organizers agreed to up the value of the prizes for each leg of the split stages. Merckx did not concern himself with the big bunch sprints, preferring to dig midway through the stages and collect adequate time bonuses from the hot-spot sprints to put him in yellow. Then on the first full day's racing he made an initial, decisive effort to show his critics that he was in France for one thing only – unquestionable overall victory.

There was no need for him to attack so early – the mountains and the time trials were what really mattered – but he had a point to make. He wanted to beat his Belgian rival, Roger de Vlaeminck, he wanted to snatch the 20-second bonus that a stage win would give him and he wanted to scare his rivals. After

Merckx and Ocana on the road to Saint-Etienne in 1971 – Merckx would lose the jersey by the end of the stage.

decimating the field – the 15 men in the break were the only ones left in the running for the *maillot jaune* after barely 72 hours of the race – he took huge risks in the sprint on the cinder track at Strasbourg. It paid off, though, and he spent the rest of the first week controlling the race first-hand, marshalling the peloton, infiltrating and forming breaks, making sure he was always close to the action. Then, when the race hit the mountains, he faltered.

A COSTLY MISTAKE

Merckx wanted to play hard and fast. He wanted to push his rivals from the start of the mountains, in order to whittle down his competition as soon as possible. His aggression on stage eight not only eliminated many of his competitors, but most of his allies as well. Even when the break he had instigated was caught, he insisted on setting the pace, single-

handedly chasing down numerous attacks, using a foolishly large gear. Then, when Ocana – a genuine threat to the jersey – attacked on the final climb, Merckx was too tired to respond. Joop Zoetemelk and Agostinho gave chase, and Merckx, refusing to slip back to the bunch, hung on for fourth place.

His bad tactics were compounded by ill fortune on the stage to Saint-Etienne, and he lost the jersey he'd been wearing since day one. In the leading group, Merckx punctured on the descent of the penultimate climb and was left abandoned on the mountainside as he waited for almost a minute for mechanical assistance. By the time he remounted he had been caught by the second group on the road, only to be cruelly dropped by two of them on the last climb. Bernard Thévenet won the stage, and the jersey went to Zoetemelk. The race had split open, and there

was a queue of riders waiting to drop Merckx into the abyss. The man to do it was Luis Ocana.

The Spaniard seized his chance without waiting for Merckx's wounds to heal. A 117-kilometre break, the last 60 of which he did solo, saw him finish almost nine minutes ahead of the defending champion and the remaining contenders. It was such a devastating ride that suddenly Ocana, who was unparalleled in the mountains, was the one who was bound to win the race. "Today Ocana tamed us all," admitted Merckx after the stage. "I cannot see how he can lose, but I'm not quitting, I can tell you that."

Forced to acknowledge another rider's brilliance, Merckx found he was better respected in defeat than he had been in previous victories.

As one who knew all too well how hard it is to lead the Tour when faced with angry rivals, Merckx was convinced that he could crack Ocana. The whole of Belgium was just as sure – a radio appeal was launched, which resulted in thousands of telegrams being sent to the national hero, each containing just one word – "Attack!"

On the undulating stage taking the peloton toward the Pyrenees, Merckx turned the race on its head.

From the moment the stage began Merckx's team-mate "Rini" Wagtmans attacked, with Merckx jumping on his wheel before the peloton had realized what was happening. For 251 kilometres the bunch pursued relentlessly, with the gap never opening further than two minutes as Merckx pressed on.

Above: Luis Ocana took the stage and the yellow jersey after a 117-kilometre break to Orcières–Merlette in 1971. Below: Agony for Ocana as he loses the maillot jaune after crashing out on stage 14.

The sprint for the stage win went to Luciano Armani (SCIC), and Merckx quickly moved up into second place. But even with the time bonuses he had picked up as well as the two-minute advantage he had made over the bunch, he was still 7-34 adrift of Ocana. He had completed the fastest stage in Tour history – averaging 45.351 kph – and had spent much of his reserves in the process, but his material gains had been small.

Merckx won the next day's time trial without much difficulty, but still complained that Ocana had an unfair advantage, surrounded as he was by French television motorbikes, which shielded him from the wind. The two men were looking forward to the Pyrenees, where they both knew the race would be decided.

THE WORST WAY TO WIN

A result came on the following day, in the worst of circumstances. Merckx was his usual belligerent self, attacking repeatedly in an effort to drop Ocana. But the Spaniard was unperturbed, holding his own, relishing the prospect of carrying the yellow jersey so close to the border with his home country, where his fans were waiting for him.

The two men were locked together as they descended together in the pouring rain. The poor road surface was running with water and looked certain to claim victims. Riders flailed down the slope, sticking out feet to slow themselves when their brakes proved useless. Merckx and Ocana fell together: the Belgian scrambled back on to his bike but, before Ocana could remount, he was hit by another falling rider – Zoetemelk, who had a front wheel puncture and was out of control, skidded into him. Ocana was knocked unconscious as yet more riders crashed into him; a gaggle of spectators ran to protect him as the race doctor rushed to help him.

But his injuries were not as bad as suspected – taken to hospital by helicopter, he was found to have severe cuts and bruises, but no broken bones. Given the circumstances, the Société du Tour understood perfectly when Eddy Merckx refused the yellow jersey at the end of the stage – he even talked about abandoning the race, but eventually decided to continue the next day, not wearing the jersey. He wanted to win, but not in this way.

Two days later Ocana returned home to recuperate, and Merckx visited him before the stage. Still wanting to justify his race lead, the Belgian turned that afternoon's stage into another epic, driving the break and winning the sprint. It extended his lead in the points' competition, and, with a win in the final time trial, he took both yellow and green jerseys home from Paris. He was physically injured from the crash, but his pride was hurt most – he hated to think that he had won by a trick of fate rather than by power and athleticism. No matter how brilliantly he rode in the final week, battling against the absent Ocana, he knew, as everyone did, that had the Spaniard not fallen the story would have been a very different one.

1972

Merckx versus Ocana, part two, was scheduled to start on 1 July 1972. The "what if" stemming from the previous race was still echoing in the ears of the three-times winner, and there was speculation that, should he win a fourth time, he would never ride the Tour again. He had won the Giro, despite having a weak team that were unable to help him in the mountains and, although Herman Van Springel would be in the Molteni line-up for the Tour, it looked as if Merckx would be left to his own devices come July.

Ocana filled the role of archetypal underdog, and found much sympathy from the French public as the moral victor of the previous race. He spent the first six months of the year preparing specifically for the Tour –

he believed that he had been the strongest man in the field last year, and wanted to prove that it had not been a one-off. In order to do that, he knew he had to mark Merckx's every move for the first week, as the Belgian would be sure to take any opportunity he could to break away before the mountain stages.

Both men made it safely with the first group in the only major break of the first week, on stage four, but Merckx had the upper hand. He had won the prologue and, with Molteni, the team time trial, and had re-acquainted himself with the feeling of the yellow jersey on his back – in place of the world champion's one that he was proudly wearing for the second time in his career. It promised to be a close-fought race in the Pyrenees.

Ocana was cruelly robbed of his first chance to really challenge Merckx on the opening mountain stage; the two had stuck together over the Aubisque, but on the next climb, the Soulor, he punctured and lost contact with the group. Oblivious to the rain and fog, he carved his way down the mountain.

Merckx noses ahead of Ocana on stage 7 to Pau, 1972.

Each time he rounded a corner he hoped that he would glimpse the others. He was slowly gaining on them, but in doing so he was taking such risks that a crash was all but inevitable. When it did happen, it was thankfully not as serious as in 1971, and he quickly remounted, losing only another minute. The Spaniard complained about the lack of sportsmanship from men who had attacked when he was down, but Merckx was quick to snap back. "I did not know Ocana had fallen. Last year when I was the victim Ocana took advantage, but I didn't cry. I've said it before – I never make gifts."

UNSYMPATHETIC MERCKX

As if to shatter Ocana's increasingly heroic image as the race brushed past his home territory, Merckx won the next stage over the Tourmalet, climbing and descending with equal panache. His eight-second margin over Ocana at the stage finish felt like

an hour to the Spaniard, although he tried to dismiss it. The stage was so arduous that the 1967 winner Roger Pingeon finished with just enough energy to strap his bike to the team car and retired not only from the race, but from the sport entirely. Merckx, meanwhile, had plenty more to dish out.

On the Ventoux stage Bernard Thévenet lifted French spirits with a fine stage win, while the two men contesting the jersey fought a private battle behind him. Ocana had tried, and failed, to shake Merckx from the lead group on the lower slopes of the climb; Thévenet stole off while the pair were engrossed in watching one another's every move and, when it came to the finale, the Frenchman was the clear winner. Merckx satisfied both pride and self-confidence with a final effort that gained him a further five seconds over his rival.

Merckx played with Ocana, never letting him forget the way he

Above: Bernard Thévenet on his way to victory on stage 11 at Mont Ventoux, 1972. Below: Merckx shares pleasantries with his latest rival, Cyrille Guimard, winner of stage 15 to Mont Revard.

had treated him the year before, letting him know how it felt to be constantly belittled by a man who could outclass him on every single mountain. Then he landed his decisive blow on the most prestigious stage of the race. Over the Col du Vars and the Col d'Izoard, Merckx rode at a relentless pace, paying no heed to Ocana as he punctured, thinking only of winning. He dropped his few remaining companions on the Izoard, taking the King of the Mountains' jersey from Lucien Van Impe in the process.

The next day was a split stage: a morning time trial, which Merckx won, and then a 151-kilometre road leg, with a flat 20 kilometres to the finish. It should have been a straightforward day. But Ocana was exhausted; he had suffered from breathing difficulties in the high mountains, and his body could respond no longer. As he trailed in off the back of Merckx's group he had to endure whistles and catcalls from the French public that had so vocally supported him in his challenge to the reigning champion. He announced his retirement from the race, leaving Cyrille Guimard, the revelation of the Tour, to move up into second place.

NEW CHALLENGE TO MERCKX

Guimard and Merckx clashed the very next day, with the Gan rider narrowly outsprinting the *maillot jaune* for the stage. But Guimard was in serious trouble with an inflamed hamstring in his right knee. With each hour of riding it deteriorated; he was given painkilling injections every morning to enable him to start each stage, until he began to damage his left knee, too, in compensating for the original injury. Merckx was also suffering, from such a painful seat that he was obliged to ride for 40 kilometres out of the saddle at one point. Guimard was forced to abandon, while Merckx, with the benefit of a 10-minute advantage over new second-placed rider Raymond Poulidor, found a new saddle and carried on. The Tour was taking its toll on everyone.

Physical discomfort and fatigue affected the race leader's judgement equally. At a crucial point on stage 19, he foolishly impeded another rider by grabbing on to his jersey, and was penalized for it. He spent the rest of the stage arguing with Jacques Goddet, the Tour Director, as he drove alongside the peloton, but to no avail. Despite this, with no challengers, and the points' competition safe too (he had lost the mountains' jersey back to Van Impe), it was a Tour won. He confirmed his superiority in the final time trial, but didn't stay in Paris to party. After stopping briefly to give Guimard the green jersey, which he surely would have won had he made it to the end of the race, Merckx went straight home to Brussels, to his wife who was expecting their second child. His dominance of the race had been no less than he expected of himself, but the strain of the repeated effort was beginning to tell. He would not defend his title in 1973.

1973

A Tour without Merckx may have been a meaningless event for his loyal fans, but for most spectators it promised to be the most exciting and open race for years. The men who had previously contented themselves with minor placings – Luis Ocana, Raymond Poulidor, Joop Zoetemelk, Cyrille Guimard – were finally able to rid themselves of Merckx's presence and race for the jersey.

Ocana, the only man to have truly tested the Belgian, was quick to take on responsibility for the race – having been so close to victory in 1971 he knew how good it felt. But he could never ride the Tour without incident – a dog ran into the peloton on stage two, felling him, and causing another 10 riders to crash on top of him. Another dent in his morale came when his Bic team manager Maurice de Muer threatened the entire squad with expulsion from the team if they did not work solely for Ocana.

Realizing that he needed to earn the services of his *domestiques*, the

Spaniard took on a primary role in the winning move on the stage from Roubaix to Rheims; then, the moment the race hit the mountains, he attacked.

It was a split stage, made up of two rough races. When Ocana made his move, it was not a violent one – it was a smooth, considered acceleration that nonetheless destroyed the group. Only Zoetemelk could keep pace with him, and even he didn't last long; the prospect of another 151-kilometre stage after lunch made the one-in-eight climb seem even more punishing. Frenchman Bernard Thévenet had an untimely crash, quickly got back on his bike and was just able to regain the chasing group in time to contest the sprint for second place.

He sought his revenge that afternoon, breaking away in the last kilometre of the rain-soaked stage, taking back a handful of seconds for his pains. Ocana was in yellow, but there was still a long way to go.

Pandering to the commerical interests of the race sponsors,

Above: A determined-looking Luis Ocana battles with Juan Manuel Fuente on the Izoard, 1973. Below: Ocana is congratulated by members of the press after victory in the first time trial stage at Thuir.

organizers Jacques Goddet and Felix Letivan had sacrificed the comfort of the riders for the benefit of the French towns and villages that wanted the publicity of the race passing through their streets.

The peloton was completely shattered after just a single week of racing and, when faced with the Col de la Madeleine, the Telegraphe, Col du Galibier and the Izoard on day eight, it fell to pieces.

Thévenet, Jose Manuel Fuente and Ocana escaped at the base of the Telegraphe, and were joined by Zoetemelk and the other pretenders. Fuente kept on digging and digging, but succeeded only in dropping the weakest of his companions, while the man in the *maillot jaune* remained unmoved.

Twelve kilometres from the summit of the Galibier he changed tack altogether, dropping back to sit on Ocana's wheel then, after cresting and descending the 2,646-metre peak, he tried again as they went over the summit of the Izoard, briefly gaining five seconds.

OCANA VERSUS FUENTE

Fuente punctured with 37 kilometres still remaining, but Ocana did not wait for him. He was confident enough of his own strength, and after leading his countryman for most of the previous two climbs felt no debt to him. The pair had fallen out already at the Spanish tour and Fuente's lack of cooperation was more than Ocana could take. "OK, so I attacked when he punctured, and that wasn't the gentlemanly thing to do, but how else do you treat such a gangster?" he said.

The 20-kilometre ascent to the finish line held no fear for Ocana, but it spelt the end of the race for many exhausted individuals.

A dozen riders were expelled for hanging on to the doors of their team cars and being towed up the climb – an offence that would normally result in both a fine and a time penalty – but a price that many were willing to pay if it meant getting to the finish before the time cut. Despite making life difficult for the riders in order to please sponsors, the race

directors offered no leniency. There was no direct confrontation, but as the race progressed with average speeds nearing a post-war low, it was clear that the peloton were unable, and unwilling, to cope with the monstrous stages and transfers that were being imposed.

Ocana's lead over Fuente had now risen to almost 10 minutes, but he was still not satisfied. In an echo of Merckx in 1971, he wanted to prove not only that he was the best in the race, but that he was better than the man who was absent.

Ocana won the next *contre-la-montre*, and the mountain stage that finished in Luchon, Spain, further heaping humiliation upon Fuente, who eventually lost his second place to Thévenet. On the final day of the race, the *maillot jaune* won the morning's time trial, and Thévenet the race to Paris.

All in all, it had been a stunning performance from Ocana – remarkably, only three men finished the race within half an hour of him – but for all of his six stage wins and

his easy victory, he would have given anything to have beaten Merckx by the smallest of margins.

1974

From the start of the 1974 season, Eddy Merckx made it clear that he was hell-bent on winning the Tour. He needed just one more stage victory to equal André Leducq's record 25 wins, and one more overall win to equal Jacques Anquetil's five. With Luis Ocana out of the race – he had fallen and injured his elbow at the Tour de l'Aude a fortnight earlier – it was a fully achievable goal.

HOLDING OUT FOR THE JERSEY

It was difficult for Merckx to follow the conventional wisdom that a potential winner should not try to hold the *maillot jaune* from start to finish. Confined to a Radio Luxembourg tribune during the previous season's race, Merckx came to the 1974 race with wins in the Swiss tour and the Giro d'Italia to prove that his appetite was undiminished, and he opened the race with his usual confidence, winning the prologue. Luckily there was a team-mate at hand to relieve him of the jersey; Frenchman Jospeh Bruyère, who finished third in the short time trial, found his way into the first stage's winning break and took over the race lead. Even with Bruyère up the road, orchestrating a tactical coup for their Molteni team, Merckx couldn't sit back. He snatched back 12 seconds in the intermediate sprints, and started laying the groundwork for the moment when he would retake the jersey that he had only temporarily lent out to his friend.

INTER-TEAM FRIENDSHIP

Making its first venture across the Channel, the Tour reached Plymouth on its second stage, a 14-lap circuit race. Merckx controlled the race while Britain's Barry Hoban bounded past him in a bid to collect sprint bonuses and cash prizes as often as he could. Naturally Hoban had designs on the stage, but was

Ocana destroys the rest of the field during the final time trial at Versailles, 1973.

badly positioned when the Molteni men wound up the pace for the final lap. Merckx was less concerned with a stage win than with making alliances that could be useful later. Holland's Henke Van Poppe, convinced that Merckx was leading out Patrick Sercu, piggybacked the move and then sprinted to victory. The two Belgians were long-standing friends and had ridden together in the Six Days – traditional winter track races – there was no secret that they would indulge in some inter-team cooperation if it was to their mutual benefit. It didn't quite work, but back on French soil a day later Sercu won the stage after Molteni had held a tight rein on the bunch all day, a feat he repeated the next day. Merckx duly reclaimed the jersey, but little attention was paid. Gerben Karstens, who was second on the stage, had forgotten to go to dope control, after the race. Belatedly remembering that he was due to present himself within 30 minutes of the stage finishing, he rushed back to the race headquarters, only to have a 10-minute time penalty and a £140 fine slapped upon him.

The consequences for the Dutchman would be disastrous – a genuine contender for the overall competition, a 10-minute deficit before the race reached the mountains would nullify any challenge he could muster. Rather than offer private thanks that one of their rivals had been effectively eliminated on a technicality, the peloton rallied round, calling for the penalty to be quashed. As a stand-alone incident they may not have been so sympathetic toward Karstens – it was a self-inflicted problem after all – but it came on the back of a truly thoughtless step by the Union Cycliste Internationale (UCI).

The same man that handed Karstens his fine had tried to penalize Regis Delphine the previous day, for the same reason. It was only when he had tried to find the rider, or a representative of his team, that he discovered the Frenchman was laid up in the local hospital, yet to regain consciousness after crashing when crossing the finish line. Riders' Union President Cyrille Guimard gave the ultimatum: we won't ride unless Karstens is reinstated to second place overall. The rule book wielders capitulated. Faced with a strike they had little choice – no riders meant no race, and, barring world wars, the Tour stops for no one. Karstens responded eloquently

Above: Good friends – Merckx and Sercu share a joke during the early stages of the 1974 Tour. Below: Raymond Poulidor on his way to winning stage 16 to St-Lary-Soulan.

by winning the stage, Merckx took back the jersey by virtue of inter-mediate bonuses, and everything returned to normal.

One day into the mountains and Merckx took command, winning the stage to Aspro Gaillard. The next day was more difficult. Gonzala Aja (Kas) attacked on the Mont du Chat, dropping everyone but the venerable Raymond Poulidor. The 38-year-old Frenchman, who had been on the verge of retiring for so long, suddenly found himself challenging Merckx, and leading him by 1-35 at the top of the climb. It was a glorious, if short-lived moment. The yellow jersey was not to be beaten, however. He made up the deficit on the descent, bringing Mariano Martinez (Sonolor) with him and then, after catching his breath in the newly formed group, outsprinted them all for the stage victory.

TERROR THREATS IN SPAIN

A third day in the Alps was more than Merckx needed to show that this was his Tour. His former rivals – Poulidor, Thévenet, Herman Van Springel and Joachim Agostinho – simply faded away, leaving only the Spanish climbers of Kas to worry him. On stage 11 the race leader found himself in the impossible position of being in the stage-winning break with three men from an opposing team. The numerical disadvantage might have been overcome, had it not been for a mistake of his own making.

The stage finished after the Galibier, and Merckx knew that he would need to use his peerless descending skills if he were to take the stage. He asked his mechanics to fit his bike with a 55-tooth chain ring, so that he could go downhill so fast that no one would dare try and keep up with him. They did as he requested but, instead of taking the customized bike, Merckx decided to use one of the spare bikes at the last moment. When Vicente Lopez-Carril broke away over the summit of the Galibier, Merckx was relying on the descent both to drop his two Kas team-mates, and to catch

up with Lopez-Carril. He simply ran out of gears, and was unable to reach the necessary speed. It was a rare mistake, but fortunately for Merckx he was in a position where he could afford to make it.

Another Molteni rider, Joseph Spruyt, had his moment in the sun, winning the stage over the Ventoux, while Merckx sat back and watched. He knew the forthcoming stage to Seo de Urgel, on the other side of the Spanish border, would be crucial. A sizeable group stayed together over the major climbs and, as they reached the finish town, it was only the stage win that was to be contested. Martinez decided to lead out the sprint, but as he rounded the final corner he skidded and fell. Merckx, who had been on his wheel, somehow twisted his bike around the prone rider, and as the rest tumbled

he charged for the line. He had all the luck, even if he didn't need it.

There was more glory for Raymond Poulidor, who won the stage to St-Lary Soulan, pulling himself further toward the podium. But the race had more to contend with than a rejuvenated Frenchman. As the Tour slept that night, six official vehicles were blown up by a Spanish terrorist group, the Internationalist Revolutionary Action Group, who threatened to kill any Spanish riders who would not quit the Tour. "We advise the Spanish cyclists to leave the race if they do not wish to be treated as conscious representatives of Francoism. Tonight's action was only a warning," read the message.

Both the Kas and Casera teams defied the menace. Only two concessions were made: Lopez-Carril swapped his conspicuous Spanish

Left to right: Raymond Poulidor, Eddy Merckx and Vicente Lopez-Carril on their lap of honour in Paris, 1974.

champion's jersey for a standard one, and a police motor bike was assigned to guard any Spanish rider that escaped from the safety of the bunch.

But the threats could not fail to play on the riders' minds, and there was little inclination to attack Merckx the next day. The field capitulated, and Merckx equalled another record. He won another time trial and then, when Patrick Sercu was disqualified from the final day's sprint, Merckx was awarded another stage, taking his total for the race to eight – as many as Charles Pélisser had won in 1930.

Poulidor finished second overall; another runner's-up prize to go with the two he had already collected behind Jacques Anquetil. He would always be known as the man who nearly won, while Merckx was the man who always did.

Tour Legends
Eddy Merckx

> **"I always had and still have that special desire in me to be the best. That's why I accept, and why I am proud of, the nickname they once gave me: The Cannibal."** Eddy Merckx

Merckx on his way to winning stage 14, Gap–Mont Ventoux, 1970.

EDDY MERCKX (BEL)
b. 17/6/45 Meensel-Kiezegem

SEVEN PARTICIPATIONS
FIVE VICTORIES
34 STAGE WINS

1969 FIRST OVERALL
KING OF THE MOUNTAINS
WINNER POINTS COMPETITION
SIX STAGE WINS: stage 6, Mulhouse–Ballon d'Alsace; stage 8 part 1, Divonne (time trial); stage 11, Briançon–Digne; stage 15, Revel (time trial); stage 17, Luchon–Mourenx; stage 22 part 2, Créteil–Paris (time trial)

1970 FIRST OVERALL
KING OF THE MOUNTAINS
EIGHT STAGE WINS: prologue, Limoges; stage 7 part 1, Valenciennes–Forest; stage 10, Belfort–Divonne; stage 11 part 1, Divonne (time trial); stage 12, Thonon–Grenoble; stage 14, Gap–Mont Ventoux; stage 20 part 2, Bordeaux (time trial); stage 23, Versailles–Paris (time trial)

1971 FIRST OVERALL
WINNER POINTS COMPETITION
FOUR STAGE WINS: stage 2, Mulhouse–Strasbourg; stage 13, Albi (time trial); stage 17, Mont de Marsan–Bordeaux; stage 20, Versailles–Paris (time trial)

1972 FIRST OVERALL
WINNER POINTS COMPETITION
SIX STAGE WINS: prologue, Angers; stage 5 part 2, Bordeaux (time trial); stage 8, Pau–Luchon; stage 13, Orcières-Merlette–Briançon; stage 14 part 1, Briançon–Valloire; stage 20 part 1, Versailles (time trial)

1974 FIRST OVERALL
EIGHT STAGE WINS: prologue, Brest; stage 7, Mons–Chalons sur Marne; stage 9, Besançon–Gaillard; stage 10, Gaillard–Aix les Bains; stage 15, Colomiers–Seo de Urgel; stage 19 part 2, Bordeaux (time trial); stage 21 part 1, Vouvray–Orléans; stage 22, Orléans–Paris

1975 SECOND OVERALL
TWO STAGE WINS: stage 6, Merlin-Plage (time trial); stage 9 part 2, Fleurance–Auch (time trial)

1977 SIXTH OVERALL

Thévenet: The Giant Slayer

Eddy Merckx was a giant of cycling but he could not keep winning the Tour for ever. He equalled Anquetil's record of five victories, but could not better it. Then he raged in disbelief as he slowly weakened, unable to stop Bernard Thévenet from leading a new generation in the fight for the yellow jersey.

1975

The fact that Eddy Merckx came to the 1975 Tour as five-times winner and reigning world champion did not stop the more vicious members of the Press corps questioning his motivation and his ability to win a record sixth time. He had missed the Giro owing to tonsillitis, and had failed to win the Dauphiné Libéré – one of his preferred warm-up events.

His former adversary Luis Ocana, now riding for Super Ser, had never fully recovered from the bronchitis that ended his race 12 months earlier. The key to winning the Tour has always been the ability to recover from racing across the hardest terrain day after day, and the Spaniard's physical frailty simply would not allow him to do that. If anyone was going to beat Merckx it would be someone younger, a star in the making, and not one of the old guard.

It took less than nine minutes for the first rider of the new generation to get the better of Merckx. Francesco Moser won the prologue, and took

the yellow jersey into Belgium for the opening road stage. The six-kilometre course was twisting and technical, over cobbles and tram lines – many riders held back a little, not wanting to risk a crash. But not so Merckx: he rode to win, and when he didn't he got angry. He rode so aggressively on the next

Above: Thévenet and Joop Zoetemelk on the Pla d'Adet, 1975. Below: Merckx shows signs of strain after arriving in Puy de Dôme. Previous page: Thévenet in yellow on Bastille Day, 1975.

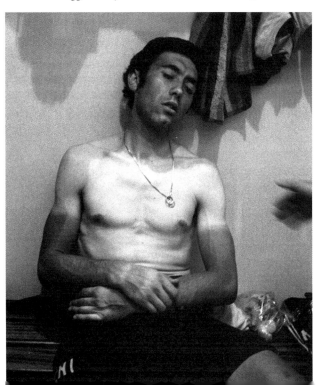

morning's half stage that he split the bunch, only to be outsprinted by Cees Priem. So in the afternoon he did it again, forcing the break and then losing the stage, this time to Rik Van Linden.

Realizing there were too many young hopefuls hunting for stage wins in the first week of the race, Merckx sat back and waited for the next time trial. His patience paid off: in just 16 kilometres he distanced Moser by 33 seconds. Even if the Italian did win the next day's stage, Merckx was back in charge. There was another time trial two days later, and, despite puncturing within five kilometres of the finish, Merckx still won. Bernard Thévenet was second, but no one paid much attention; they were too busy lauding the man who they were sure was on his way to winning his sixth Tour de France.

THÉVENET TO THE FORE

Into the High Pyrenees, and the top of the general classification shed all the men who were there by virtue of their sprinting prowess. It was time for the big men to step forward and see if yellow jersey Merckx really was as strong as he still appeared. The Tourmalet and the Aspin would soon draw out the real contenders.

Lucien Van Impe was first across the summit of the Tourmalet, leading Ocana by the narrowest of margins, with Merckx and his Molteni team-mate De Schoenmaecker and Thévenet following close behind. Prologue winner Moser was already way off the pace before the leaders reached the peak of the climb, and could not bridge the gap as they re-grouped on the descent.

A shorter, less arduous climb, the Aspin was more significant because of its place in the route. The riders were noticeably growing tired, and the Tourmalet had reduced the leading group to the most talented climbers. Again, Van Impe was first to attack – he had boldly stated his intention to win the stage before the race started that morning – whittling the group down to eight as they dropped back down for the final climb of the day, to the Pla d'Adet.

On the tortuous final section of the climb all scmblance of cohesion in the group disappeared. Riders weaved across the road, seeking water from the spectators and any kind of relief they could find from the gradient. Then, urged on by the riotous French crowds, Thévenet attacked. Believing the Peugeot rider to be his main rival, Merckx chased after him, only to give Joop Zoetemelk a springboard to make his own move. As the Gan rider opened up a gap, only one man could match him. And it wasn't Merckx.

Thévenet worked his way across to Zoetemelk, and managed to hold him almost all the way to the line. Merckx – along with Van Impe – lost a minute; his belief that Thévenet was the danger to his lead borne out as the Frenchman moved into second overall.

SPECTATOR HITS MERCKX

On the longest stage of the race, 260 kilometres from Albi to Super Lioran, Merckx reminded the peloton of just why he was in the yellow jersey. He was first over the Côte du Plomb du Cantal, and, although he let Michel Pollentier escape for the stage win, he was sure to finish ahead of the field, making a one-second gain and proving that he was still on top of his game.

Within 48 hours, that single second seemed worthless. On the stage to the Puy de Dôme in the Massif Central Merckx lost 34 seconds to Thévenet, and 49 to Van Impe, but this wasn't just down to his speed. The pair had dropped him with four kilometres to go, and as he dug deep within his reserves to hold on to the jersey in the final kilometre – he had 1-32 in hand over Thévenet – a spectator lunged out into the road and punched him in the liver.

Wincing in pain, Merckx stumbled over the line before vomiting. The physical hurt, coupled with the emotional blow of being dropped by Thévenet again, would prove a turning point.

Thévenet finally took the *maillot jaune* the next day. First Merckx tried to escape on the descents – there

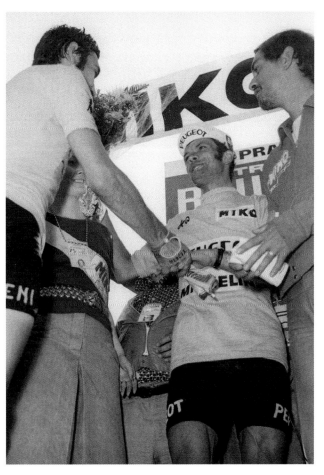

Merckx congratulates Thévenet after victory on stage 15 virtually ensures a first win overall for the Frenchman in 1975.

were five mountains to be scaled, and four times they dropped back to the valley. Then he spent himself countering Thévenet's repeated attacks, and launched his own, final move. He stayed away over the Col d'Allos, but the time gap remained stubbornly small. Thévenet punctured on the rocky descent, as did Moser. They quickly borrowed wheels from team-mates, and each managed to regain the minute they had lost.

Up ahead, Merckx was on the final climb, but he was beginning to lose his rhythm. One by one, the others began to catch up with him. First Gimondi, then Thévenet, then Zoetemelk, then Van Impe; Merckx had no answer but to gasp the thin air and hope that the others were suffering as much as he was, and that they might slow down enough for him to stay in contact. Thévenet took the stage, and the jersey, leaving Merckx to face the all too realistic prospect of defeat.

At just 107 kilometres, the next day's stage was short and sharp.

Merckx still clung to the idea that he could escape on the descents and reclaim the jersey. He attacked as the race dropped down from the Col de Vars, forcing Peugeot to expend valuable energy reeling him back in. The riders came together again on the valley roads, then, at the very foot of the Izoard, as Merckx waved for assistance from his team car, Thévenet attacked.

Later on, Merckx said that he had punctured – others said he was having difficulty breathing. Whatever the reason, he was in no position to chase the yellow jersey. Only Zoetemelk, up the road from an earlier move, could stay with Thévenet as he came past, and then only for the first half of the climb. It was Bastille Day, there was a Frenchman in yellow, and he was on his way to a stage win that would seal his overall victory in the Tour.

Merckx had lost the race, but he would not accept defeat meekly. The next day – the longest of the race – he crashed at the base of Col du Telegraphe, landing on his face. Disoriented and confused, he was told by the race doctors to abandon the event, but, despite vomiting with pain, he refused. He completed the stage, riding over the Madeleine, the Aravis, the Col du Colombière and finally to the ski station at Morzine-Avoriaz with bloody legs and a face sprayed with local anesthetic. He even attacked Thévenet on the descents, outsprinting him by two seconds at the finish. "I have never known such a sport as Merckx," said Thévenet afterward.

Merckx was taken to hospital, suffering from a broken cheekbone, but returned the next morning to complete the race. He was unable to perform at his best, but still managed third place in the mountain time trial. He wore his world champion's jersey and, together with Thévenet in the *maillot jaune,* was welcomed on to the Champs Elysées by 500,000 French fans.

The Frenchman had ridden absolutely superbly, and even without Merckx's crash would have certainly won the Tour. And Merckx?

Well, he had proved that even without the yellow jersey on his back he was still a champion.

1976

Thévenet had shown himself to be a rider in Merckx's mould, and the prospect of bringing them back together – one motivated by an entire nation lining the course and cheering his name, the other by pride, revenge and an insatiable desire for victory – had been relished all year. So when Merckx pulled out of the running it seemed that the new French hero would have the race all to himself.

But as he soon found out, no sooner had one rider been promoted from new kid to established star, than someone newer and younger came along to threaten his lead.

In Freddy Maertens, Belgian fans found someone to fill the Merckx void temporarily. The Flandria rider not only surprised the field by winning the prologue, but went on to double the impact by taking the first road stage in a mass sprint, followed by a victory in the stage three time trial, and a further sprint-win on stage seven.

This last stage was hampered by striking workers at the start line who had strewn newspapers across the road in an attempt to disrupt the race. The peloton had to dismount *en masse* and wheel their bikes across the sea of newsprint. A group of quick-thinking spectators gathered up the papers and sold them to onlookers, collecting a total of 531 French francs, which they promised to donate to the unluckiest rider in the Tour at the end of the event.

It took until the slopes of the Alpe d'Huez, at the end of an eight-hour stage, to undo Maertens. He had made the selection over the Col du Luitel, but when the attacking started on the final 14-kilometre climb he was one of the first to be dropped. He was in good company – Luis Ocana and Thévenet both lost contact as Lucien Van Impe and Joop Zoetemelk engaged in a

Above: Freddy Maertens crossing the line for the sixth of his eight stage victories, a feat which made the green jersey undeniably his in 1976. Below: Roger Delisle pushes hard on the climb to Pyrenees 2000 to win the stage by seven minutes.

two-man race up the mountain. The Dutchman easily won the sprint, but the jersey went to Van Impe.

DELISLE GETS LUCKY

There was more of the same the following day, the second summit-finish of the Tour: Maertens lost a further five minutes, Zoetemelk won the stage and Van Impe kept the jersey. This time Thévenet held things together, despite crashing on the way down from the Izoard. Now there were six riders all within two minutes of Van Impe – they would either have to sit quietly, recovering their energy before attacking him, or go for broke the next day, hoping he would crack before they did.

By mutual consent the leaders opted for the former plan, waving José-Luis Viego (Super-Ser) down the road as he made off on a 180-kilometre lone break. They were so relieved to see him go that they did nothing to chase, allowing him not only to win the stage, but to do so by 22-50. He moved up from 77th to 43rd place, still half an hour behind the yellow jersey.

With legs well rested from what was little more than a training ride, followed by an official rest day, the Pyrenees promised to be the backdrop for the most exciting racing of the Tour. Zoetemelk had to test Van Impe to see if there were any weaknesses in his superlative

climbing. When eighth-placed Roger Delisle, Thévenet's Peugeot team-mate, attacked just after the halfway stage, neither Van Impe or Zoetemelk responded. The enemy in the group was more threatening than the man disappearing up the road. Or so they thought.

Over the top of the Col de Jau the Frenchman had stretched his lead to almost five minutes – suddenly he was *virtuel maillot jaune*, and the bunch realized that he was serious about keeping his lead. The chase was launched and, for a short while, the gap shrank. By this time, however, Delisle was within sight of the final climb and, with counter-attacks from the group disrupting their own progress, he prised his advantage back again. When the remaining chasers – including most of the main contenders for the general classification – finally reached the finish line at the newly completed ski station Pyrenees 2000, Delisle had been there for seven minutes. To add further insult, several riders – Thévenet and former yellow jersey Maertens among them – collided and fell just 300 metres from the line, losing an additional 17 seconds and even more pride.

VICTORY FOR VAN IMPE

Van Impe was angry that he had been caught out by Delisle and had lost the jersey. Now he needed to formulate a new tactic to win it back, and without taking Zoetemelk with him. He used his head first, then his legs, to create exactly the opportunity he needed. A decent-looking break went away, and it was now the Peugeot team's responsibility to hold it in check. Van Impe sat in, watching as Delisle's men struggled to keep the leaders within reach as they began the climb of the Portillon over six minutes ahead of the bunch.

Sensing that the time was right, Van Impe jumped away, clearing the summit a full 90 seconds ahead of the yellow jersey group. He was investing all his efforts in this one solo move. He had no time for looking back over his shoulder to see what reactions he had provoked.

He caught the break on the Peyresourde, but didn't stop working there. He rode straight through them, pulling Ocana out of the group as he passed. On the descent he punctured, lost 30 seconds and was caught by Walter Riccomi. The Italian and the Belgian worked together to get back to Ocana and, once the three were reunited, they were easily able to maintain their advantage.

On the final climb, the Pla d'Adet, it took just one hairpin for Van Impe to drop the pair – they had spent so long at the front of the race that they could not respond to his attack. Behind him, Delisle was falling to pieces, and even though Zoetemelk was riding strongly he was far too late to make a difference now. Van Impe won the stage, took the jersey and found himself back exactly where he had been on stage 11, only this time with a healthy three-minute advantage over the Dutchman, and almost 10 minutes ahead of Deslisle, the next man in the standings.

Lucien Van Impe pushes himself up the Pla d'Adet to take the yellow jersey on stage 14, 1976.

The final day in the mountains had no impact on the leaders but, much to the chagrin of the French public, saw the end of Thévenet's hopes of defending his title.

Delisle and Van Impe waged war against each other from early on, and succeeded in costing the 1975 winner another seven minutes. Thévenet retired from the race three days before reaching Paris, and was later diagnosed with viral hepatitis. The disease had robbed him of his strength, leaving him unable to respond to even the slightest change

than just one superman. And if the French had lost Thévenet, at least they still had Raymond Poulidor. The 40-year-old was in the top three again, behind Zoetemelk – his eighth podium placing since finishing third in 1962. It wasn't just Van Impe who was a hero.

1977

The organizers of the Tour de France never like to make things easy. Since the 1976 Tour had been won by an expert climber – Lucien Van Impe – the *parcours* in 1977 was designed to favour those a little more susceptible to gravity. There were only two mountaintop finishes, and a greater number of kilometres *contre-la-montre*, including three individual time trials in the final week of racing. Any man who wanted to win the race would have to be a tactician with a loyal team of *domestiques* to protect him across vast expanses of rolling roads, yet still be able to hold his own on the climbs. The fewer mountains there were, the harder the pure climbers would attack when they came. To make things worse, they started on day three.

West Germany's Didi Thurau, riding for TI-Raleigh, put his track-pursuit experience to good use on his Tour debut, winning the 5,000-metre prologue ahead of team-mate Gerrie Knetemann, and the irrepressible Eddy Merckx. He wore it well, getting into the 31-strong group that led the peloton home on the first road stage and, finding that he rather liked leading the biggest race in the world, decided he would try and keep it at least as far as stage 13, when the race would cross into Germany.

THURAU WEARS IT WELL
Stage two took the riders over the Aspin, the Tourmalet and the Aubisque. First over the top of the Aspin was Spain's Luis Balague; it was a hopeful attack that had seen his lead stretch to over six minutes at the foot of the climb, only to shrivel to less than 90 seconds by

in pace. It was a supremely sad exit to what had been for him a painful and disappointing race.

Van Impe could afford to breathe easy now but, as all riders know, no matter how big the advantage, the race is not won until the final corner has been negotiated and the finish line crossed. While he was riding cautiously to avoid disaster, his countryman Freddy Maertens was itching to get on to the flat stages and get back into the superb form that he had displayed in the first week of the race. He won two more stages, and was absolutely untouchable in the points' competition. He attacked with Ferdi Bracke 40 kilometres from the finish of stage 21, hoping to gain a reasonable advantage before the downhill run into Senlisse.

Conditions were far from ideal – tyres wouldn't grip on the rain-soaked tarmac, and as the pair shot round a corner they skidded together and crashed. Bracke was up and away immediately, but Maertens – bruised and cut, though not seriously

hurt – could not follow because his bike was damaged. The bunch had reached him before he got a spare bike, so he joined in with the pack as they hunted down the one remaining man on the road. The rain was falling more and more heavily, but there was no stopping them now. Bracke was swallowed up as he entered Versailles, and as the bunch slowed to round the final, tight bend of the finishing circuit Maertens moved into position. His torn green jersey flapping from his shoulders, he sailed across the line – his seventh stage win of the race.

Maertens won the morning time trial on the final day, equalling Merckx's record of eight wins in one Tour, and narrowly missed out on his ninth when he finished second to Gerben Karstens on the race up and down the Champs Elysées.

While no one was ever going to replace Eddy Merckx in the hearts of the Belgian fans, Van Impe and Maertens had shown that their country's talent pool was deeper

Raymond Poulidor is presented with a bust of himself in 1976 after completing his 13th Tour at the age of 40.

the time he reached the peak. He was caught on the descent and, as if to reprimand him for his move, the yellow jersey contenders took control of the pace on the Tourmalet.

A group of 15 broke clear on the lower slopes, but the initial selection was not enough. The pace increased, and Merckx, Ocana, Michel Laurent and Thurau were dropped. The chasers were two minutes down at the summit, but Merckx, utilizing his famous descending skills, brought Thurau and Laurent back to the leaders before the final major climb. Both escapees and pursuers were tired now; they grouped together to conquer the Aubisque and complete the remaining 50 kilometres of the stage. It would have been different had the race ended at the summit, but thanks to the organizers' anti-climbing bias the front group of 14 was an unruly rabble of climbers, *rouleurs* and, of course, giants of the road like Merckx. Honours were decided by a two-kilometre lap of the motor-racing circuit at Pau, where Thurau cemented his lead with another stage win.

There were a quiet few days before the first long time trial – the Tour skirted into the Basque country, where the heat was so oppressive that only the eternally optimistic breakaway merchants sought any action. The serious contenders were much more concerned with the long-term outcome: the 30-kilometre test against the watch was their next big target.

Thurau was not above mind games; he deliberately chose a gear one up from Merckx's for the time trial, and confidently stated his intention of winning the stage. When he did so by 50 seconds even he was surprised, while all of his other rivals – including Thévenet – had lost more than a minute.

Thurau was not quite so successful in the team time trial two days later. Despite having world champion Hennie Kuiper in his squad, they were beaten into third place behind Merckx's Fiat team and the Peugeot outfit. No matter, though, the West German was still holding on to the

jersey, getting closer every day to his goal of wearing it in front of his home fans at the end of the second week.

BRINGING IT BACK HOME
Both the Belgian and the German fans were in for a treat as the Tour swept through their home countries later in the race. However much the Walloons and the Flandrians had been hoping to welcome Merckx home in yellow, they could not fail to be delighted at the sight of his team-mate and countryman Patrick Sercu blazing down the finishing straight, not in his customary sprint, but at the end of an incredible 170-kilometre lone break. The next day, as the race crossed into Germany, he won again – this time in his favoured style, the mass finish – while Thurau lapped up the applause from his

Germany's Didi Thurau leads the race into his home country, 1977.

delirious home fans. It wasn't all smiles though: points' leader Rik Van Linden had lodged a complaint against Peugeot's Jacques Esclassan, claiming that the Frenchman had denied him second place on the previous stage thanks to a hand-sling from a team-mate. The race jury spent several hours interviewing riders and other witnesses, before deciding they must give Esclassan the benefit of the doubt. A worthy decision, soured only by the fact that they could have eliminated doubt entirely, if they hadn't left the video recording of the sprint behind in Belgium.

Eleven riders were within five minutes of Thurau, and Merckx was only 51 seconds adrift. It would take just one blow to knock him from the top – the trick being to choose the right moment. The first Alpine stage, to Morzine, was the first part of a

With Merckx's wheel to follow on the way down, Thurau was confident that the gap would soon narrow. But the Belgian had blown completely; Thurau could not afford to wait for him on the remaining part of the climb – he would have to get back under his own steam. He caught the tail-enders of the chase group as they crested the climb and, as he had hoped, they all regrouped before the final climb, but without Merckx. Van Impe took the prime to increase his lead in the mountains' competition; Thurau was rewarded for his gutsy ride with the stage win, and Thévenet stayed comfortably in yellow. But Merckx was now more than three minutes down on the general classification and had little strength even to try for a stage win.

WATERTIGHT DEFENCE

The Madeleine proved to be Merckx's final undoing. Stomach problems compounded his precarious grasp of the leaders, and he lasted only one kilometre of the climb before dropping back. No sooner had the group got the first big climb behind them than they started the second, the Col de Glandon. Hell for most of the peloton, this was Van Impe's playground. He flew away, gaining 90 seconds by the summit to chasers Thévenet and Zoetemelk. Not content, he extended his lead on the descent; with the Alpe d'Huez the last obstacle between him and not only the stage win but also the jersey – he was just 33 seconds down at the start of the day – he could suppress the pain for another 11 kilometres to the summit.

Thévenet had no choice but to lead the chase – it was his jersey that Van Impe was stealing. Kuiper and Zoetemelk clung to his wheel; if they were to remain in the race they had no other choice. They were bonded together by the common need to bring Van Impe back.

The plan worked. The Belgian climber began to tire, gradually slowing as the three men behind him maintained their speed. When it became clear that they would catch him, Kuiper attacked from the

split day, and not a good prospect for those sitting at Thurau's heels. That afternoon's mountain time trial was a much better option.

After leading the race for almost 3,000 kilometres, Thurau was spent. The psychological trophy that had delayed the onset of fatigue, to wear the jersey into Germany, had been achieved, and suddenly his colossal effort caught up with him. He slumped to 15th in the 14-kilometre stage, losing the jersey to Bernard Thévenet, while Joop Zoetemelk posted fastest times at all the intermediate time checks and won the stage by a clear 45 seconds.

He was down, but Thurau was not out. The next day Antonio Menendez set off on a glory ride,

only to be caught, and then to go again after the group had negotiated the first mountain. The others allowed him to go – it hardly mattered who rode themselves into the ground while the others concerned themselves with who, of the genuine contenders, might be vulnerable later that day.

The first damage was done on the penultimate climb, the first-category Forclaz. The two previous race winners, Thévenet and Van Impe – now in yellow and polka-dot jerseys respectively – joined forces to break the race apart. Thurau and Merckx were the first to fall off the back, but with only six kilometres left on the climb there was still a chance that they would regroup on the descent.

Van Impe looks anxiously back up the road for help as his bike lies damaged after his fall on Alpe d'Huez, 1977.

group, dropping Zoetemelk and drawing Thévenet away with him. As they neared Van Impe the support vehicles were directed out of the way, but on the narrow hairpins there was little room for manoeuvre. Van Impe was balked and fell, damaging his bike. As he was assisted by his team car, Kuiper rode past, then, as he tried to rediscover his rhythm, Thévenet came by. Neither paused for breath as they went.

Before this stage, Kuiper had been a mere 49 seconds behind the Frenchman. Now he was opening a gap on the road, to 44 seconds, as he passed under the *flamme rouge* with one kilometre to go. His deceleration to celebrate his stage win allowed Thévenet to claw back three seconds. His overall lead had gone from 11 seconds to eight, only now it was over Kuiper.

The world road race champion had only one more chance to overturn Thévenet's lead: the final long time trial at Dijon. Setting off in reverse order, the *maillot jaune* would have intermediate time checks *en route*, enabling him to compare his performance directly with Kuiper's; the man ahead would be riding blind. The Dutchman struck early, so fast in the opening kilometres that Thévenet could not match him. But the third-category climb halfway along the route proved too much – he'd had only one card to play, and he had used it up at the beginning of the stage. Thévenet was ahead at the top of the climb, and finished the 50-kilometre stage 30 seconds up.

On the final day in Paris Didi Thurau reminded the peloton of how things had all started, winning the six-kilometre morning time

Thévenet takes advantage of Van Impe's misfortune and forges ahead of the Belgian on Alpe d'Huez, 1977.

trial as he had done the prologue. Thévenet helped himself to another few seconds over Kuiper, but the times were academic; he had won his second Tour, despite the fact that he had not won any mountain stages, and had only one time trial to his name. As the organizers had hoped, neither the climbers nor the sprinters had had an easy time of it, but then neither had they. A series of positive dope tests had landed several riders, including Joop Zoetemelk and Luis Ocana, with fines, time penalties, and suspended sentences. Despite their protests, they were obliged to hand back their prize money and seek redress in secondary testing and the appeals procedure. Ten years after Tom Simpson's death, it was a timely reminder that the dope-ridden underbelly of the Tour was still as murky an area as ever.

Tour Legends
Bernard Thévenet

"I got my team-mates together and told them I would go for victory. I would take the yellow jersey in the mountains or drop in the attempt. It was this year or never." Bernard Thévenet in 1975

Left: Thévenet on the podium after stage 15, Nice–Pra Loup, 1975. Main picture: Stage 15 and Thévenet is well on the way to claiming the yellow jersey from Eddy Merckx.

BERNARD THÉVENET (FRA)
b. 10/1/48 Saint-Julien-de-Civry, Saône et Loire

11 PARTICIPATIONS
TWO VICTORIES
NINE STAGE WINS

1970 35TH OVERALL
ONE STAGE WIN: stage 18, Saint-Gaudens–La Mongie

1971 FOURTH OVERALL
ONE STAGE WIN: stage 10, Saint-Etienne–Grenoble

1972 NINTH STAGE
TWO STAGE WINS: stage 11, Carnon-Plage–Mont Ventoux; stage 17, Pontarlier–Ballon d'Alsace

1973 SECOND OVERALL
TWO STAGE WINS: stage 7 part 2, Gaillard–Méribel-les-Allues; stage 20 part 2, Versailles–Paris

1974 DID NOT FINISH

1975 FIRST OVERALL
TWO STAGE WINS: stage 15, Nice– Pra Loup; stage 16, Barcelonnette– Serre-Chevalier

1976 DID NOT FINISH

1977 FIRST OVERALL
ONE STAGE WIN: stage 20, Dijon (time trial)

1978 DID NOT FINISH

1980 17TH OVERALLL

1981 37TH OVERALL

Chapter 8: 1978–1990

Hinault, Lemond and Fignon

Cycling, and the Tour in particular, reached a higher level as a whole new generation of riders started carving out their reputations. Three men now battled for supremacy – France's belligerent Bernard Hinault and intellectual Laurent Fignon, and the supremely gifted American Greg Lemond. Their diverse backgrounds may have dictated the differing ways they approached the Tour, but their overriding need to win united them as true champions.

1978

Bernard Thévenet was plagued by illness after winning his second Tour. He was struck down in succession by food poisoning, kidney problems and fevers; if he had been unable to defend his 1975 win because of an excess of post-tour celebrations and after-dinner speaking during the winter, he looked unlikely to be able to defend his 1977 win owing to poor health.

The Tour did not start well for anyone. The weather was so bad during the prologue that organizers decided the results of the 5.2-kilometre time trial would not count toward the general classification. Then Jan Raas and his TI-Raleigh manager Peter Post fell out with the *commissaires* over dress regulations. Raas won the stage nevertheless, wearing his illegal skin suit beneath the standard team jersey. The next day he outsprinted Freddy Maertens (Flandria) to take the yellow jersey that had not been awarded after the prologue, and the race got under way in earnest.

After three days of conventional road racing, the peloton hit the next of the organizers' "diversions". The results of the stage-four team time trial would not count directly in the overall standings, but instead bonuses would be awarded to riders in the first six teams. At 153 kilometres there was plenty of scope for things to go wrong; Thévenet and the Peugeot team missed their *soigneurs* at the feed station, and finished the stage in a state of total exhaustion.

The Flandria team were having a much better time of it – Sean Kelly and Freddy Maertens were winning stages in turn, and it seemed the Belgian would take his third stage win of the week in the first individual time trial. He led at each intermediate time check, steadily increasing his lead over Frenchman Bernard Hinault, until just past halfway. Then, in the final 25 kilometres, he collapsed, turning a 27-second lead into a 56-second deficit by the time the stage was over. Hinault moved from obscurity into fourth place.

Above: Bernard Hinault, Joop Zoetemelk and Michel Pollentier jostle for position on the Tourmalet on stage 11 during the 1978 Tour. Previous page: Laurent Fignon leads Greg Lemond (left) and Bernard Hinault (right) on stage 18 to La Plagne in 1984.

HINAULT MAKES HIS NAME

Winning the time trial was enough to place Hinault with the real race contenders, along with Hennie Kuiper, Lucien Van Impe and Michel Pollentier. When Pollentier attacked on the stage to Pau, Hinault was quick to follow; and while the new French hero was forging his reputation at the front of the race, Thévenet was struggling at the back, wondering how he had once been able to win. The break did not shatter the peloton completely, but it certainly weeded out the weakest men, and Thévenet was among them.

On the Tourmalet the next day Thévenet abandoned the Tour, while up ahead Hinault was riding away with Pollentier and Mariano Martinez. Several others, including Joop Zoetemelk, chased after them, and over the long ride to the Pla d'Adet the riders split and regrouped as they tried to work out which combination would be strong enough to stay away. At the foot of the final climb Zoetemelk made his move and he was clear in an instant. Pollentier tried to hang on, but could not and was overtaken by Hinault and Martinez. Before the summit the pair caught up with and dropped the Dutchman, as did Pollentier. Martinez won the stage, Hinault moved to 1-05 behind leader Joseph Bruyères, and Pollentier took the climber's jersey.

Hinault wasn't quite in yellow, but he was already taking control of the race. The next day riders were obliged to get up at 5 a.m. to get to the stage start: something they regarded as the organizers' negligence toward their comfort in favour of taking the race to every town that would pay for it. Led by Hinault, the entire peloton dismounted at the end of the morning stage, and walked across the line in protest. The crowds whistled and booed, angry at being denied the spectacle they had waited hours to see, but the riders remained completely unmoved. Co-organizer Felix Levitan gave the stage's prize money to charity, while the riders, satisfied that they had made their point, rode on in the afternoon.

Bruyères was expected to lose the lead on the mountain time trial to the Puy de Dôme but, thanks to a brilliant ride and to Hinault's poor decision to change bikes for the final climb, he held on to the yellow jersey for another day. As if to make amends, Hinault won the following day's stage in a mass sprint, when tactically he would have been better saving himself for the next day's mountains. When they came, they were even more dramatic than predicted.

DESCENT INTO THE DEPTHS

All the big name riders made sure they were in the first main break of the stage. Pollentier, defending his King of the Mountains' jersey, crested the Col de Luitel just ahead of the group, and then with a breath-taking descent swept down to the foot of Alpe d'Huez with a minute in hand. And he didn't slow. The combined efforts of Zoetemelk, Hinault or Kuiper could not catch him. Pollentier experienced the most glorious moment of his career as he accepted the applause for winning the stage, and then stepped onto the podium to receive the yellow jersey, though he did not keep it for long.

At the mandatory post-stage dope control Pollentier said he was having difficulty producing a urine sample – not unusual after riding 240 kilometres in the heat. But as the liquid finally flowed, doctors realized it was coming from a plastic bulb under his arm, being fed into a tube through his shorts. Pollentier was immediately stripped of his jersey and his winnings and thrown off the race as a dope cheat. From the highest point of his career, Pollentier had sunk to the lowest place imaginable.

After the shock of the Alpe d'Huez stage, Zoetemelk found himself in yellow, with Hinault 14 seconds behind. It remained that

Above: A shame-faced Michel Pollentier packs his bags, thrown off the race for trying to cheat a dope control, 1978. Below: Hinault battles through the swirling dust on stage 9 in Belgium in 1979.

way until the final time trial; each man watching the other for the slightest flicker of an attack, neither being able to shake the other. In the race against the clock, however, there was no chance to play games. Hinault won the stage easily, beating Zoetemelk by more than four minutes – an undisputable win to end a controversial, unforgettable race.

1979

Nothing pleased the home crowd more than the prospect of a Tour with a truly charismatic French favourite, and Bernard Hinault was more than willing to put his reputation on the line in a bid to defend his first Tour title. And who was there to challenge him?

Zoetemelk was riding his ninth Tour, and although he had never finished outside the top ten he had never won either. Both Bernard Thévenet and Didi Thurau had lost the youthful edge that had spurred them on to greatness in the middle of the decade. The jersey was Hinault's for the taking.

After a slow start – he could only manage fourth place in the prologue, and violent storms dissuaded him from trying anything too risky on the first road stage over the Pyrenees – Hinault settled into his Tour rhythm on stage two. It was a mountain time trial, just 23 kilometres long, but so arduous that only the best riders could complete it in under an hour. Hinault rode so fast that the five slowest riders were eliminated, for being more than 25 per cent outside his time. He was taking no prisoners with him to Paris.

Another 12 riders abandoned the next day, although Britain's Paul Sherwen, who had finished outside the time cut, was reinstated as an acknowledgement of his gutsy ride; he had crashed, and spent so long chasing the broom wagon on his own that the organizers relented and gave him a second chance.

THE BEST FORM OF DEFENCE

At the other end of the race, Hinault was at the centre of the action, in a 12-man group that broke away on the Peyresourde, then in the eight-man group that tackled the Aspin in

the mist and rain, and then unfazed when he punctured on the gravel descent. Try as they might, they could not drop him. Hinault was not just there to defend his jersey; he was determined to win.

He took the hot-spot sprint at Ponzac, and then, as the finish line came in sight, he didn't sit back to let the also-rans compete for the stage; he went straight to the front, not to lead out a team-mate who had served his purposes all day, but to win the stage himself. He sprinted from the front, checked over his shoulder, and then kicked again. The others were too intimidated to do anything but watch him go.

Zoetemelk regained some ground in the team time trial, only to see Hinault claw it back by dint of continuous effort in the intermediate sprints on the flat stages, stealing back a handful of seconds whenever the opportunity arose. At the next, mammoth, 90-kilometre team time trial, the roles were reversed, with Hinault's Renault squad bettering the Miko-Mercier men by over a minute. But the fourth twist of the Tour was the most cruel.

TEARS ON THE FINISH LINE

Stage nine ended on the Roubaix velodrome, the finishing circuit of the queen of the classics, Paris-Roubaix. The stage route mirrored the one-day epic in character – it was long, dusty, and covered vast stretches of cobbled roads where mechanical failure or plain bad luck might be deciding factors in the outcome of the race. Just before the halfway point of the stage, Zoetemelk saw a move to go, and immediately jumped on it.

And that was exactly the moment when Hinault punctured. Suddenly he was cornered into defending; he had 100 kilometres in which to chase down the Dutchman.

A group of striking steelworkers lined up across the road at Denain but, following stern threats from the French riot police, a gap opened up to allow the riders through. Hinault was getting no closer to the lead group, but there was still a chance

that he could retain the jersey, if he could limit his losses. Then he punctured again, 10 kilometres from the finish line. He came into the velodrome 3-45 down on Zoetemelk's group, clothed in the yellow jersey that was no longer his.

The crowd were angry, booing him as he completed the last lap of the track. He climbed off his bike in tears, disappearing from the track as fast as he could, not wanting to see Zoetemelk step onto the podium to take his place as the new race leader.

Hinault suffered again on the very next time trial, but this time he channelled his anger directly through his pedals – despite another puncture and the derisory whistles of the Dutch supporters, he won the stage convincingly and moved back to within 90 seconds of Zoetemelk. Both now knew that the race would be decided in the Alps.

They started their Alpine campaigns cautiously, sitting tight in the main group while a breakaway of non-threatening riders stayed clear to the finish of the first mountain stage. Hinault was the first to signal his intentions, boldly sprinting away from Zoetemelk at the finish line in a massive gear to pull back three

Above: Hinault is engulfed by the Press as he tries to escape from the Roubaix velodrome, 1979. Below: Safely back in yellow, Hinault leads Zoetemelk (green jersey) on the ascent of Alpe d'Huez.

seconds and to strike fear into the hearts of anyone who thought he had over-extended himself in the opening week. The Dutchman was in the *maillot jaune*, but it was Hinault controlling the mind-games. He didn't let an opportunity slip, taking bonus seconds at every hot-spot sprint he could, bringing the gap down to less than a minute.

It was the mountain time trial that finally ended Zoetemelk's reign. The conditions were appalling, just as Hinault liked – he knew that they would affect his rivals much more profoundly than it did him. In the brutal 55-kilometre test from Evian to Morzine-Avoriaz he not only negated his 49-second deficit, but managed to push Zoetemelk down by another 1-48.

Zoetemelk was shattered. He had lost his best chance in nine attempts at winning the Tour, and yet again he was obliged to chase the leader. He stayed with him for the majority of the next stage, wincing as he contested the hot-spot sprints when there was no need.

When a promising break went, including Lucien Van Impe and Claude Criquielion, Hinault went with it, forcing them immediately to rethink their strategy. He didn't stop when he caught up with them, either. He didn't even make eye contact. He just rode on, taking Van Impe with him.

A momentary lapse in concentration allowed the Belgian to sneak away to win the stage, but Hinault's virtuoso performance had brilliantly earned him a further minute over Zoetemelk.

His only display of weakness came on stage 18. It was the final summit-finish of the race; Zoetemelk had no choice but to attack. On slopes mostly populated by Dutch fans, the man in second place put on a brave show, making up 47 seconds on Hinault. The Frenchman may have been irritated, but he wasn't worried – he snatched the time back in the final time trial, winning his second Tour, one of the toughest of recent years, in the style of a true champion.

1980

Bernard Hinault lined up at the 1980 Tour with a Giro d'Italia win to his name already. He was in search not only of his third consecutive win, but also the legendary Giro-Tour double, achieved only by Fausto Coppi, Jacques Anquetil and Eddy Merckx. Joop Zoetemelk was back for more: the irrepressible Dutchman now had Jan Raas and Gerrie Knetemann, both former world champions, to aid him in his bid to unseat Hinault.

Casual observers often underestimate the vital role played by team tactics in the Tour de France, but this time it was clear that the combined powers of Zoetemelk's Raleigh squad were going to be a force to be reckoned with. Hinault won the prologue, but the Dutch team hit back with a stage win from Raas on

day one, then a clear-cut victory in the next day's team time trial. Henk Lubberdink delivered them another win on stage three, while the yellow jersey went from rider to rider as the main contenders bided their time. With no major climbs until the end of the second week, the *maillot jaune* became a reward for the courageous, or flighty – those who knew that the first flat stages were their only chance of making an impression.

Hinault won the first individual time trial of the race, and both he and Zoetemelk hauled themselves up the general classification into the first six. Something triggered in the defending champion's mind: time to start taking this race apart.

As far as he was concerned, the more miserable the conditions, the better – he had won Liege-Bastogne-Liege in April in the worst conditions in living memory, and now, back

Always well-intentioned, Johan Vandevelde does his best to look after Joop Zoetemelk on stage 18 to Saint-Etienne in 1980.

in the northwest corner of France, he was ready to roll.

Blinding rain and treacherous cobbles held absolutely no fears for Hinault. Over almost 240 kilometres the peloton rattled across the *pavé* and the puddles, but Hinault and his breakaway companions pressed on relentlessly. He took the stage and struck his second blow against his main rival.

DUTCH INVASION

Allied with his Dutch superteam, Zoetemelk and Raleigh won the team time trial while, a minute down, alarm bells sounded from the Renault camp. Hinault was suffering from tendinitis behind his left knee, the consequence of his ferocious effort on the stage to Lille.

Now it was someone else's turn to capitalize on that winning feeling. Jan Raas won another couple of mass sprints, then Cees Priem took the honours for Raleigh. Subsequently, as if to lead by example, Zoetemelk himself took on the mantle of defending team honour in the next time trial.

The Dutchman won the stage by a comfortable margin – Hinault did enough to take the jersey, but could do little more than that as he struggled to limit the aggravation that might possibly damage his knee further. "You don't think I'm going to quit while I've got the jersey do you?" he said.

But, ironically, that's exactly what he did. Before the start of the first mountain stage to Luchon, his *directeur sportif* Cyrille Guimard met with race organizers Jacques Goddet and Felix Levitan, to tell them that Hinault would no longer be riding.

Zoetemelk declined to wear the jersey that day – he hardly wanted it while it was still warm from Hinault's back – but six and a half hours later, he pulled it on with no little sense of pride.

Frenchman Raymond Martin made a solo ride to glory and ended it by taking the stage, but Zoetemelk rode with immense dignity and good sense to finish fifth and thus stepped right up to the top of the general classification on his own merit.

Much as Zoetemelk made a popular leader – it was his 10th Tour, and after five second-places he finally had a firm grasp on the race lead – he was not the *patron* Hinault was. On the first Alpine stage he sat and watched as a pair of lowly riders, Jos de Schoenmaecker and Alberto Fernandez, broke away. He concerned himself with keeping Hennie Kuiper, his nearest rival, in check, with his team riding single file ahead of him, no thought other than to protect his lead.

Then somehow, as exhaustion coincided with a jumping gear, Vandevelde swerved across the road. Suddenly unable to control his bike, he swerved again and brought Zoetemelk crashing down. The team mechanics immediately produced another bike for him to ride, and with a huge effort he caught up, avoiding disaster. Immediately he crossed the line Vandevelde ran to him, "I'm so sorry, Joop," he said. Had it been Hinault, the rider at fault would have been hidden in a hotel room, praying that his unintended victim didn't find him, but Zoetemelk didn't use his fists in the way Hinault did. "Don't worry, it's one of those things," he reassured his team-mate. For once, the nice guy had kept the lead.

Second-placed Hennie Kuiper lost more time on the stage to Morzine and, although the ride was a severe test for Zoetemelk and his team-mates, he came through without damage. Conscious of what could have been, Vandevelde re-doubled his efforts to protect his leader, keeping him safe while Raymond Martin took over from Kuiper as nearest challenger.

It was not until he had won the final time trial that Zoetemelk dared to believe what the result sheets told him – he had finally won the Tour. And if the event had not been as dramatic as in the previous year, that didn't matter. It was reward not just for three-and-a-half weeks' racing, but for a full decade of trying – proof that, sometimes, perseverance is what it takes to make a winner.

1981

Hinault had not scored the Giro-Tour double he coveted in 1980, but he had bounced back with victory in the world championship, and had won such a diverse range of events in the first part of 1981 that some thought he might well burn out before July. The tendinitis that had ended his previous Tour had made it clear that he was not, physically at least, indestructible. So would Zoetemelk be able to beat him all the way to Paris?

The race began in a similar fashion to the one 12 months earlier: the prologue going to Hinault, and the team time trial to Raleigh, putting Gerrie Knetemann in yellow.

Three days later another team time trial, this time over 77 kilometres, put them in an even more commanding position. But then the climbing started and, when the finish line at the Pla d'Adet reared up, there were some unexpected faces at the front of the race.

Above: Hinault on his way to victory in the prologue at Nice, 1981. Below: Australia's Phil Anderson makes Hinault work hard on the stage to St-Lary-Soulan.

Of course Hinault was there, but so too were 1976 winner Lucien Van Impe and brash young Australian Phil Anderson. With no pretences of competing in the general classification, Van Impe was doing what he knew best, climbing and climbing fast. Behind him Hinault was keeping him in sight, with the 23-year-old antipodean sitting on his wheel as if it was second nature. Thanks to his placing in the previous stages Anderson took the jersey, disrupting the established pattern of the race in typical Australian style. "It was good for cycling," acknowledged Hinault as he saw the young man pull on the *maillot jaune*. He'd let him have a day in the sun before putting the Tour back in order.

Hinault claimed the jersey after the next time trial, with Anderson finishing a highly creditable third. Still not satisfied, the Frenchman took more time out of the Australian with some well-timed sprinting for both intermediate and stage-finish bonuses, but the Peugeot rider was

so delighted with his Tour debut that he had no complaints. He stuck doggedly to Hinault as the race crossed northern France, into Belgium and toward Mulhouse for the next time trial. Proving that Van Impe wasn't the only rider who could make a comeback at the Tour, Belgian Freddy Maertens (Sunair) was getting his fill of glory, sprinting to victory for his third and then fourth stage win as the race came to his home.

DEFEATED BY THE ALP

Despite being caught for two minutes by Hinault in the Mulhouse time trial, Anderson was holding on to second place overall. It was a gutsy, tenacious performance, but it couldn't last. When the Australian cracked, he cracked completely, losing 17 minutes over the final 100 kilometres of the stage to Alpe d'Huez. Worse for him, he lost the white jersey to Peter Winnen, the Dutchman who had beaten Hinault himself for the stage win.

The *maillot jaune* had not yet won a road stage. When he found himself alone on the final climb of the next stage with his former team-mate Jean-René Bernaudeau, now riding for Peugeot, he knew he had no choice but to set the record straight. The two men had been more than team-mates, they had been friends. Now they were so far apart in the overall standings that the competition was purely for the stage, and for revenge.

Hinault didn't attack outright. He rode harder and harder, not looking at Bernaudeau. He didn't even glance when his rival dropped back – he just kept on riding. There were no more whispers about whose Tour this was now.

The final time trial of the race could have been little more than a victory parade for Hinault, but he couldn't pass up an opportunity to do even more damage. The stage win took his tally for the year to five, and extended his winning margin to 14 minutes over Lucien Van Impe. It was hard to imagine there had ever been any doubt.

1982

The Giro-Tour double was back on again. Bernard Hinault had won the Italian race in convincing style, with his main rival Giovanni Bataglin unable to start owing to a broken collarbone. Now they would meet at the Tour.

Hinault had carried his form well over the month between the two Grand Tours. He won the prologue then lost the jersey to Ludo Peeters as the Belgian chanced his luck with a late break on the first road stage. It didn't take long for the general classification to take shape though; a day later Phil Anderson was in the yellow jersey after winning the stage on a tough, hilly course, while Sean Kelly and Hinault closed to within a minute of him.

And while Hinault protested that the race would not start properly until they reached the mountains, he was not above joining in the sprint for the intermediate bonuses, winning them frequently. Only three days into the race and the defending

Bernard Hinault hitches a ride on a motorcycle after getting stuck behind protesting farmers on stage 16, 1982.

champion, the *maillot jaune* and the *maillot vert*, Kelly, were battling for a handful of seconds here and there – no bonus was too small.

Anderson maintained his pole position, while Hinault and Kelly traded second place. It seemed that the team time trial would be more significant than ever: a chance for Peugeot to augment Anderson's lead. But the riders never got the chance to find out. The stage was cancelled when striking steelworkers blocked the road in a bid to gain media attention. Most riders were frustrated by the interruption to the race, but Kelly didn't complain too loudly. He knew that his Sem-Loire team would have fared badly on the stage, and they had been spared the ordeal.

It was only a brief respite. Organizers rescheduled, squeezing in a team time trial on the morning of stage nine. Kelly's team did just as badly as he had feared, and he dropped to 10th place, while Hinault moved to within 30 seconds of Anderson. When they raced against the clock again, this time on their own, the truth came out. Hinault was so much faster than his Australian rival that he finished the stage with a two-minute lead in the general classification, with stage winner Gerrie Knetemann moving into second place.

And now for the mountains. The first Pyrenean stage was not too arduous – a downhill finish enabled a group of 18 riders to stay together over the climbs. Hinault should have won the stage, but he mistimed his move, and was overtaken by Kelly, a better sprinter. Finding himself boxed in, he could do nothing as the group swallowed him up. He didn't make the same mistake again. As Swiss climber Beat Breu led a small group away to St-Lary Soulan, Hinault controlled the chasing group, making sure that when he dropped Anderson there was no way for him to come back.

A WINNER IN EVERY SENSE

Hinault was in a winning mood now. On the Martigues time trial he pushed himself so hard in the final

1.5-kilometre climb, the last section of which was 1 in 7, that he collapsed at the finish as a scrum of reporters engulfed him. His lead was now over five minutes and, while he was getting stronger, Anderson was beginning to fade.

The Australian got into more trouble during the first day in the Alps, losing contact with the yellow jersey group on the penultimate climb, allowing Joop Zoetemelk to overtake him in the standings. He slipped back even further the next day, and was left to hope that he could find something in his legs to carry him over the toughest stage of the race, 244 kilometres from Alpe d'Huez to Morzine.

Anderson managed to get on terms with Hinault, and stuck with him all the way. But to be delighted in keeping up was to acknowledge that there was no chance of getting ahead of the man in yellow – a sad admission from a rider who had worn the jersey himself for 10 days. Or perhaps it was just Australian realism – Hinault went on to win the final time trial and stretch his lead even further. Then, in a move that was as dangerous as it was spectacular, the *maillot jaune* discarded the tradition of rolling across the final line in Paris, soaking up the applause. Instead he contested, and won, the 125-man sprint for the stage win, ending the race exactly as he had started it, raging at the front. It gave his rivals plenty to think about for the next 12 months.

1983

It was Bernard Hinault's right knee, rather than the man himself, that made the headlines in the run-up to the 1983 Tour of France. Since winning the Tour of Spain in May he had failed to complete a stage race, because he was suffering from tendinitis – the same condition that had forced him to abandon the 1980 Tour. Doctors told him that to ride without fully recovering would make a disaster of the Tour, and could even cost him his career. The race would

just have to go on without him.

There were many riders in contention for the race lead in Hinault's absence: Sean Kelly, Phil Anderson, former winners Joop Zoetemelk and Lucien Van Impe. The route was entirely within the French borders, but even without the long transfers that result from doglegs into neighbouring countries, it was a tough course. In the first week there was a 300-kilometre stage from Roubaix to Le Havre, and a 100-kilometre team time trial. The race favourites spent the first few days stretching their legs and taking stock of the field while lesser riders battled for stages. But Kelly knew he could not afford to wait until the mountains to stake his claim on the jersey – he could not climb well enough. First he took the green jersey, then the next day the yellow, thanks to some canny sprinting at the intermediate hot spots.

It wasn't enough. Stage 10 took the peloton over the first Pyrenean *cols* of the Tour, and there was no thought of easing in gently, with two *hors* and two first-category climbs in 198 kilometres. One of the *cols*, the Tourmalet, was the highest point of the race and the scene of Kelly's demise. Fourteen minutes down

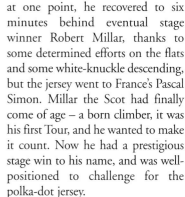

Above: Laurent Fignon is willed on by the partisan crowd during the time trial to Avioraz, 1983. Below: Kim Andersen of Denmark congratulates Sean Kelly after the Irishman claims the yellow jersey in Bordeaux.

at one point, he recovered to six minutes behind eventual stage winner Robert Millar, thanks to some determined efforts on the flats and some white-knuckle descending, but the jersey went to France's Pascal Simon. Millar the Scot had finally come of age – a born climber, it was his first Tour, and he wanted to make it count. Now he had a prestigious stage win to his name, and was well-positioned to challenge for the polka-dot jersey.

HOLDING OFF THE INEVITABLE

After such a difficult stage, many were hoping for a chance to recuperate. While the next day was not so difficult physically, it provided just as many upsets. Simon crashed and broke his shoulder blade just 46 kilometres into the stage. He only made it to the finish line, some 131 kilometres later, thanks to the constant attentions of team-mates Millar, Stephen Roche and Phil Anderson. Then, after the stage, Joop Zoetemelk admitted that he had failed a dope test following the earlier team time trial; he was docked 10 minutes and his challenge for the jersey was over.

Anaesthetized and exhausted,

Simon drew strength from the *maillot jaune* that rested on his broken shoulder. He was sufficiently well to let Robert Millar concentrate on his own interests – taking over the lead in the King of the Mountains' competition— in the Massif Central. He lost more than three minutes to second-placed Laurent Fignon (Renault) in the 15.6-kilometre time trial, and another 13 seconds on the next road stage. Each day in yellow was a bonus now – he knew he was on his way out. The next day, to Alpe d'Huez, there were seven mountains to be scaled. Simon made it over two of them before conceding that his Tour was over.

With or without Simon in the race, Fignon was acknowledged as the man to beat now. Peter Winnen and Jean-René Bernaudeau took off on the final climb, with the Frenchman even briefly becoming leader at one point. But Fignon clawed his way back, finishing fifth on the stage, while Winnen, who was trailing Bernaudeau in the overall competition, outsprinted him at the line. "In my first Tour de France, this is the happiest day of my life," beamed Fignon as he took the *maillot jaune* for the first time.

NEW LEADER, SAME TACTICS

The Renault squad were well-drilled in defending the jersey – they had done it often enough for Hinault. Bernaudeau's early efforts were soon quashed, but as the day dragged on he became more persistent. Eventually he got away, again becoming *virtuel maillot jaune*, only for Fignon to make good his losses on the final slopes of the stage, and then drop him.

Old-timer Lucien Van Impe, now 36, may not have had it in him to be the overall challenger he once was, but he hadn't forgotten how to dance up a mountain.

He won the time trial to Avoriaz by such a margin that he moved into third place overall. Meanwhile, Fignon started the stage well, but conceded 1-44 to Van Impe by the end of the uphill 15-kilometre ride. He almost had the Tour now – all he had to do was win the final time trial to validate his title.

In second place at the halfway time check, Fignon needed every decibel of the crowd's support in the *contre-la-montre*. He had to prove that he was not wearing the yellow jersey by default, and he did it in those final 25 kilometres. He finished more than 30 seconds up, and even had time to sit up and salute the crowd as he finished – something usually reserved for road stages. Pre-stage favourite Stephen Roche could only manage third place but, even with Fignon overshadowing him in the competition for best young rider, he had shown that he was on course to become a great rider. Fignon had already achieved that distinction: at 22, he became the youngest man to win the Tour since 1933.

1984

France had not just one, but two former winners with their sights set on the *maillot jaune* in 1984, each representing a different side of the national character. Defending champion Fignon had earned the nickname "The Professor", with his metal-rimmed glasses and his urbane Parisian upbringing. Hinault on the other hand prided himself on being a man of the French soil, not ashamed to use brute force and aggression to combat Fignon's carefully thought through race tactics. Whatever else happened, the fans could not fail to be enthralled by the spectacle.

Hinault got the better start, winning the prologue by three seconds. He found something lacking in his team La Vie Claire soon after, as they lost a minute to Fignon's Renault squad in the team time trial. They were equally at fault when three men who had set off on a publicity-seeking move at the beginning of stage five, found themselves leading the race by more than 17 minutes by the time the day was over.

Both Fignon and Hinault had a team-mate in the break, so there was no incentive to bring them back to the bunch. The lethargy of the peloton had its price – it took another 12 days' racing to prise Vincent Barteau out of the yellow jersey.

Until then, they, and all the other big riders, had to concentrate on watching one another while making sure that neither Barteau, nor anyone like him, was allowed to pull off the same trick again.

Fignon won the first long time trial, pegging back five minutes on the yellow jersey. Hinault, very

Fignon attacks Hinault at the head of the peloton on stage 11 to Guzet Neige, 1984.

much the second-favourite now, was 33 seconds slower.

On the longest stage of the Tour – a truly tortuous 338 kilometres to Bordeaux – Hinault reverted to his tried and tested tactic, making up 40 seconds in the intermediate sprints while the peloton rode at 30 kph between each hot spot. He felt he needed a little buffer before the mountains started and the ultimate trial of strength began.

Scotland's Robert Millar had earned himself a deserved reputation as a climber in the previous Tour, but even without the advantage of anonymity he was still unmatchable on the first Pyrenean stage.

He drove the winning break, and then crushed the few riders able to stay with him on the final climb, winning by 41 seconds. Behind him Fignon put another minute into Hinault, while Barteau rode valiantly to lose only a little more time than the four times Tour winner. It was time for Hinault to attack.

ATTACK AFTER ATTACK

Of course, Hinault should have waited for a suitable moment to show his colours, but the next day he went with the first move to his liking instead. He then proceeded to spend 16 kilometres off the front by himself, in a crosswind, with no time bonuses to be gained and no hope of maintaining the lead. With Fignon, the yellow jersey Barteau and the world champion Greg Lemond, Renault were not going to tolerate such behaviour and, to Hinault's disgust, brought him back but did nothing to break up the race. "If they had attacked with me we would have got rid of a lot of the opposition. As it is, don't blame me if someone like Herrera wins the Tour," he said.

Fignon answered Hinault in the most eloquent fashion, outsprinting him for second place on the 14th stage and soundly beating him in the next time trial. They were now in second and third place behind Barteau, within 10 minutes of his

Fignon celebrates victory at Cranz Montana on stage 20 in 1984.

time. The *maillot jaune* was finally within their reach.

The stage to Alpe d'Huez finally deposited Fignon back at the top of the general classification. Both he and Hinault were certain that this would be Barteau's last day in the yellow jersey and, to make sure, they started attacking early. Hinault was first, bridging to Patrocinio Jimenez on the Col du Coq. Fignon was soon back with him, only to be forced into a second chase on the Cote de Lafrey. This time Fignon rode past his rival, and chased into the valley after Colombian Luis Herrera. Eventually Hinault caught the pair, and immediately counter-attacked as they reached the foot of the mighty Alp. He made good progress, gaining time over Fignon, but had not figured Herrera into the equation. The Colombian had no loyalty to either Frenchman, and the overall race for the jersey was of little concern to him. He just wanted the stage win. Irrespective of who stayed with him longest, he was going to reach the summit first.

Taking Fignon, Millar, Angel Arroyo and Beat Breu with him, Herrera soon overhauled Hinault. None of them could stay on his wheel around all of the 21 hairpins, but Fignon held on longest, winning the jersey, and gaining three minutes on Hinault. The next day settled the race once and for all.

Robert Millar had taken the King of Mountains' jersey, but knew there were several men hoping to deprive him of it before the race reached Paris. By digging his heels in to defend challenges from Pedro Delgado, he succeeded in helping Fignon's cause. Hinault had already been dropped once, only to fight his way back before the feed. Then, as the peloton slowed *en masse* to pick up *musettes* and to refill pockets and stomachs, he attacked again. The impolite timing of his move showed just how desperate he was – his former Renault team-mates, now defending Fignon's lead, were quick to teach him the error of his ways, bringing him back and spitting him out of the lead group.

On the final climb to La Plagne, Fignon finally achieved what he had failed to do in his Tour career to date. He won a high mountain stage at the summit of a famous climb, and proved that he was a complete rider – not just a lucky one – thoroughly deserving to be winning the Tour. As success follows success, he won again on stage 20, pushing Hinault another minute down the standings and the final time trial gave him a fifth stage win to add to his total for the race. It confirmed his position as the undisputed French hero of the summer, and elevated him to the ranks of multiple Tour winner at the age of just 23. It had been a thrilling race and, with Fignon and Hinault respectful, if not friendly, rivals, the golden era of French cycling was poised to continue for some time yet.

1985

Laurent Fignon did not defend his title in 1985 —a knee operation had left him unable to compete. So it seemed that the way was clear for Hinault to claim his fifth Tour victory, and assume his place with the sport's greats, Jacques Anquetil and Eddy Merckx. His likely rivals included Phil Anderson, Robert Millar and Pedro Delgado, and, interestingly, his own La Vie Claire team-mate, Greg Lemond.

If Hinault were to play it right, he could utilize the American's talent to his own benefit, and for the greater good of the team.

Hinault won the opening prologue as a matter of course; it was in Brittany, his home territory. Lemond's challenge evaporated when his chain jammed on the final section of the route, reducing him to walking pace. He was unperturbed, as was Hinault, when the jersey passed to Erik Vanderaerden the next day. Neither of them was particularly concerned with the minutiae of the opening stages.

La Vie Claire won the team time trial, on conventional road bikes, and without losing a man over the 76.5-kilometre course. As Hinault

Hanging out: Hinault poses alongside his four previous winners' jerseys on a rest day during the 1985 Tour.

climbed off his bike, he was mobbed by fans, all pressing to catch a glimpse of their hero. Hinault panicked and lashed out, catching a photographer on the chin. Before he could do any more damage he was bundled into a police car and driven back to his hotel. The French Press were in overdrive, and Hinault wasn't even in the yellow jersey yet.

After the fracas in Fougères, the gendarmes were better prepared for Hinault's inevitable return to the top of the general classification after the individual time trial at the beginning of the second week. Oblivious to the downpour, thousands of fans lined the route to see their man destroy the competition, finishing more than two minutes clear of his closest rival. He was given a police escort to the podium to collect the *maillot jaune*. The uniformed men by his sides were probably as excited at standing next to him as the fans they were protecting him from.

VILLAINS AND HEROES

The first day in the mountains was an eventful one, but not because of the main protagonists. Didi Thurau,

hero of the 1977 Tour, had been penalized for taking pace in the time trial, and took umbrage at the *commissaires'* decision. Before the stage to Pontartlier started, he sought out the chairman of the jury, Raymond Trine. He had his fingers around the Belgian's throat and was threatening to put him in hospital when the whistle blew for the race to start. Immediately Thurau dropped the official and chased off after the bunch. It was not until the stage had finished that the *commissaires* were able to catch up with him and expel him from the race.

A far more heroic tale was unfolding on the route itself. Paul Sherwen, the long-suffering Briton riding his last Tour, crashed in the first kilometre, before the race had left Epinal. While he lay on the floor struggling to find his bearings, Hinault was already at the front, setting the pace for the day.

Sherwen had two team-mates to help him ride back to the bunch, but eventually he waved them on, worried that all three of them would finish outside the time cut.

Sherwen rode solo for six hours,

over six *cols*, only to find that as he reached the final one the Tour caravan was coming back down the other way, assuming that he had abandoned. The vehicles moved aside to let the solitary rider and the single accompanying motorbike pass. He finished more than an hour after stage-winner Jorgen Pedersen, 23 minutes outside the time cut. His courage was rewarded, however, and he was reinstated in the race.

The crises and heroics of stage 10 were soon forgotten as Hinault decided that the next day was the one where he would eliminate any doubts about his ability or desire to win a fifth Tour. He attacked with ace climber Luis Herrera, driving the two-man break for 75 kilometres to gain a further minute on second-placed Lemond. It was a brutal display, but still nagging voices in peloton could be heard – how long until Hinault cracks?

Hinault "only" came second in the next time trial, but it was still a strong enough performance to increase his lead over the American. He was no longer winning as a matter of course, however. On the stage to St-Etienne he had been comfortably in the second group on the final descent, a minute behind Lemond's group – a seemingly safe position. But he didn't come across the line. The photographers and team personnel waited as impatient fans climbed over the barriers in search of the *maillot jaune*. Eventually he emerged, broken-nosed and bloodied, having crashed 300 metres from the finish. Again he needed a police escort to protect him from the Press and the spectators, but this time they took him straight to hospital.

BLOODIED BUT UNBOWED

Hinault refused to quit. Given the same time as the rest of his group by the *commissaires* (because the crash happened in the final kilometre), he was still in the yellow jersey. Along with other injured riders, including Phil Anderson, he rode gently the next day, allowing Skil's Frederic Vichot to win the stage after a day-long 200-kilometre solo break.

Hinault was able to control the race on the flat but in the Pyrenees, where the climbing stressed his bruised respiratory system, he found that only the power that he wielded over the team could save him. Unable to breath properly, Hinault was dropped on the Tourmalet, while Lemond stayed with the leaders. Suddenly the American was threatening his team-leader, poised to attack from the group and supersede his place in the general classification. La Vie Claire's director Paul Koechli was incensed. Lemond said afterward, "Koechli said to me, 'How dare you attack Hinault when he's in difficulty?'" Koechli denied the charge, and the official team line was that Lemond was given the freedom to break away, but simply wasn't strong enough. The Tour was not yet ready for an American takeover.

Lemond was stuck between defending his second place from Stephen Roche, and not threatening Hinault's lead. He genuinely believed that he could win the Tour, were it not for the team's overriding need to see Hinault in yellow in Paris for a fifth time. He made up another 15 seconds on his ally-turned-rival on the stage to the Aubisque, and then, to underline his superiority in the second part of the race, he won the final time trial, beating Hinault.

Above: Bruised but not broken, Hinault climbs into the team car after breaking his nose during stage 14, 1985. Below: In 1985, Greg Lemond and Hinault exchange banter on the run-in to Paris.

"Now I know I can win a Tour de France," he said.

That Lemond had the ability to win the Tour was certain, but that Hinault had done so five times was now an undisputed fact. And to do it back to back with victory in the Giro d'Italia, with a broken nose and a stitched forehead further bolstered the reputation of the last great French patron of the Tour de France.

1986

Bernard Hinault and Greg Lemond had come to an uneasy truce in 1985, but Hinault would not be allowed to pull rank on the American again. Now the two were obliged to ride for one another as befitted their overall standings: whoever was in the strongest position would be protected, even if it cost the other man valuable resources. And Laurent Fignon was back in the race, so there was every chance they would have to work together to fight an external opponent too.

Hinault knew that he would have to adapt his approach to the race if he were to beat both Lemond and Fignon. He sat tight for the first week of the race, and they did the same, conserving their efforts for the decisive stages. The first of those came on the ninth day, the first long individual time trial.

The "race of truth" put Hinault clear of Fignon by several minutes, a devastating margin for the Parisian, but for Lemond the result was less clear. A puncture had slowed him, and his second place on the stage was not an accurate reflection of his performance. Jorgen Pedersen, the Danish rider who had started the day in yellow, rode the time trial of his life to keep the jersey for another day, while Stephen Roche moved into second place overall thanks to his third place on the stage.

Hinault was 31 now. He knew that he was as strong as ever on the flats, but that he would not be able to stay with the specialist climbers in the high mountains. So he chose his moment to attack carefully,

exploiting his rivals' weaknesses for his own benefit. On stage 12, to Pau, he enlisted the help of his La Vie Claire *domestiques*, keeping in the front group over the first climbs. Then, when they reached the flat 50-kilometre section to the penultimate climb, he initiated his plan.

One by one the La Vie Claire riders attacked, mercilessly wearing down Hinault's opponents, forcing them to chase repeatedly. Once the group's collective spirit was broken, Hinault made his move, taking two team-mates and Pedro Delgado with him. Eventually only Delgado remained and, with a pre-stage advantage of seven minutes over the Spaniard, Hinault was hardly concerned by his company. The Frenchman took the yellow jersey, while Fignon retired from the race, and Lemond came home best of the rest at 4-37.

Now that Hinault was in yellow, Lemond's first concern was to make sure he was kept out of trouble. But the priority was to keep the *maillot jaune* with the team, so he could legitimately ride for himself if Hinault came unstuck. There was no way the team could lose.

LEMOND ECLIPSES HINAULT

The magic of wearing the yellow jersey had gone to Hinault's head. He felt invincible – he had a five-minute cushion over second-placed Lemond, a team-mate, yet he still wanted to attack. He spent most of the next day off the front, only to succumb to the mountains on the final climb, where first Andy Hampsten and then Lemond rode away from him. Of the two Americans, Lemond proved the stronger, winning the stage, and taking back all but 40 seconds of Hinault's lead.

When Lemond finally took the jersey it was, technically at least, as a consequence of defending Hinault. He marked Urs Zimmerman all the way to the line on stage 17, preventing the Carrera rider from taking the lead himself as Hinault trailed in behind them. The battle for supremacy was fought out once and

for all the next day on the Col du Galibier, the Col de la Croix de Fer, the Col du Telegraphe and finally the Alpe d'Huez.

Neither Hinault, nor most of the peloton, could accept that Lemond was leading their Tour. The Frenchman attacked on the descent of the Galibier and was already 20 seconds ahead before Lemond realized the danger. Looking after his own interests, Zimmerman joined Hinault in pursuit and, when they caught Lemond, Hinault attacked again until, eventually, the two men were isolated in their duel. They remained locked together to the line, where Hinault finally conceded, grasping Lemond's hand and raising it above his head as they reached the finish. Lemond gave Hinault a push across the line, and with it the stage win. It was the gesture of a man who knew he had won the race.

Hinault won the final time trial. Lemond crashed, but would not

Greg Lemond chases down Urs Zimmerman on stage 17 to Le Granon, 1986.

have beaten him anyway. Hinault won the climbing competition as well – his long attacking moves had seen him cross many summits ahead of the bunch so that, even as a weaker climber than in his heyday, he became King of the Mountains. The Hinault era had not ended without a fight, but it was time to lead in the new stars now. Lemond was not only a gifted rider, but an innovator, and the legacy he began in 1986 would touch the entire peloton.

1987

In seven attempts, Hinault had won the Tour five times, had been forced to abandon once and had been beaten by Fignon once. In his eighth Tour, not only had he been defeated by Lemond, he had been vanquished. He retired, unwilling to play a supporting role in the race where he had taken centre stage for so long.

Lemond himself was injured and unable to defend the title, which left Urs Zimmerman, the final man on the 1986 podium, as default favourite. Laurent Fignon was acting as chaperon to Systeme-U's new hope, Charly Mottet, and Ireland's Stephen Roche, who had won the Giro d'Italia in the early summer, was also tipped as potential winner, provided he could recover sufficiently between the two Grand Tours.

For a week the contenders bided their time, saving themselves for what they knew would be the first major selection on stage 10. An unforgiving 87.5-kilometre individual time trial, it would spread the field across 20 minutes between the potential winners and the *lanterne rouge* who would waste no more energy that was needed to stay within the time cut. Roche won the stage, despite calling it "ridiculous", and Frenchman Charly Mottet took the jersey.

With no obvious leader, the race ambled on as far as the foot of the Pyrenees before any decisive action was taken. The peloton was tiring, and the men chasing the jersey were getting nervous. First to strike were Jean François Bernard and Erik Breukink. Roche, Robert Millar and Pedro Delgado staked their claims the next day, dropping Breukink like a stone and bringing the first five men within five minutes of the yellow jersey.

FIGNON: DOMESTIQUE DE LUXE

If Fignon no longer believed he had a chance of winning the race, he knew that his experience could be vital for his team-mate Mottet. They were halfway through stage 15 when the heavens opened. The peloton cowered under the black skies, knowing that they had to bring back the early breakaway.

As they strove to catch the leaders, a gap opened up in the line – the tiny Colombian climbers could not hold the pace. Seeing his chance, Fignon seized control, ordering the four Systeme-U riders to attack and take Mottet clear in the momentary confusion. The PDM team joined in the action, enabling the group to maintain its position ahead of the field and secure Mottet another minute's worth of breathing space in the *maillot jaune*.

The next day Mottet paid for his efforts. He was dropped on the

final climb, losing the time he had gained on stage 15. He held on to the jersey for just 48 hours longer, until the time trial to the summit of the Ventoux, where Jean François Bernard finally overhauled him.

That evening Bernard admitted that he had gambled everything on the Ventoux climb. He would not be performing any more heroics, merely hoping that a tight defence from his Toshiba team would keep him in yellow. So when he punctured early on in stage 19, he knew his chance was over. By the time he had received mechanical assistance every one of his challengers had disappeared into the distance, leaving him to crawl in four minutes after Pedro Delgado. Roche claimed the jersey with his second place, only to cede it to the Spaniard the next day.

There were two further mountain stages yet to be contested, plus the final time trial. With only 25 seconds between first and second place there was no time for admiring the Alpine views. Roche knew he must attack, and attack he did, staying away with a select group for 50 kilometres before being caught. He was then dropped by Delgado, finding himself a minute down with five kilometres remaining. He somehow managed to win back all but five seconds of this deficit, only to

Above: Heavy rain causes chaos on stage 15, 1987. Below: Ireland's Stephen Roche on his way to victory in the time trial at Futuroscope.

collapse across the line and be instantly rushed away by paramedics.

Buoyed by his performance, and having recovered from the oxygen debt, Roche took on Delgado again the next day, this time beating him by a handful of seconds. He knew that when it came to the race against the clock, he should beat the Spaniard, but given that it was only 38 kilometres long he wanted to minimize the last remaining obstacle between him and the *maillot jaune*. He had enough flat-out speed to ride the technical sections of the course without danger, and took the jersey by 40 seconds. He became the fifth man to win the tours of Italy and France in the same year, and later in the season took the world title, too, making a unique triple.

1988

With both Greg Lemond and Stephen Roche absent, Laurent Fignon signed up for the 1988 Tour de France with hopes of contending the overall competition. His old foe – now race commentator – Bernard Hinault was quick to dismiss him as past his best and, when he was dropped on the team time trial on the first day and abandoned by his team, it was clear that the Systeme-U management thought the same.

Aside from Fignon's abject failure in the first day's racing, the Tour got off to a quiet start. Canadian Steve Bauer had two spells in yellow, initially for just 24 hours, having broken away in the last 20 kilometres of stage one for a glorious solo victory, and then following another well-timed escape, this time on the descent into Nancy on stage eight.

After a long 10 days, the race finally reached the mountains. It was worth the wait: Colombia's Fabio Parra pulled off a magnificent stage win, while behind him all and sundry rode their hearts out, some to stay in contention for the jersey, others just to stay in the race. After 184 kilometres of the 232-kilometre stage, the Tour began for real. At the foot of the first-category Pas de

Morgins climb, Parra, Charly Mottet, Pedro Delgado, Urs Zimmerman and a host of other strong riders joined forces to drop the hangers-on. Bauer soon caught on to the back of the group, but others were not so fortunate. Fignon missed the move and, by the summit, was already 11 minutes down. By the time the stage finished, the gap had almost doubled; Jean François Bernard also lost time. The Frenchman who would replace Bernard Hinault in the hearts of the French fans was as elusive as ever.

Fignon abandoned the next morning, Bastille Day, without starting the stage. In doing so he avoided the punishing 21 hairpins of Alpe d'Huez. It was here that Steve Bauer saw his hopes of finishing the Tour in yellow disappear out of view as Pedro Delgado rode away from him. Zimmerman and Breukink were unceremoniously dumped from the top 10, leaving the Colombians Herrera and Parra, along with Dutchmen Steven Rooks and Gert-Jan Theunisse squaring up to take their places.

TROUBLE IN ALL ITS GUISES
Delgado confirmed his place at the top of the standings by winning the mountain time trial, all but catching Bauer, who had started three minutes before him. He had two more Pyrenean stages to finalize his campaign and, being Spanish, he had plenty of support *en route*. He didn't go with the break on the stage to Guzet Neige – he didn't have to – and as the race unfolded he was certain he had made the right decision. Holding the escapees within a safe distance for a while, Delgado's group were some eight minutes behind on the final climb.

As Robert Millar locked on to Phillipe Bouvatier's wheel to prepare for the final sprint, he did not lift his eyes above waist height. Neither did Bouvatier. He was mesmerized by the leading cars, which were following signals from the gendarmes to clear the finishing straight of vehicles. Both men went off course toward the car park and, by the time they realized their mistake, Massimo

Ghirotto had won the stage. In addition to the honour of winning at the famous peak, the victor of the stage also took home a brand new Peugeot. Ghirotto gave the car to Bouvatier – a selfless gesture, but not one that could make up for the loss of the stage.

Delgado had two more quiet days to enjoy the *maillot jaune* before the biggest scandal of the race erupted, threatening to take him and his jersey with it.

The organizers of the race announced that Delgado had tested positive for Probenicide. Then they changed their minds. Delgado had given a urine sample that contained traces of Probenicide, which was on the waiting list to be banned by the Union Cycliste Internationale – due to be added in eight days' time at the next committee meeting. Had Delgado been tested under International Olympic Committee regulations he would have been positive, but in these peculiar circumstances he got off the hook. He admitted he had used Probenicide and, technically, he was at liberty to do so. The drug acted to help kidneys clear uric acid from the body but, more dubiously, could be used as a

Still holding the Crédit Lyonnais lion he was awarded on the podium, Pedro Delgado steps out of the drug testers' caravan on stage 18 at Puy de Dôme, 1988.

masking agent for other substances. Whatever his critics hinted at, his supporters remained loyal: King of the Mountains Steven Rooks stated that, should Delgado be fined and penalized 10 minutes, he would do his utmost to ensure that he was allowed to ride off the front in order to gain those 10 minutes back the next day. To make matters more embarrassing, Delgado's second test was clear. According to protocol, no announcement should have been made until after the counter-analysis had been made – if the organizers had followed the rules, nothing would have been said. All they could do was condemn anyone bringing the race into disrepute, and hope that nothing else would go wrong in the final week.

Delgado finished the Tour untroubled. The festivities on the Champs Elysées temporarily drowned out any whispers and, with more than seven minutes over his nearest rival, he had clearly been the strongest man in the race. Unfortunately for him, however, there will always be an asterisk next to his name in the Tour's hall of fame.

1989
The missing men came back to retake their race in 1989. Fignon arrived at the prologue in sparkling form – something the French public had not seen since he won the race in 1984. And Greg Lemond, who had almost died after being shot accidently while on a hunting trip two years previously, was back on his bike. But Delgado never even got a chance to pit himself against such adversaries; humiliatingly, he missed his time slot at the prologue, and the clock passed two and a half minutes before he reached the start ramp. Eight kilometres later and he was officially in last place, 2-54 behind stage winner Erik Breukink.

Laurent Fignon was one rider who knew how it felt to have your race fall apart on the first day – it had happened to him 12 months previously. Learning from the

experience, he commanded Super-U to a comfortable win in the team trial, setting himself up as first real favourite for the overall. Then, two days later, in the 73-kilometre individual *contre-la-montre*, Lemond proved that his was the greatest comeback of the era. The man who had cheated death won the time trial by 38 seconds from Delgado, taking a five-second lead over Fignon in the overall.

Those five seconds were fragile, and Lemond knew it. He made it clear he was not concerned with the jersey, for now at least; he was still unsure of how his body – still full of pellet shrapnel – would cope with the high mountains. At the first test, he faltered. Fignon made up those few seconds on the last of four ascents on stage 10, reversing their positions and now seven seconds ahead of the American. Suddenly France loved him again.

14 July was no normal Bastille Day this year: it was the 200th anniversary of the Revolution, so when the race leader and the world's number-one-ranked rider, Charly Mottet, escaped together there was not a soul in France who did not cheer them on. For 40 kilometres the pair worked side by side until, finally, Lemond and Delgado – aided by a vicious headwind, brought them

back. "The Tour can be won anywhere, why not on a flat stage?" said Fignon after the event. But Lemond disagreed. He was saving himself for the next time trial. If he was unsure of his climbing with the pack, he knew that this was one area where he still reigned. It was a mountain time trial, but the American was able to produce his best effort. He beat Fignon by a minute, retaking the jersey in readiness for the second round of mountains, the Alps.

The first Alpine stage was not the most difficult, with only a short uphill finish after two proper climbs, but that was enough to see Fignon drop back another 13 seconds, while Lemond held on with Mottet and Delgado. The pendulum swung back in his face the next day.

SO NEAR YET SO FAR

Both men made it into the chasing group on the stage to Alpe d'Huez – the leaders were interested only in the stage win, and posed no threat to the jersey. Inevitably the real contest began on the famous slopes of the most infamous of mountains. Fignon attacked first, but Lemond pulled him back. Then Lemond attacked, and Fignon brought him back in turn. They took a few moments to recover, then Fignon

Above: Fignon attacks Lemond on stage 10 in 1989; the Frenchman gained enough time to retake the yellow jersey from him. Below: Lemond celebrates after the dramatic finish in Paris.

attacked again, just as they caught breakaway Robert Millar. Lemond did not move. Delgado gave chase, Lemond capitulated, riding alone to the summit and losing a minute to Fignon. The Frenchman had the jersey once again, but he knew that, with another time trial to come, he must build up an advantage that would be unassailable.

On the short stage to Villard, Fignon produced a ride to merit his inclusion in the pantheon of Tour greats. He attacked 23 kilometres from the finish, crossing the summit of St Nizer with a slender margin, and holding it all the way to the line. With no one willing to cooperate, Lemond lost another 24 seconds.

The pair were inseparable on the final mountain stage. Along with Delgado, Gert-Jan Theunisse and Marino Lejaretta, they rode unrelentingly to Aix les Bains, maintaining an average of 60 kph on the final, slightly downhill 20 kilometres. Unable to break away, Lemond did the next best thing, and outsprinted Fignon for the stage win. With just 50 seconds between them, the Tour was far from over.

Lemond had won the jersey twice and lost it twice in the space of three weeks; Fignon had held onto it at the second time of asking. Now for the final test – a 25-kilometre time trial to the Champs Elysées. In a longer event Lemond would have been confident of winning the stage and the jersey, but somehow the pre-destined *parcours* would balance Fignon's advantage exactly with Lemond's time-trialling one.

Lemond set off second to last, leaving Fignon to wait at the start ramp for two agonizing minutes before beginning his ride. At the 11.5 kilometre time check Lemond was 21 seconds up on Fignon; it couldn't have been closer. Then, once he had completed his 26 minute 57 second ride, it was Lemond's turn for the torture of waiting. The clock continued to tick as Fignon gasped for every breath, willing himself to stay within reach of his target. As the clock passed Lemond's time, a stunned silence washed across Paris.

Lemond whooped in ecstasy while Fignon lent across his handlebars and wept: he had lost the Tour by eight seconds.

1990

As if to prove that his miracle Tour win was not just a one-off, Greg Lemond completed the 1989 season by winning the world championships. But, for the first half of the following season, he was rarely seen competing in his rainbow jersey and, when he did appear, he looked overweight and out of condition. Fignon was recovering from injury, but would surely be the most motivated man of all after his heart-breaking defeat the previous year. Former winners Stephen Roche and Pedro Delgado were also ready for a crack at a second title, but it seemed no one could rise above the masses to earn the mark of pre-race favourite. Only the race itself could determine that.

Lemond finished second in the prologue, giving him a 15-second advantage over Fignon before the real racing started. The Frenchman was not happy, and made a point of criticizing Lemond's tactics to anyone who would listen. Lemond was not afraid to answer back. "I've ridden four times, won twice, been placed second and third. I think it's better that you say nothing and look at your *palmares*," he said.

While the two men continued to argue via the Press, others used more immediate methods to air their grievances. On stage three, the organizers were forced to re-route the *parcours* mid-stage as French farmers attempted to hijack the Tour as a vehicle for their protests against Eastern European and British imports. An extra 200 gendarmes were called up to protect the race from burning tyres and felled trees.

There was chaos in the bunch too – Fignon got stranded in the second group, then punctured, then crashed as he fought to regain the leaders. His problems were compounded the next day when he was held up behind a mass pile-up

and lost a further 44 seconds. He hadn't seen the front of the race since it left Futuroscope, the venue of the prologue, and after less than a week's racing he abandoned.

Canadian Steve Bauer was in yellow, and with some 10 minutes over Lemond he knew that the first individual time trial could hurt, but not destroy, his grip on the lead. But the American had a disappointing ride, making up only 32 seconds, while his team-mate Ronan Pensec moved into second overall. He took over the jersey on the first mountain stage – coincidentally on his 27th birthday, leaving Lemond to chip away at his deficit on each stage they rode.

TACTICS VERSUS ENTHUSIASM

The Alpine stages ended the hopes of some riders, while other lesser-known men found themselves thrust into the spotlight. Gianni Bugno won the stage to Alpe d'Huez, and Claudio Chiappucci took the yellow jersey after the mountain time trial. The little Italian spent the rest of day with a permanent grin splitting his face, only to find that defending the lead in the Tour was no

Lemond in the yellow jersey at the front of the peloton as riders race down the Champs Elysées, 1990.

laughing matter. He was outnumbered and outmanoeuvred the next day and lost five minutes, allowing both Lemond and Erik Breukink to move up to within three minutes of him. He lost more time the next day, and suddenly it became a question of when, not if, he would lose the race.

Realizing the danger he was in, Chiappucci didn't wait for someone else to make a move. On the first day in the Pyrenees he attacked partway up the Aspin, dropping both Lemond and Breukink and opening up a lead of more than four minutes. But he had gone too soon. The ascent of the Tourmalet saw his lead drop to a minute, and he was caught by Lemond before they reached the valley floor. On the final climb Lemond easily dispensed with the Italian, dropping him for two minutes in three kilometres, finishing second on the stage to Miguel Indurain, Delgado's *domestique*. Chiappucci made a gallant effort to limit his losses and was rewarded with another day in yellow, although his lead was now just five seconds.

Lemond survived a scare the next day as the Z team rescued him when he punctured one kilometre from the summit of the last climb before a 60-kilometre run into Pau. He had to wait until the final time trial to topple Chiappucci from the top of the general classification. This time around organizers had scheduled the test for the penultimate day – after last year's high-tension finale, they had decided they preferred the carnival atmosphere of the race up and down the Champs Elysées to the nerve-wracking prospect of the jersey being won and lost in the dying seconds of the Tour.

Lemond had founded his two previous Tour wins on his superlative time-trialling – he did not doubt he would beat Chiappucci by the six seconds he needed to win the event for a third time. Within three kilometres of the start he was *virtuel maillot jaune* and, thanks to the fact there was still a road stage to Paris to be ridden, this time he got to complete the Tour safe in the knowledge that the race was his.

Tour Legends
Bernard Hinault

"As long as I live and breathe, I attack."

Bernard Hinault

Main Picture: Hinault on stage 11, Pontarlier–Avoriaz, 1985. He grits his teeth and retains the yellow jersey. Right: Hinault on stage 2 in 1978, Brussells–St Amand-les-Eaux.

BERNARD HINAULT (FRA)
b. 14/11/54 Yffiniac, Brittany

EIGHT PARTICIPATIONS
FIVE VICTORIES
28 STAGE WINS

1978 FIRST OVERALL
THREE STAGE WINS: stage 8, Saint-Emilion–Sainte-Foix-la-Grande (time trial); stage 15, Saint-Dier-d'Auvergne–Saint-Etienne; stage 20, Metz–Nancy (time trial)

1979 FIRST OVERALL
WINNER POINTS COMPETITION
SEVEN STAGE WINS: stage 2, Luchon–Superbagnères; stage 3, Luchon–Pau; stage 11, Brussels (time trial); stage 15, Evian–Avoriaz (time trial); stage 21, Dijon (time trial); stage 23, Auxerre–Nogent-sur-Marne; stage 24, Le Perreux–Paris

1980 DID NOT FINISH
THREE STAGE WINS: prologue, Frankfurt; stage 4, Spa-Francorchamps (time trial); stage 5, Liège–Lille

1981 FIRST OVERALL
FIVE STAGE WINS: prologue, Nice; stage 7, Nay–Pau; stage 16, Mulhouse (time trial); stage 20, Bourg d'Oisans– Le Pleynet; stage 22, Saint-Priest (time trial)

1982 FIRST OVERALL
FOUR STAGE WINS: prologue, Bâle; stage 14, Martigues (time trial); stage 19, Saint-Priest (time trial); stage 21, Fontenay-sous-Bois–Paris

1984 SECOND OVERALL
ONE STAGE WIN: prologue, Montreuil–Noisy-le-Sec

1985 FIRST OVERALL
TWO STAGE WINS: prologue, Plumelec; stage 8, Sarrebourg–Strasbourg (time trial)

1986 SECOND OVERALL
KING OF THE MOUNTAINS
THREE STAGE WINS: stage 9, Nantes (time trial); stage 18, Briançon–L'Alpe d'Huez; stage 20, Saint-Etienne (time trial)

Tour Legends

Greg Lemond

"Today is the greatest moment of my whole life."

Greg Lemond on winning in 1989

Right: Lemond crossing the line first ahead of Laurent Fignon on the crucial stage 19 in 1989. Opposite page: Fignon celebrates taking the yellow jersey at L'Alpe d'Huez in 1984.

GREG LEMOND (USA)
b. 26/6/61 Lakewood, California

EIGHT PARTICIPATIONS
THREE VICTORIES
FIVE STAGE WINS

1984 THIRD OVERALL

1985 SECOND OVERALL
ONE STAGE WIN: stage 21, Lac de Vassivière (time trial)

1986 FIRST OVERALL
ONE STAGE WIN: stage 13, Pau–Superbagnères

1989 FIRST OVERALL
THREE STAGE WINS: stage 5, Dinard–Rennes (time trial); stage 19 Villard-de-Lans–Aix-les-Bains; stage 21, Versailles–Paris (time trial)

1990 FIRST OVERALL

1991 SEVENTH OVERALL

1992 DID NOT FINISH

1994 DID NOT FINISH

Tour Legends
Laurent Fignon

"I am ready to cope with fame." Fignon, 1983

LAURENT FIGNON (FRA)
b. 12/8/60 Paris. d. 31/8/2010

10 PARTICIPATIONS
TWO VICTORIES
NINE STAGE WINS

1983 FIRST OVERALL
ONE STAGE WIN: stage 21, Dijon (time trial)

1984 FIRST OVERALL
FIVE STAGE WINS: stage 7, Alençon–Le Mans (time trial); stage 16, Les Echelles–La Ruchère (time trial); stage 18, Bourg d'Oisans–La Plagne; stage 20 Morzine–Crans-Montana; stage 22, Villié-Morgon–Villefranche-sur-Saône (time trial)

1986 DID NOT FINISH

1987 SEVENTH OVERALL
ONE STAGE WIN: stage 21 Bourg d'Oisans–La Plagne

1988 DID NOT FINISH

1989 SECOND OVERALL
ONE STAGE WIN: stage 18, Bourg d'Oisans–Villard-de-Lans

1990 DID NOT FINISH

1991 SIXTH OVERALL

1992 23RD OVERALL
ONE STAGE WIN: stage 11, Strasbourg– Mulhouse

1993 DID NOT FINISH

Chapter 9: 1991–1997

Indurain Joins the Greats

The sparkling era of battles between Hinault, Lemond and Fignon had brought a tension to the Tour that was sometimes too agonizing to watch. Now, as the 1990s approached, the event saw one man emerge as a peerless champion. From 1991–1995 there was only one thing for the peloton to race for – second place behind Miguel Indurain.

1991

Greg Lemond was favourite in 1991 and faced a truly international collection of competitors – his long-time rival Laurent Fignon, who hoped that the home advantage would do him some good; Italians Gianni Bugno and the ever-unpredictable Claudio Chiappucci; a pair of former winners Pedro Delgado (Spain) and Irishman Stephen Roche, and a host of other outsiders. It promised to be a hard-fought race, with various loyalties and allegiances shaping the way the riders competed. No one was prepared to wait until the mountain stages to see who was on top form.

The first road stage of the race was a 100-kilometre loop around Lyon, with a team time trial to follow in the afternoon. Halfway through the morning stage Lemond and Erik Breukink infiltrated an early break, with the American taking full advantage of the intermediate sprints and snatching sufficient time bonuses to put him into the *maillot jaune*. He wore it for just 42 minutes (the Ariostea team narrowly bettered Castorama in the second part of the day's action), but this was long enough for him to assert his strength without putting the onus on his team-mates to defend the jersey on the windswept roads of northeast France. That he left in the capable hands of World Cup leader Rolf Sorensen.

The Danish rider wore the yellow jersey well, but lost it cruelly just three days later. He crashed a few kilometres from the end of stage five, breaking his collarbone. Ignoring the searing pain, he dropped his twisted bike, swapping with team-mate Bruno Cenghlialta, and grimaced all the way to the line. He was immediately taken to hospital – missing out on the ceremony of collecting the jersey – and was unable to continue the race.

The loss of the *maillot jaune* was disquieting. It highlighted the inherent danger of bunch-racing on roads that were becoming increasingly burdened with traffic-calming devices. Many riders thought it best to wait until the time trial to show their cards. It was a long race against the clock – 73 kilometres – and would leave no place to hide. Banesto's second-string rider Miguel Indurain won the stage, but all eyes were on Lemond. The American, just eight seconds adrift, put more than a minute into his rivals, securing the yellow jersey and sending the bookies into a frenzy

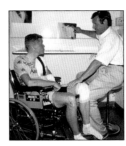

**Above: Rolf Sorensen is shown his X-rays by a doctor, 1991.
Below: Greg Lemond cracks on the Col du Tourmalet. Previous page: Indurain confirms his first Tour victory by winning the final time trail, 1991.**

as they shortened the odds on him winning still further.

LEMOND IN TROUBLE

Could anyone beat Lemond? The answer came much sooner than expected, on the first major climb of the first mountain stage of the race.

Frenchman Charly Mottet bridged across to the breakaway group on the descent of the Soudet, while Lemond was cut off from his team-mates in the chasing group. On to the second main climb, the Somport, and the leading group was soon down to three men – Mottet, Luc Leblanc and Pascal Richard. Lemond found no one willing to help him try to bring them back, and was instead left to face a constant, irritating stream of small attacks and digs from his companions on the road. Leblanc took the jersey, Mottet the stage and, in a final affront to the American, Indurain attacked in the finishing moments to pull back eight seconds – not a huge time gap, but a particularly poignant one, as it exactly matched Lemond's winning margin in 1989.

This was a dramatic end to what had been a long, difficult day. Àngered by what they regarded as the organizers' and the Union Cycliste

Internationale's (UCI's) petty ruling, the peloton had remained at the start line for some 40 minutes, refusing to race. The reasons had been twofold: firstly, they were protesting against the exclusion of the Swiss rider Urs Zimmerman. He had made the transfer from Nantes to Pau in a team car as he did not like flying, and had been excluded as a result of not taking the official transport. Once this matter had been resolved (eventually his team manager was excluded instead), the riders turned their attention to the compulsory wearing of helmets. Two thirds of the field left theirs with team officials by way of protest, risking a collective statutory fine of 41,000 Swiss Francs to the UCI.

Lemond had little time to recover from the shock of losing the jersey before he found himself in even deeper trouble. It was the hardest stage of the race, and at its highest point – at the summit of the Tourmalet – he began to crack.

He was just a few seconds behind the leaders over the 2,115-metre peak but, by the time he had clawed his way back and finally made it through to the front of the group, Indurain was gone.

Joined by Claudio Chiappucci in the lull before the next mountain, Indurain sensed that the timing was right. With complementary objectives – the Spaniard wanted the yellow jersey, the Italian the stage win and the points' jersey – the pair soon built a healthy lead. Lemond's group splintered, and the first casualty was Luc Leblanc. The yellow jersey was going backwards and Indurain went forwards, with Lemond marooned somewhere in between. "I spent all day bridging gaps," he said after the stage. "Since the first day everyone's ridden to make me lose, and they got me in the end."

ENTER THE NEW HERO

Crossing over to the Alps provided Lemond with just the change of air he needed. A seemingly insignificant fourth-category climb on a transition stage put the frighteners on Indurain and his Banesto squad, when three

Above: Miguel Indurain in the first time-trial from Argentan to Alençon during the 1991 Tour.

of his remaining rivals for the overall competition got into a threatening break. It wasn't until second-placed Mottet instructed his RMO team to get on the front and dig Banesto out of a hole that the group was brought back. Realizing that Indurain was tired, Lemond attacked the moment the bunch regrouped. A handful of seconds would do nothing to change the overall classification this time, but at least a little pride had been restored.

Although a Spaniard was in yellow, it was the Italians who were having the best of the day-to-day action. The stage to Alpe d'Huez – a prestigious climb with an unusual flat kilometre from its peak to the finish line – was to be no exception. With just 125 kilometres of riding in prospect, the specialist climbers knew that the final ascent would arrive while their legs were still relatively fresh, and Banesto boss Jose Echavarri made sure his men did not repeat their mistake, and held the breakaways in check all the way to the foot of the Alps. Italian national

champion Gianni Bugno exploded out of the bunch the moment they hit the climb, drawing out Indurain, polka-dot-jerseyed Chiappucci and a select few others. Lemond and Laurent Fignon had been dispensed with. The old guard battled up the climb while the front-runners fought among themselves for the stage. The result was just as it had been on the previous mountain stage. The plucky Italian – in this case Bugno – took the stage, with Indurain close on his wheel, increasing his chances of wearing yellow all the way to Paris.

The Col de Colombière, on the final mountain stage of the race, was the fatal blow to Lemond's Tour campaign. He would start the race on a further two occasions, but this was the last time he would finish it. The riders contesting the podium places were happy with their lot. Unless Indurain cracked, they would bide their time and let the stage play out as the other, lesser riders wanted. But Lemond could not even do that, losing eight minutes as the new rulers of the peloton rolled in within

dislodge him from the *maglia rosa* – the pink jersey – worn by the race leader of the event. Indurain's victory proved that his form was at least as good as it had been the previous year. The only remaining question was whether he would be able to repeat his success so soon after competing in the Italian race.

According to the custom of the Tour de France, the route of the 1992 race was chosen to reflect a particular aspect of the times: on this occasion, it was a celebration of the European single market.

Following the prologue and road stage, based in and around San Sebastian, the peloton was scheduled to skim round the Pyrenees and take a long plane transfer up towards Flanders, where the race would perform a whistle-stop tour of Belgium, Holland, Germany and

seconds of stage winner Thierry Claveyrolat.

Indurain may have ridden defensively through the Alps, but in the last time trial it was only right that the final man to start, the race leader, should win the stage. He did so with an unnerving display of force, underlining his dominance of the discipline. There was only one place left for Lemond to strike; a symbolic move in the Parisian suburbs, as the bunch eased its way to the Champs Elyseés for the traditional 10-lap finale. The American was first to the Arc de Triomphe, a feat that was rapidly overshadowed by a high-speed crash involving Djamolidine Abdujaparov. The points' winner came down just metres from the finish line at 65 kph, and was left prone on the tarmac as the bunch skidded around him. With assistance, he managed to cross the line some moments later to finish the race technically. The blood-splattered green-jersey wearer was taken directly to hospital, while up on the podium three young riders – Indurain, flanked by Bugno and Chiappucci – stood with heads held high. The Lemond era was over, but no one could predict the reach of the new era that had just begun.

Above: Gianni Bugno (left) and Claudio Chiappucci (right) flank Miguel Indurain in Paris, 1991.

1992

A generation gap had opened during Indurain's first Tour win, and it had widened even further 12 months on. The ageing process could be over-ridden in a one-day, or even a one-week race, but in a Grand Tour, where an individual's performance relied heavily on recovery from repeated efforts, there was no place to hide.

The young riders who had topped the previous year's podium – Indurain, Chiappucci and Bugno – were just reaching the peak of their physical powers, and now had the experience to quell nerves that might previously have made them commit tactical errors.

Bugno, who had graduated from the red, white and green of Italian champion to the rainbow stripes of World Champion, had laid careful plans for the season, which he hoped would culminate in victory at the Tour. Chiappucci had also spent the first half of the year preparing for July, and had already raced head-to-head with Indurain at the Giro d'Italia. Even with the advantage of a rapturous home crowd, he had not been able to match Indurain in the time trials, nor make sufficient in-roads on the climbs to be able to

Luxembourg. A few days later, a summit finish at Sestriere would see the riders cross briefly into Italy for 50 kilometres, at the end of what promised to be one of the hardest stages of the entire Tour.

A TEMPORARY SETBACK

Back in San Sebastian the prologue results were startling. Indurain won but, more surprisingly, 21-year-old Alex Zülle came within two seconds of him and Lemond was pushed out of the top 10 altogether. The unheralded Swiss rider made a well-timed move during the first road stage, taking a time bonus on the very first intermediate sprint, and with it the yellow jersey. A day later another young hopeful sprang from the bunch to take custody of Indurain's jersey – Richard Virenque – while the old guard slipped back.

The Tour returned to French soil for the team time trial – a chance for the most cohesive teams to lift their leaders up the general classification. An intermittent feature in the race, the event concerned Indurain; he knew that his Banesto squad could not hope to beat the likes of Chiappucci's Carrera team, or Bugno's Gatorade outfit.

His premonitions proved to be well-founded and he lost time to both his rivals on the stage. However, he faced an even ruder shock two days later, when Chiappucci formed an alliance with Greg Lemond – their sole intention being to do damage to the Spaniard's race.

It was a miserable day, pouring with rain, and given the *parcours* – from Roubaix to Brussels via the Oude Kwaremont and the Muur de Grammont – it was hardly ideal

Above: Greg Lemond (left) struggles to keep pace with Claudio Chiappucci (right), 1992. Below: Chiappucci evokes memories of the great Fausto Coppi during his lone assault on the stretch to Sestriere.

territory for a climbing specialist and a former Tour winner to flex their collective muscles. Across the treacherous, cobbled roads that make up the traditional early-season classic races, it was a brave move, or perhaps one inspired by the prospect of taking on Indurain in the mountains. This was perhaps their only chance to handicap him before the Alps.

CHIAPPUCCI'S EPIC

After a week of surprises and upsets, normality resumed – a distorted version of it, at least – in the first time trial. Indurain won by three minutes, a fitting riposte to the pair of riders who had stolen a minute on general classification in Belgium. During this time the yellow jersey remained safely on the shoulders of Frenchman Pascal Lino. He held on to it through the first mountain stage, returning it

to Indurain on one of the most dramatic stages of the Tour for a number of years.

Italy was the last of the seven countries to host the race and, 40 years on from Fausto Coppi's lone ascent to Sestriere, this would be a prestigious stage for an Italian rider to win. With real pretensions for the overall prize, Claudio Chiappucci knew that this could be the day that transformed him from charming but inconsistent climber to a real man of the peloton. If he was going to win, he wanted to do it in style.

Chiappucci attacked on the first climb of the day, the Col des Saises, speeding away and prising a group free from the bunch. Indurain and Bugno did not respond – surely it was far too early for race-winning breaks to be forming on a 250-kilometre stage? The Italian climber had an agenda, however, and wanted to see who would dare to come with him. It took until the next climb, the Cormet de Roseland, for Banesto to group at the front of the bunch and start its team duties. Nothing further happened until the next climb – the third of five – when, rather than gain on the breakaways, the bunch succeeded in dropping Greg Lemond. Tired and saddle-sore, he was in no state to contest the race.

The leading group had broken up by now and, with more than 100 kilometres to ride, it seemed inevitable that they would be picked off by the bunch. But Chiappucci attacked again, reaching the head of the race before the top of the snow-covered, 2,800-metre-high Col d'Iseran and increasing his lead further still on the descent. He crested the fourth climb alone, with a sufficient time advantage to make him the *virtuel maillot jaune*. Behind him Bugno was getting agitated. He wanted to get up to Chiappucci, but he could not afford to take Indurain with him. It was a classic lose-lose situation: attack and offer Indurain a tow to Chiappucci, or stay where he was and let his countryman waltz into the lead unchallenged. As Bugno made his move, Indurain jumped on his wheel. Two more men joined them – Franco Vona and Andrew Hampsten – and the four rode together, slowly eating into the time gap, closing Chiappucci down.

On to the final climb and the lead was fragile, but Indurain was still biding his time. With five kilometres to go Chiappucci was suffocating in a mass of fans, willing him onward. But victory was far from secure; suddenly, Indurain decided he had had enough of his companions, and took it upon himself to chase the lone figure high up the mountain. In just

Below: Chiapucci celebrates after crossing the line first at Sestriere, 1992.

one kilometre the Banesto team leader had regained 24 seconds, and was only a minute behind Chiappucci. *Tifosi* were running madly alongside their hero, not allowing him to let up for a fraction of a pedal stroke. Then, just as Indurain seemed to be within touching distance of his rival, he cracked. Unbelievably, the time gap began to open up again – if Chiappucci was suffering, Indurain was suffering more. Deliriously, Chiappucci passed the *flamme rouge* and, sure that he was safe from any late comebacks from Indurain, he began celebrating way before crossing the line. It was an epic victory and, although Indurain had succeeded in gaining the yellow jersey, Chiappucci had convincingly earned his place in the annals of the sport.

VICTORY SEALED

Such a race-defining stage left the main contenders happy to let someone else make the running on the next day of the race. Placed eighth overall, rider Andy Hampsten took up the mantle, attacking on the penultimate climb of the stage, catching the early break and, slowly but surely, riding them all off his wheel. Further back Bugno was in trouble and Lemond, in too much pain even to sit straight on his saddle, finally conceded defeat and abandoned the race.

Hampsten's win at Alpe d'Huez was enough to leave him third overall, and Chiappucci was the only threat left. Tactically, Bugno's capitulation made life much easier for Banesto, as there was now only one man to mark. The race was out of the mountains, and all that most competitors could hope for now was a stage win. Old-hand Stephen Roche took one over the hills of the Massif Central, French riders Thierry Marie and Jean-Claude Colotti gave the home fans something to smile about, while Indurain rolled down the start ramp of the final time trial to take the prize home to Spain. His win in the *contre-la-montre* was a solid performance, showing that he had strength in reserve after

the mountains, and Bugno earned himself a place on the podium with the ride of the day.

The Tour reached Paris on the same day that the Barcelona Olympics started. As the torch burned in Spain, the country's greatest cyclist took his second Tour de France, and completed the Giro-Tour double. Chiappucci was again crowned King of the Mountains, and swapped places from 1991 with Bugno on the steps of the podium. The points' jersey went to France's Laurent Jalabert. It had been a tough race, and Indurain had proved beyond doubt that he was the man of the decade. In a battle of survival, over thousands of kilometres and countless hills and mountains, he could outlast everybody.

1993

There was something more than a little familiar about the start of the 1993 Tour de France. Indurain was the obvious favourite, Chiappucci, the thorn in his side and, when the race opened at Le Puy de Fou, Indurain defeated Alex Zülle in the prologue.

So far so good – the riders who had so recently been the new boys were now the established favourites, and there were more young hopefuls waiting to join their number.

On the opening road stage Mario Cipollini scored the victory that had eluded him 12 months earlier, marking the first in a series of mass sprint-finishes, in which Wilfried Nelissen took enough time bonuses to wear the yellow jersey up until the team time trial.

The arduous 81-kilometre stage was absolute purgatory for many riders. Unlike an individual time trial, where those not competing for the stage or overall win can ride tempo, here they have to go flat out for an hour and a half in order to keep their team leaders well positioned in the general classification. Despite all this, it was Cipollini who ended up in yellow at the end of the day, thanks to a superb team performance

from GB-MG, who had spent the past three days leading him out at the stage finishes.

Indurain had looked on with an air of detachment during the first week. His only thoughts were to stay out of trouble, and to make sure that none of his rivals tried a pre-emptive strike before the mountains.

As usual, it was in the first individual time trial that he showed them exactly what it was they were going to have to beat. In 59 kilometres he put more than two minutes into Gianno Bugno, while the man who had come close to him in the prologue, Alex Zülle, was unable to mount a challenge because a freak accident on the previous day's race had left him bruised and cut.

A spectator had stepped out to take a photo of the peloton and, in doing so, had dropped a plastic carrier bag. As the Swiss rider went past, the bag had got caught in his spokes and floored him. It was the kind of

Above: 'Super' Mario Cipollini wins the sprint for the line on the first stage at Sables d'Olonne, 1993. Below: Alex Zülle suffers after his freak accident.

bad luck that no one would wish upon a rival, but even without it Indurain would surely have won the stage at the Lac de Madine. And Chiappucci, Indurain's primary rival? He lost more than five minutes.

ROMINGER RAISES HIS GAME

There were just two big Alpine stages in the 1992 Tour, and Switzerland's Tony Rominger won both. He had been so disappointed with his result in the time trial that he had resolved to make amends, and did so with some style.

Even Chiappucci, the agile-looking Italian who had scaled the mountains so quickly the year before, was unable to keep up with him. The only man to hold his wheel was the seemingly unperturbed Indurain. Over the course of 48 hours, no fewer than 20 riders either abandoned the race or finished outside the time cut – including the star of the first week, Mario Cipollini.

Organizers were not afraid to fine anyone caught holding on to his team car, and so get a quick tow up to the man in front, but Rominger and Indurain pushed on relentlessly.

Chiappucci lost more than 14 minutes on the stage to Serre Chevalier and, despite fighting back the next day to finish just behind Rominger and Indurain, he knew he had lost the race, and even a place in the top three. There was simply nothing the peloton could do – a collaborative effort from the best in the world was not enough to unseat the man in yellow.

Each time someone attacked – Robert Millar, Zenon Jaskula – Indurain responded with unfaltering patience, quietly but purposefully reeling them back in, gently pointing

out to them the error of their ways.

The peloton was demoralized. The riders were halfway through the most important race of the year, and all that was left was a race for second place. Rominger had only Indurain as competition for the climber's jersey, although it was of no interest to the Spaniard because he was already in the *maillot jaune*. The *rouleurs* and the sprinters came out to play for a few days while the rest commiserated with one another. They still had the Pyrenees to contend with.

Motivation to attack in the mountains was hard to find. The only interested parties were those on the hunt for a day of glory; on this occasion it was Oliverio Rincón who decided to go out on a limb.

The Colombian got into the

Above: Indurain with Tony Rominger (left) trailing in his shadow during the 1993 Tour.

early break, and then ditched his companions on the penultimate *col*, with 30 kilometres to go. The brow-beaten peloton was immobilized by Indurain's supremacy and his devoted team of *domestiques*, who sheltered him for much of the stage and quashed any contender's hopes of attacking him. Rincón had been involved in the action over an incredible nine successive climbs, and the race he fought out with his fellow breakaways barely impinged on the men behind him. All they could do was hold the pace that Banesto was setting and hope that Indurain might finally crack the next day.

With just one remaining summit finish in the race, the next stage was the only chance that anyone had of breaking Indurain. Rominger was the first to try his hand, attacking on the Col de Portillon, some 65 kilometres from the finish. The yellow jersey went with him, sparking a counter-move from Chiappucci and Massimo Ghirotto on the descent. The Italian pair hovered half a minute ahead of the chasers for some time, before finally deciding to sit up and wait for them halfway to the finish line.

Tactically, making an early move had been the right thing to do – it was the only chance the riders stood of making up sufficient time on Indurain if he got into trouble. It had failed, however, and the race now was to win the stage. Again it was Rominger who succeeded in opening up a gap – wearing the polka-dot jersey and with two mountain stages to his name already, he was in the form of his life – and again it was Indurain that went with him.

Zenon Jaskula joined them as they made their way up the last climb to Saint Lary Soulan.

Jaskula wanted to jump away, but the crowds were so densely packed along the final kilometres of the climb that there was no room for him to get past the others. He changed

his plan, and sat tight until the final straight. Then he attacked as the road dipped down to the line. Rominger followed him, and Indurain rolled across the line behind them. In some 80 hours of racing, that three-second gap between second and third place was the most the peloton could do to damage him. As he said rather disingenuously after the stage: "I think I can say now, that, barring major accidents, I've won the Tour."

RACING FOR SECOND PLACE

If the Tour had been reduced to a battle for the minor podium places, at least it was an interesting subsidiary to "Big Mig's" parade. The expected challenge from Chiappucci had not materialized – he took the final Alpine stage, but was way out of contention for second place. Instead, as the race came out of the mountains, Alvera Mejia, Jaskula and Rominger were separated from Indurain by less than a minute. They expected the final time trial to follow much the same pattern as the rest of the race had – the Spaniard out ahead of the field, with the best of the rest competing for the position of "first loser". For

Above: Chris Boardman celebrates victory in the prologue at Lille in 1994. Below: Roadside tables laid out for a British tea party as the tour passes en route from Dover to Brighton.

once, not everything went according to plan.

Mejia lost time as expected, but Jaskula outdid himself, finishing third on the stage. Ahead of him was Indurain, but quicker still was Rominger. The only man to have come close to the *maillot jaune* in the mountains finally got the better of him in the time trial, despite having a puncture and having to swap his aero-dynamic lo-pro bike for his normal road bike in the last kilometres of the stage. After three weeks in the saddle, Indurain was finally beginning to show signs of tiring. At last, a tiny sign of human frailty, an indication that he could, in theory, be beaten in the Tour. All eyes would be on Tony Rominger next year.

1994

British fans were in for a double treat in the 1994 Tour, with the race being routed – via the Eurotunnel – to southern England for two stages in the first week of action. Added to that, Olympic pursuit champion Chris Boardman was making his Tour de France debut and, when he

won the prologue, there was real hope that he would bring the yellow jersey back to Britain, if only for those two days. But the racing had barely begun before a needless accident blackened the event, and almost ended the careers of two riders.

With Boardman's lead a comfortable 15 seconds over Indurain, there was little chance of him being threatened by the sprinters, even with the time bonuses they could score on the early road stages. So all that the fast men had to think about was getting to the line first and collecting the flowers for a stage win.

As usual, there were thousands of fans clamouring to get a view as their heroes wound up to 70 kph in the final straight. The road was wide, with barriers on either side to protect the riders and the spectators from one another. A sea of arms and faces spilt over the barricades, and one fan who could not see to get a photograph persuaded a gendarme to take the picture from inside the barriers. Watching the peloton come toward him through the lens, the official did not realize the speed with which it was approaching and, as he moved to get a better view, he stepped into Wilfried Nelissen's path. There was nowhere for the Belgian to go –

he crashed to the ground, bringing others with him. Nelissen and Laurent Jalabert were both immediately taken to hospital, the latter with serious facial injuries. Though both men returned to race the next season, Nelissen never quite recovered. "Jaja" came back to have a hugely successful career, but he had lost his nerve for the big bunch sprints and was to find a new, less dangerous way of winning races.

LE TOUR EN ANGLETERRE

The stage before the channel crossing was a team time trial. With Greg Lemond in the team, Boardman hoped that GAN had the experience to defend the yellow jersey, so that he could ride into East Sussex as leader of the Tour. But in this discipline, it is the strength of the whole team and not that of the individual riders that determines the result. The squad was beset by bad luck, with several punctures in the last desperate minutes of the 66-kilometre race. And Boardman, wanting more than anything to hang on to the jersey, could not keep the team together. He was so strong that each time he came to the front of the group they would struggle to hold his wheel, losing both rhythm and position. They lost

Above: Laurent Jalabert is a blood-stained crash victim in Armentières, 1994. Below: Eros Poli cruises over the line in Carpentras after conquering Mont Ventoux.

more time from his effort than they were gaining. The jersey passed on to Johan Museeuw, and Boardman arrived in the UK in his regular team kit.

There was one other Briton in the Tour, Sean Yates. Coming from Kent, he had the home advantage, and knew all the roads on stage four of the race. Over a million spectators came to watch *Le Tour en Angleterre* that day. As is the tradition, when the peloton reached the Ashdown Forest, Yates was permitted to sprint off the front, stop, kiss his wife, who was waiting for him at the roadside, and rejoin his colleagues as they came past.

Yates did even better when the race returned to French soil. He took the yellow jersey for one glorious day after escaping on a leg-breaking 270-kilometre stage. No Briton had worn the golden fleece since 1962 and then, suddenly, two of them had in the space of a week. For the moment at least, Indurain and his rivals were forgotten. The reminder came right on time, at the first individual time trial of the race.

Over 64 kilometres Big Mig averaged more than 50 kph – faster than the winning team MG-GB had achieved in the team time trial the

previous week. Rominger got to within two minutes of him, but the rest were nowhere. If there had been any doubts about Indurain's capabilities before the race started, his critics were silent now.

The antics of the sprinters and the *rouleurs* were relegated to history the moment the Tour hit the Pyrenees. Boardman pulled out of the race at the first feed station on stage 11 – he had not been expected to complete the Tour on his first attempt – and Chiappucci, the darling of the *tifosi*, fell to pieces. His Carrera team-mate, Marco Pantani, took on the role as chief irritant to Indurain, attacking at the foot of the Hautacam.

As calmly as ever, Indurain pressed onward and upward, taking Luc Leblanc up to the Italian's wheel. As they regrouped Leblanc made his own move, and again Indurain followed him. Tony Rominger held on to his place as second overall, but his time deficit was already close to five minutes – exactly what it had been in Paris the year before – and the race was less than two weeks old. He and Chiappucci had been struck by the same stomach bug and, while they were fighting with cramps and diarrhoea, Indurain proved as impervious to the infection as he was to everything else.

POLI TAKES VENTOUX

Chiappucci withdrew from the race overnight and, with a far-from-fit Rominger, Indurain was left without an obvious rival. He allowed the charming young Frenchman, Richard Virenque, to take the victory on the stage to Luz-Ardiden. Virenque also took the King of the Mountains' jersey. Rominger bravely finished the stage, but was too ill to start again the next morning. For two days those racing for the yellow jersey called a truce as the Tour trundled on toward the Alps. The peloton sat up and took slow, deep breaths as it prepared for Mont Ventoux.

The stage went right over the mountain and down to Carpentras, rather than finishing at the summit

as was customary. This changed its character entirely – it was no longer purely the domain of the climbers. After 60 kilometres bowling along the valleys, the biggest, friendliest man in the bunch decided to take on the rest of the pack. At almost two metres tall, Eros Poli was not meant to go uphill fast, but he could speed across flat ground by dint of sheer power. He seemed such an unlikely prospect for the Ventoux that he was left alone, and reached the climb after ploughing a lonely 100-kilometre-long furrow. His lead was enormous – 25 minutes – but he was beginning to tire. He put his head down, not daring to look at the winding road ahead of him, and began to climb.

It was excruciating to watch. Poli was grinding metre after metre along

A flag-flying British fan cheers on Piotr Ugrumov, Bjarne Riis and Nelson Rodriguez on the way to Val Thorens, 1994.

the climb, losing one minute in every kilometre. Indurain had come to the front of the bunch, not aiming to catch the Italian, but to break his rivals. Creeping over the top of the climb, Poli had just five minutes left to his lead. It was downhill all the way to the line, and on this side of the mountain his size was a definite advantage. Behind him a few hopefuls made off from Indurain's group as the gradient of the descent eased, but what did the two big men care? Poli had defied convention to take the most memorable victory of his career; and Indurain? – well, he'd just had another day at the office.

REVENGE FOR UGRUMOV

No one even thought about challenging Indurain anymore. Instead, Pantani was seeking to win a stage for his sadly missed team leader, Chiappucci, Virenque was delighting in wearing the polka-dot jersey and was keen to do it justice in the Alps, and all the riders in the top 10 were wondering just how they had managed to get there. Now they were racing to the top of Alpe d'Huez and, discounting Indurain's lead, nothing was certain. And if the shock of seeing Poli haul himself to victory over the Ventoux had not been bizarre enough, two riders – Australian Neil Stephens and Raul Alcala – had actually dismounted partway up the climb to settle an argument the old-fashioned way, with their fists. Stephens was left with a broken nose and a host of ONCE team-mates physically restraining him from chasing after the Mexican; just one more sign that this was not an average Tour.

Pantani had not made a conscious effort to chase points in the climbing competition, and had no chance of taking the jersey from Virenque. He still wanted to out-perform him, though, and did so on Alpe d'Huez. Boosted by Poli's win, several would-be winners pushed hard from the first, small climb, and arrived at the bottom of the final ascent in a tattered group. Roberto Conti made a solo escape around the famous hairpins, leaving his erstwhile companions to fall in behind him. Indurain rode along majestically, with Pantani and Virenque desperate to eke out a little time on the final section of the climb.

Indurain did the same thing again the next day on the short, sharp stage to Val Thorens. Mexico's Nelson Rodriguez sacrificed good manners for a stage win, blatantly sitting in for the duration of the 80-kilometre winning break and then cruising past an exhausted Piotr Ugrumov in the sprint. Action at the tail end of the race was equally unsavoury – 68 riders finished outside the time cut by four minutes. Perhaps some of them were hoping to be thrown out, so they could go home and get some rest, but the organizers turned a blind eye and told them to start again the next day.

Ugrumov had learnt his lesson on Alpe d'Huez, and decided to try a different tactic the next day. He made sure that when he attacked no one came with him, preferring to climb the Col de la Colombière without help, or hindrance, from anyone else. With a clear advantage at the top he knew the stage was his this time – the 20-kilometre descent to Cluses was a deserved opportunity to take it all in. Two minutes behind him, Indurain was doing his own thing, powering along as Pantani tried to draw his fire. Big Mig did not respond; he didn't need to. He simply stuck in his groove, slowly dropping his rivals, until it was only Pantani and Virenque who could hold the pace to the summit. Unable to keep up on the descent, the Italian didn't hang on much longer. Then, just for good measure, Indurain tweaked his gears and sprinted away from Virenque at the line – a rare piece of showmanship from the ringmaster of the circus.

JOB DONE FOR INDURAIN

The final shake-down in the general classification came on stage 19, the mountain time trial to Avoriaz. Over three increasingly difficult *cols*, the course required riders not only to climb brilliantly, but also to descend without fear, and to do so quite alone. It was a disaster for Virenque. Lacking the concentration to time-trial at the best of times, he was thrown completely by the bad weather at the finish of the stage. His characteristic daring on the descents cost him dear as he was obliged on two occasions to pull to a near halt on the slippery corners. Pantani was no more stylish, but he was effective, taking second on the stage behind Ugrumov, the pair of them pushing Virenque off the podium. Meanwhile Indurain chose to ride cautiously, not wanting to risk his place in history as the third man to win four consecutive Tours for the sake of a stage win. Some of his biggest potential rivals had been waylaid by illness, but even on top form they were unlikely to have been able to compete with the Spaniard.

1995

Hoping to add to the drama of the race, the Societé du Tour organized the prologue of the 1995 Tour as a nocturne – a race after dark.

As usual the first to ride were the no-hopers, the water-carriers, the ones who were there to help their leaders and not themselves. From this unsuspecting, self-sacrificial bunch it was Jacky Durand who posted the quickest time over the short Saint Brieuc course.

As the evening wore on the real contenders began to warm up, worried by the impending clouds and eventual rain that the early starters had avoided. Last man to start, Miguel Indurain, was taking no chances – he decided to ride his conventional road bike, without tri-bars, and to worry about the general classification later. This was not an option for prologue specialist Chris Boardman, however. He had won this stage last year, and it was his job to do so again.

Boardman screamed out of the start house and into the rain at precisely 9.25 p.m. Ninety seconds later he crashed horribly, breaking an ankle and a wrist as he hit the ground. Unbelievably he immediately attempted to climb straight back on his bike, and actually managed

Below: Wearing the world time-trial champion's jersey, Chris Boardman begins his fateful ride of 1995 in the prologue at St Brieuc. Opposite page: Indurain in fine shape during the time trial in 1995 after being made to work hard for victory by Bjarne Riis.

a turn of the pedals before being overcome with pain. He was carried from the scene by his *directeur sportif* Roger Legeay – his race was over in less than two minutes.

Last year's crash victims suffered mixed fortunes on their return to the Tour; Wilfried Nelissen also came off in the prologue, but managed to continue, whereas Laurent Jalabert blazed along the comeback trail in true style, taking the yellow jersey on stage two. The Tour was in danger of becoming a farce two days later, when Jaja became the victim of a crash on a roundabout two kilometres from the finish, with the unlucky Nelissen joining him on the tarmac. The Frenchman remained unbowed and, with a spare bike hastily passed down from the team car, rode on to the finish.

After four years of Indurain using the time trials to lever open a gap in the general classification, Big Mig stunned the peloton by doing something very unexpected 24 hours before the first *contre-la-montre*. On the hilly stage to Liège, when Johan Bruyneel attacked, Indurain powered across the gap and pulled the Belgian up the dragging climb of Mont Theux. Then, when Bruyneel refused to co-operate, he towed him all the way to the finish. The ONCE rider could hardly believe his luck as he was delivered to the line to take the stage and the yellow jersey. Indurain had no material gain from this effort bar a 50-second time advantage, but the psychological blow he had dealt his rivals was worth more than the stage win. Besides, he knew he was due for one of those tomorrow.

RIIS POSES A THREAT

Indurain was almost on the receiving end of an upset in the next day's time trial. The course was not technical, but ended with a 500-metre uphill, so riders were required to pace themselves throughout. Were it not for his careful preparation, Indurain might have lost the stage to former yellow-jersey wearer Bjarne Riis. The Dane started off so fast that he was well ahead of Indurain at the

intermediate checkpoints, but when he hit the final climb his hard-won advantage did him no good at all. His lead evaporated as he struggled to the line – proof that it takes more than brute strength to win a time trial.

With Indurain in the leader's jersey, the only chance left to the riders in the peloton was to make a long, early break, and so become *virtuel maillot jaune* for a few kilometres. Alex Zülle did just that on the first Alpine stage, spending an epic 70 kilometres off the front on his own. By the time he reached the lower slopes of the climb to La Plagne, the stage finish, he was sure of victory. All he had to do was to bear the pain and weave up the final climb. A few minutes later the chase group passed the same spot, and Indurain decided he had had enough. He simply dropped the lot of them. Bearing down on the young Swiss rider he felled his rivals, and even climbing

specialists Richard Virenque and Marco Pantani lost more than two minutes to him.

Zülle had moved up to second overall thanks to his win and, with his ability to time-trial, perhaps here was someone who could finally unseat Indurain. But he would have to attack him in the mountains, and with a week and a half to go it was too early for him to try anything yet. He shadowed Indurain religiously on the stage to Alpe d'Huez, and was roundly applauded for being able to stay with him on the climb. It was Pantani – already a quarter of an hour behind – who rose to the challenge of the mighty Alp. Indurain wisely watched him go as he danced up the mountain ahead of him; unlike Eddy Merckx, Indurain had no appetite for stage wins when there was the overall classification to consider. But for a superstar in the making like Pantani, a solo ascent of

Alpe d'Huez, round the 21 hairpins, through the writhing crowds and on to glory was his golden opportunity to make pure magic.

JAJA STORMS THE BASTILLE

For poignant moments in the recent history of the Tour, 14 July 1995 is certainly among the more memorable. Laurent Jalabert, wearing the points' jersey, had come out of the mountains feeling strong and, on the French national holiday, decided it would be a fine chance to attack. He maintained a 100-kilometre glory ride that, at one point, put him back in yellow – on the road at least.

With help from his ONCE team-mates he broke up the race, forcing Banesto to give chase when the gap got too wide. With a final, short, one-in-five climb two kilometres from the finish, Jalabert attacked again, dropping his fellow-breakaways once and for all. The

In Memoriam: Fabio Casartelli's bike is carried on the roof of his team's car, 1995.

terrifying crash at Armentières 12 months earlier had not killed him; it had in fact made him stronger, and what better way to prove it than with a stage win on Bastille Day?

On the first Pyrenean stage Marco Pantani treated fans to a repeat performance of his Alpe d'Huez victory while, yet again, the yellow-jersey wearer remained unmoved by his attack, preferring instead to wait until near the end of the stage to assert his authority. ONCE did their utmost to provoke him, but it was Bjarne Riis who actually managed to put some daylight between himself and the race leader on the Port de Lers. He was caught at the summit, and the predicted outcome was borne out – Pantani took the stage, with Indurain reminding his competitors exactly where their place was.

Stage 15 of the Tour should have been the most spectacular day of the race and, knowing this, Richard Virenque went on the attack. He rode solo over the Tourmalet and the Peyresourde, punishing the chase group, totally unaware of the tragedy

that was unfolding in his wake. On the descent from the Portet d'Aspet, Fabio Casartelli, Italy's Olympic champion, had crashed into the concrete barriers on the side of the road. He was taken by helicopter to hospital in Tarbes, but died soon afterward.

With half an hour separating the last men from Virenque, organizers hoped to keep the news from the riders until they reached the finish and could be told properly. But riders who had been involved in the crash, such as Johan Museeuw, knew how serious it was, and it was not long before the terrible news trickled through the peloton.

As Virenque pressed on towards victory, his pursuers rode on pointlessly behind him, tear-stained and trembling in shock. The King of the Mountains finally found out what had happened as he stood on the podium – a tragic end to what should have been a joyous day.

Casartelli's team, Motorola, paid tribute to their lost friend as best they knew how. After consulting his wife, the Societé du Tour decided to

Above: Casartelli's Motorola team-mates cross the line in unison on stage 15, 1995. Below: In his own way, Lance Armstrong pays tribute to his Italian colleague after winning in Limoges.

continue the race, with the Italian's bike mounted on top of his team car, a single black ribbon attached to the frame. At the end of the next stage, the peloton halted before the finish to allow the Motorola riders to cross the line alone. Then, two days later, when racing had resumed, Lance Armstrong escaped from a stage-winning break and, as he crossed the line, he raised both arms and pointed to the sky. It was a gesture that would be repeated in years to come.

A sombre peloton arrived in Auphelle for the final time trial. Indurain's victory elevated him to rarefied status – only Jacques Anquetil, Eddy Merckx and Bernard Hinault had won the Tour on five occasions, and none had done so in consecutive years. His style was not to everyone's liking: winning the Tour with exceptional time-trialling never wins as many fans as doing it by daring on the open road. But whichever way you look at it, Indurain won the Tour five times because he was the best rider of his generation, and it's hard to do more than that.

1996

Six is the magic number as far as the Tour is concerned. Eddy Merckx had failed to win a sixth Tour after being hit by a spectator, but Indurain didn't inspire that kind of wrath in his rivals' supporters.

The year looked like having another race for second place. The Spaniard had won the Dauphiné Libéré – a traditional pre-Tour indicator of form – without much difficulty and approached the Tour as odds-on favourite. He named Alex Zülle, Tony Rominger and Bjarne Riis as his main challengers, but of those only Rominger had come close to him in previous years.

Hoping for a less predictable outcome, or at least a less predictable path to that outcome, organizers routed the first time trial straight up a first-category climb to Val d'Isère – but after the first mountain stage. And it worked; the legend came undone four kilometres from the summit at Les Arcs and, suddenly, the Tour was no longer Indurain's to defend. It was an open race and, of all the pretenders who had long coveted Indurain's yellow jersey, it was Riis, the architect of his downfall, who stood in the strongest position.

The Indurain era ended on Saturday, 6 July. The 200-kilometre stage encompassed a windswept and foggy Col de la Madeleine less than halfway through; the conditions discouraged any early breaks. Riis attacked on the descent, only to change his mind and sit up once he had established a lead of over a minute. Although Indurain held the

The mountain stage to Sestriere is cut to just 46 km after the snow line drops 500m overnight, 1996.

pace of his rivals, he was suffering, and they knew it. The composed face and the controlled torso were replaced by a look of panic and a desperate hunch. And then Indurain cracked. He needed energy, and he didn't know where to get it from. He waved to every car and motorbike that he could see, and took a bottle of energy drink from Aitor Garmendia, Alex Zülle's team-mate. Then Gewiss-rider Emmanuele Bombini took pity on him and broke the rule prohibiting feeding in the final kilometres of a stage. Bombini was fined and Indurain was penalized 20 seconds – a cruel insult considering he had already lost more than three minutes to stage-winner Luc Leblanc. Indurain's reign was over, but the 1996 Tour was just beginning.

WHAT NEXT FOR RIIS?

Evgeni Berzin won the mountain time trial for Gewiss the next day, strengthening his grip on the yellow jersey. The following mountain stage had to be cut to just 46 kilometres because of the atrocious weather, and Berzin was confident that he could hold on to it even longer. But he had not counted on the unstoppable Bjarne Riis.

Starting at the foot of the Mongenèvre – the peloton was spared the ascent of the Galibier and Val d'Isère after the snow line came down 500 metres overnight – the truncated stage was a painfully fast affair. Riis attacked on the first of the two remaining climbs, jumping four times before he finally shook off the bunch. He had gained 20 seconds by the summit, and Berzin proved too weak to defend his lead.

It was now down to someone else to take on the Dane – and who better than Miguel Indurain? His move in the final few kilometres saw Berzin dropped, edging Indurain a small step back upwards in the general classification. In isolation, the event would have been just as expected from Indurain, but in the context of his race to date it was a brief reminder of what used to be.

Into the Pyrenees, and Riis wanted to seal his victory. He was not going to ride conservatively, but he was not going to take any unnecessary risks either. He saw the stage to Hautacam as pivotal, and laid his plans accordingly. There was only one real climb – the one to the line – so he waited until the early breakaways were safely reeled in before setting to work.

Riis' young team-mate Jan

Above: Riis invites Indurain on to the podium at Pamplona, 1996. Below: Riis on his way to victory along the shortened stage to Sestriere.

Ullrich was charged with the job of pace-making, and duly took to the front of the group at the speed determined by his Danish leader. Then, suddenly, the yellow jersey dropped back through the group as if he had overestimated his own abilities. He fell as far as the middle of the group and stopped. As he had eased off, he had taken the chance to inspect the state of the other riders, to see who – if anyone – was likely to pose a challenge to him. The answer was clear: no one. Riis sprang forward, successfully breaking away from the group and, seven kilometres later, the race was all but his.

The final mountain stage ended in Pamplona, Miguel Indurain's home. It should have been a glorious moment for him as he rode through his village, on his way to becoming the first man ever to win six Tours.

Instead, it was a moment to celebrate past achievements, and to applaud the man who had finally brought the Indurain era to an end.

Fans got a sneak preview of what the future held – and a glimpse of the old glory days – at the final time trial. Indurain was the only rider to come within a minute of the stage winner, Jan Ullrich. Riis's team-mate was too far down in the general classification to threaten the Dane, but he had struck a resounding warning to all those already planning their campaigns for the 1997 Tour de France. Two weeks later, Indurain took a consolation prize, in the form of an Olympic gold medal, for the time trial but, as any continental cyclist will tell you, it has little value when compared to the lustre of a sweat-soaked, grease-stained yellow jersey on the road to Paris.

1997

Indurain's reign was well and truly over and, although Bjarne Riis had clearly been the superior rider in the 1996 Tour, he was too old to expect a long reign at the top.

That, however, did not prevent him going into the tour focused on defending his Tour title. He'd had a careful build-up to the race, carefully monitoring his pulse rate while competing throughout the late spring, and was not at all fazed by going into the Tour with the number one pinned to his Telekom jersey.

Riis's self-belief had been a key factor in his first Tour win – for so long, the peloton had meekly accepted Indurain's rule and had raced only for second place. If Riis had been confident that he could win in July of 1996, he was absolutely sure that he

Egged on by the crowd, Pantani digs deep as he fights his way to the finish line on Alpe d'Huez, 1997.

could do it again 12 months later.

But he didn't just pour his energy into making himself stronger and fitter. He also spent considerable time learning about the foibles of his opponents, finding out exactly how he could beat them and just where and when they could be made to feel vulnerable. The race had been routed viciously, without a rolling *moyenne montagne* stage between the Pyrenees and the Alps to allow the lesser riders to recover.

Telekom had a potential embarrassment of riches in its Tour line-up, with Riis's lieutenant, 23-year-old Jan Ullrich, good enough to rival his captain himself. And if the *domestiques* found there were times when their team leader did not need them to keep him out of trouble on the early stages of the race, sprinter Erik Zabel was keen to put them to work

setting him up for the sprints. One of the few fast-men able to get through the high mountains without draining his strength for the final flat stages, Zabel had just as much hope of defending his green jersey as Riis did his yellow one.

FAVOURITES CRASH OUT

Before the real racing started, the prologue provided Chris Boardman (GAN) with a chance to destroy the demons that had haunted him since he burst on to the pro circuit in the 1994 Tour. Winning the 7.3-kilometre pre-stage gave him a deep sense of satisfaction, and the names behind him on the leader board made interesting reading. Riis had stated unequivocally that he was Telekom's leader for the race, yet had finished 13 seconds behind Ullrich. Alex Zülle had broken his collarbone in the Tour of Switzerland less than a fortnight before and, in a desperate bid to maintain form following the operation, he had popped out one of

the screws holding the bone in place just two days before going to Rouen. Despite the horrific two weeks he had endured in the run-up to the start of the Tour, he still managed to finish fifth behind Boardman – now all he had to do was make sure he stayed on his bike for the remainder of the race.

Riis's fortunes took an ominous turn for the worse on the first road stage. A crash in the final 13 kilometres split the field; the front-runners pelted down the road while two thirds of the riders ground to a halt behind a pile of bikes and bodies. In the heap was Alex Zülle, who had not only crashed, but had landed on his already broken collarbone. So, while Riis fumed about being left behind by Ullrich – he lost another minute to his team-mate – Zülle lost more time, but got to the finish line somehow, vowing to carry on.

Accidents littered the first week of the race, with Tony Rominger the first major casualty on stage three.

Above: Belgian Tom Steels is expelled for throwing his bidon at Fred Moncassin, 1997. Below: Jan Ullrich (right) has little need of Riis's help on the Courchevel.

Zülle managed to hang on for four days, but finally conceded that he could not risk carrying on – a further fall on his collarbone might have ended his career.

Belgian national champion Tom Steels was expelled from the race after an 80-kph fracas. Elbowed in the ribs as he jostled for position in the finishing straight, he responded by hurling his *bidon* at Fred Moncassin. It was the first time a rider had been thrown off the Tour for an offence other than doping since 1911.

But at least there was good news for some riders: Cedric Vasseur attacked on stage five and soloed to victory, having spent a tortuous 147 kilometres off the front all by himself. His father, Alain, had won a Tour stage in similar fashion 27 years earlier, but Vasseur junior went one better than his dad, taking the *maillot jaune* and holding it all the way to the mountains.

After five days of glory Vasseur stepped aside for the real competition to begin. The first summit-finish of the race was at Arcalis, in Andorra and, with the Envarlia – 34 kilometres long and 2,400 metres high – to be mastered midway through the 250-kilometre stage, this was no place for *rouleurs*. The last five of those kilometres were to become one of the defining moments of the race.

Both Riis and Ullrich were safely in the front group at the foot of the Arcalis, along with specialist climbers Marco Pantani and Richard Virenque. Ullrich attacked the moment the gradient went up, and found that only Virenque had come with him. He immediately attacked again, and the Frenchman was gone. And the Dane? He was back where he had been at the time of the first move, hemmed in with the leading group and unable to offer any form of challenge or even help to his young team-mate. The two riders' roles had been reversed, and Jan Ullrich was in charge now. He took the stage, and his first yellow jersey, with warm congratulations from his former leader Bjarne Riis.

TELEKOM'S NEW BOSS

Two days later, at the first long time trial of the Tour, Ullrich had the chance to confirm his new status as race leader. With a second-category climb along the route, many riders, including the young German, rode a light climbing bike as far as the Col de la Croix de Chaubouret before quickly jumping on to a time-trial machine for the second part of the stage. The hilly course allowed Virenque and Pantani to play to their strengths, and both produced remarkable performances in their least favourite discipline. But no one came close to Ullrich. His winning margin of over three minutes was a crippling blow to anyone who cherished thoughts of even trying to contest the stage.

Into the Alps, and it was time for the climbers to take over. Alpe d'Huez, a favourite, came after a long, flat, day's racing, making it

ideal territory for a glorious stage win that would not threaten the overall classification. And who better to inflict the damage on the peloton than tiny Marco Pantani?

As riders fell off Pantani's wheel around the famous hairpins, it was Ullrich who held on longest, limiting his losses to less than a minute. Three hundred thousand people clung to the mountain side, cheering Pantani on. It was overwhelming – hands and fists flew toward him, water spraying from both sides, and it was all that he could do to find a clear path. But find it he did and, for his pains, he added his name to the list of climbers to have won a stage on the famous slopes of Alpe d'Huez.

There were two more days in the mountains and time was running out for anyone wanting to steal the yellow jersey from Ullrich. Given his impressive form so far, the riders best placed in the general classification

Jens Heppner and Bart Voskamp are locked together as they cross the line at Dijon, a move which saw both riders disqualified in 1997.

knew that he would have to falter badly if they were to make up their deficits. Never one to shy away from a turn at the front, Richard Virenque gathered his Festina team-mates around him on the stage to Courchevel, attacking on the descent from the first of three climbs.

Initially Ullrich gave chase, careering dangerously down the mountain in an attempt to gain contact with the fearless Virenque. Down in the valley he changed tack, however, waiting for his team-mates and putting them to work. The Frenchman was still ahead at the summit of the next climb, the Col de la Madeleine, but only just, with Riis working selflessly for the man who had displaced him as team leader. He brought Ullrich up to Virenque at the base of the final ascent before slipping back himself. Fernando Escartin was the final man to be dropped by Ullrich and Virenque, and the pair had the last climb all to themselves. Ullrich had no need to attack now, and he let Virenque lead the way, concentrating his efforts on holding his wheel without expending any more energy than was necessary. There was no sprint at the finish, and Virenque cruised across the line first. Barring disaster, Ullrich had won the race, and was happy to leave the stage wins to his defeated rivals.

CLIMBERS' PARADISE

If there was little suspense left in the overall positions, at least Marco Pantani was on hand to create a little drama. Having secured his place in the record books with the Alpe d'Huez victory, he now claimed to be suffering from bronchitis, unsure even if he would be able to start the next stage. Eventually he climbed out of his team bus and decided to play. The peloton was tired, and the chancers were given plenty of scope for early moves.

Each time a small breakaway formed it was allowed a little time off the front before the bunch brought it back. Then, when the riders neared the top of the final *hors categorie* mountain of the race, who should pop out of the front of the leading group but Pantani himself – with no apparent breathing difficulties.

It was an eight-kilometre descent to the line – not Ullrich's favourite type of stage finish. He took a deep breath and jumped on to the wheel of Richard Virenque as he plummeted towards Morzine, taking care to follow his well-chosen line down the road. The stage confirmed what the race had already determined: Ullrich would win the Tour, Pantani would have his fill of mountain escapades, and Virenque was not only King of the Mountains, but lord of the descents too.

The remaining stages to Paris saw Abraham Olano win a purist's time trial around Disneyland, and Bjarne Riis finally vent some of the anger that he must have been feeling about his fall from grace. He suffered an undignified tumble as he rushed to sign on, damaging his gears and missing his start time by 24 seconds

as he rushed to change his bike. Once he started riding again, he had additional mechanical problems and changed bikes once more, only to puncture this time. His Telekom mechanics leapt out of their car to change his wheel but the replacement jammed against the stays, making the bike impossible to ride. Unable to contain his frustration, Riis hurled the offending machine into a ditch, and ended up almost 10 minutes down on Olano.

The Riis incident was embarrassing to watch, but the finish of the stage the previous day had been more ludicrous. A pair of riders – Jens Heppner and Bart Voskamp – had got away on their own with 30 kilometres to go. As they approached the line with 30 seconds in hand, they each launched what they hoped to be a winning move. Somehow the two leaned together and became entangled, with Heppner's head wedged firmly in Voskamp's armpit.

Wearing the German national champion's jersey, Jan Ullrich shows his climbing strength on the slopes to Andorra, 1997.

Heppner's bike was at such a precarious angle that he could not move away without crashing. Neither man could move sideways, so they crossed the line locked together, with Voskamp slightly ahead. The *commissaires* retired for half an hour to debate the result and then, bizarrely, disqualified both. Third-placed Mario Traversoni was awarded the stage while Voskamp and Heppner were relegated to the back of the group.

Race *commissaires* were kept busy in the 1997 Tour; relegating a host of sprinters and expelling Tom Steels entirely. Erik Zabel was one of many riders to find that crossing the line first didn't always mean a win. After being chastised for failing to hold his line on stage six, he added stage seven to his tally and finished as clear winner in the points' competition. As for his old boss Bjarne Riis, he finished in a respectable seventh place, sense of humour restored in time for the end-of-race party.

Tour Legends

Miguel Indurain

"You'd see him there, with that smile on his face and you couldn't tell whether he was tired, faking it or laughing at you." **Claudio Chiappucci on Indurain**

Left: In 1991, stage 13, Indurain loses out to Chiappucci but still gets hold of the yellow jersey. **Right:** On stage 17 in 1991, Indurain maintains his grip on the yellow jersey as he approaches Alpe d'Huez.

MIGUEL INDURAIN (SPA)
b. 16/7/64 Villava, Basque Country

12 PARTICIPATIONS
FIVE VICTORIES
12 STAGE WINS

1985 DID NOT FINISH

1986 DID NOT FINISH

1987 97TH OVERALL

1988 47TH OVERALL

1989 17TH OVERALL
ONE STAGE WIN: stage 9, Pau–Cauterets-Cambasque

1990 10TH OVERALL
ONE STAGE WIN: stage 16, Blagnac–Luz-Ardiden

1991 FIRST OVERALL
TWO STAGE WINS: stage 8, Argentan–Alençon (time trial); stage 21, Lugny–Mâcon (time trial)

1992 FIRST OVERALL
THREE STAGE WINS: prologue, San Sebastian; stage 9, Luxembourg (time trial); stage 19, Tours–Blois (time trial)

1993 FIRST OVERALL
TWO STAGE WINS: prologue, Puy-du-Fou; stage 9, Lac de Madine (time trial)

1994 FIRST OVERALL
ONE STAGE WIN: stage 9, Périgueux–Bergerac (time trial)

1995 FIRST OVERALL
TWO STAGE WINS: stage 8, Huy–Seraing (time trial); stage 19, Lac de Vassivière (time trial)

1996 11TH OVERALL

Chapter 10: 1998
The Great Doping Scandal

The 1998 Tour de France should have confirmed Jan Ullrich as the next big thing in cycling, and introduced a whole new country – Ireland – to the joys of hosting the greatest race on earth. Instead, everything went pear-shaped and it turned into the most scandal-ridden event in the sport's history.

1998

While the Festina affair of the 1998 Tour de France is still remembered as one of the biggest sporting scandals of all time, some close to the events maintain that the team were simply unlucky enough to get caught. What started as a routine border check – as the team's *soigneur*, Willy Voet, drove from Belgium to France – blew up into the ugliest story in the Tour's long history.

CAUGHT IN THE ACT

Voet was on his way to catch a cross-channel ferry en route to the Tour start in Dublin. His cargo, which would supply the team for the three-week race and more, included EPO, human growth hormone and testosterone. The 52-year-old also had a little something for personal consumption; a few doses of "pot Belge" – a nasty mix of amphetamines, heroin, caffeine, cocaine and pain-killers that would numb the tedium of the long drive to meet the team. As the uniformed officer signalled for him to pull over and get out of the car, Voet's first concern was that they would search him and find the "pick-me-up" in his pocket.

Inevitably the car was searched, and Voet was arrested for smuggling drugs across the border. Humiliated and demoralized by the interrogations and the strip-searches – and perhaps because he knew that the time for honesty had finally arrived – the Belgian explained to the authorities how the team systematically doped its riders, to make sure that they performed in the races that mattered with minimum risk to their health. Left to their own devices, the management believed that the riders would be unable to work out for themselves what to take.

PLAN A – DENY EVERYTHING

In Ireland, the Festina squad feigned shock at Voet's revelations, but the team was expelled from the race after six days of racing – a long week of rumour-mongering and finger-pointing. Team manager Bruno Roussel and team doctor Erik Rijkaert were arrested for drug trafficking and incitement to consume drugs. Meanwhile Richard Virenque, erstwhile King of the Mountains, gathered the frenzied press corps to an impromptu conference in the back room of a tobacconist's shop. He tearfully protested his innocence, a stance he maintained for more than a year – even after the entire squad, including the management, had detailed Festina's programme to the authorities, and confirmed that the riders were fully complicit in, and

Above: Festina team director Bruno Roussel, 1998. Below: Riis and Ullrich do battle with the weather on the way up to Les Deux Alpes. Previous page: Marco Pantani in the middle of protests at Tarascon, 1998.

financially committed to doping.

In the shadow of the scandal and the hypocrisy, a real race was unfolding. Boardman had made the most dramatic start, winning the prologue for a third time, only to crash into a stone wall two days later as the peloton wound its way through the back roads of County Cork.

Erik Zabel, Mario Cipollini, Jan Svorada and Tom Steels were repeatedly battling for the sprints, with one exception. On stage three, when the race returned to France, a sizeable breakaway took the initiative early on, and lethargy from the bunch gave the nine men the gap they needed. Telekom's Jens Heppner took the stage, and Bo Hamburger the yellow jersey, levering open the general classification for all and sundry. Even in the first time trial previous unknowns were putting themselves into contention; while defending champion Jan Ullrich won the 58-kilometre stage as expected, Americans Tyler Hamilton and Bobby Julich both excelled, with the latter moving up into third overall as Ullrich claimed the jersey.

As the race edged toward the Pyrenees the *rouleurs* took their chances. Heroics from the likes of Jacky Durand and Andrea Tafi were welcome relief to a race that seemed unable to extricate itself from the

continuing scandal, with each new revelation pushing it further into the mire. Two Tour stories were unravelling in parallel.

The first mountain stage, finishing with a 15-kilometre descent into Luchon, was not going to separate the contenders. Instead, the first *hors categorie* climb, the Aubisque, saw Rodolfo Massi and Cedric Vasseur escape over the summit. As race leader, Ullrich took the initiative when he needed to – on the final climb to the Peyresourde – and watched to see who would come with him. While fewer than a dozen riders were able to match his acceleration, one man, Marco Pantani, could better it.

The tiny Italian not only gained time on the ascent, but pulled back further time on the other side of the mountain as he chased after the one remaining breakaway rider Massi. While the slower riders were struggling to complete the stage, Pantani was using it as a warm-up.

Slightly shorter and flatter than the previous day's racing, stage 11 was always going to be about the final climb to the Plateau de Beille. With 150 riders left in the race, most decided to ease themselves in gently. Rolling across the series of early climbs *en masse*, the peloton did little more than watch as Roland Meier headed off into the hills. There was a momentary panic when Ullrich punctured a kilometre from the final climb, but the surge of adrenalin was enough to see the German push on straight back to the bunch, and plough his way through the field just as the gradient reared up and broke it to pieces.

Pantani sensed that it was time to attack and, although Ullrich made a huge effort to chase, his move simply compounded the splintering of the peloton, losing his *domestiques* in the process. The "pirate" was gone, and all that Ullrich could do was to provoke a group of six riders to limit his progress on the final 12 kilometres. With no one willing to commit to the isolated *maillot jaune*, Ullrich found a little help from Leonardo Piepoli. As the German took his

wheel and tried to recover a little, Pantani pressed on, passing and dropping Meier, and claiming back more than 90 seconds from the race leader by the end of the 16-kilometre ascent. The jersey was resting only loosely on Ullrich's shoulders.

PLAN B – COME CLEAN

Temporarily out of the mountains, the Tour was still in deep trouble. Cees Priem, *directeur sportif* of the Dutch team, TVM, and four of his riders, were arrested and subsequently released after it was revealed that the team truck had been searched and found to contain EPO way back in March. All nine Festina riders were taken into custody in Lyon, with most being held overnight. At the race itself, French television reporters took their film crews round to the back of a team hotel and rifled through the rubbish bins. The riders decided it was time to make their feelings known.

Reigning French champion Laurent Jalabert became spokesman for the peloton. "They are treating us

Laurent Jalabert (left) and Luc Leblanc speak to the Press on behalf of the peloton, 1998.

like beasts," he said. Tempers rose higher when the Union Cycliste Internationale (UCI), announced new "health checks" without consulting the riders. On top of this, there was still no decision from the Societé du Tour about the ultimate fate of the TVM squad, with Jean Marie Leblanc saying he could not throw them off the race without firm evidence against them.

While the riders sat on the bonnets of the team cars and all across the road, Willy Voet, Bruno Roussel and Erik Rijkaert were at another sitting. Facing Judge Patrick Keil in Lille, the three men at the heart of the Festina scandal met for the first time since Voet's arrest and were forced to compare statements in the presence of the judge. Satisfied with what he had seen, Keil released Voet from jail and allowed him to go home. The remaining riders were also released and, among the public confessions, some of them found a little sympathy from the fans they had deceived for so long. Tales of short-sighted Alex Zülle being stripped and left in a cell without his glasses, along with revelations about the institutionalized doping at Festina, cast the more vulnerable riders as victims of the system rather than hardened cheats. Confusion touched every aspect of the Tour.

Eventually the riders agreed to race. After leading the two-hour protest, it was Jalabert, along with younger brother Nicholas and Bart Voskamp, who animated the stage, even putting Jaja in the *virtuel maillot jaune* at one point. After 130 kilometres off the front of the bunch, the anger which had fuelled the attack ran dry, and Jalabert senior pointedly sat up and waited to be caught. The resulting bunch sprint was little more than a relief to those who had feared that the race was never going to reach Le Cap D'Agde.

Stage 15, from Grenoble to Les Deux-Alpes, was a classic mountain *etape*, cresting the highest point of the race, the Col du Galibier, before sweeping back down into the valley and finishing on a nine-kilometre climb to the line. It was destined to be an epic stage from the start, with

heavy rain and temperatures dropping to 8°C at the finish. An attack on the final ascent seemed like the only sensible option – going off early would leave a solo rider far too exposed, both to the elements and to the collective might of the peloton.

On the first climb of the stage, the Croix de Fer, Pantani fell, but quickly remounted and regained the group. The adrenalin from the crash, and the potential danger along the rest of the route seemed to build him up until he could contain himself no longer. By the time the group got to the Galibier, some of the other climbers – Fernando Escartin and Luc Leblanc – were edgy, feigning moves and testing Ullrich's lieutenant, Bjarne Riis. When Escartin finally got clear it was Pantani who went with him, and made one unstoppable effort. By the summit he was almost three minutes ahead of Ullrich, 10 seconds away from being leader on the road. The German's resolve was washing away with the torrential rain – the descent only served to increase Pantani's advantage and then Ullrich punctured.

Marco Pantani celebrates a convincing victory on stage 11 to Plateau de Beille.

Ullrich was freezing cold, exhausted and demoralized. He capitulated. He was still four kilometres away from the finish, being coaxed slowly along by Bjarne Riis, when Pantani won the stage and took the *maillot jaune* from his back.

Both the first- and the second-placed riders knew that the Tour had been won. The final mountain of the race was the 2000-metre-high Col de la Madeleine and, with some 44 kilometres of fast descent into Albertville from the summit to the finish line, the only question was whether Ullrich would make a final move of defiance, or if Pantani would put on a show of his own.

Approaching the foot of the climb the German pre-empted his rivals, screeching away from the group without so much as a glance back. It was a move that separated those who were truly Tour-winning material from those scrabbling for a foothold on the podium. Only Pantani could keep up with him; Bobby Julich and Fernando Escartin resigned themselves to losing more time to the duo.

PLAN C – WALK OUT

All the way up the 10.5-kilometre climb Ullrich urged his companion to share the work, to help him open up the gap. But Pantani, smug in yellow, wouldn't play. He made full use of his advantage, tagging along behind Ullrich without wasting his energy. Then, as they crested the summit, he turned the screw.

Mentally fresher, and more than confident of his descending prowess, the Italian dived down toward Albertville, daring Ullrich to stay with him. To his credit, Ullrich rose to the challenge, touching speeds of almost 100 kph and refusing to let go, not after working so hard to reach the top of the climb at the front of the race. The gradient eased in the final section of the stage and, knowing that they were both in unassailable positions, the pair rode together to the finish. Race etiquette dictated that Ullrich should take the day's spoils, and Pantani was so taken by the spirit of the *maillot jaune* that he was only too happy to oblige. The real prize was safely his.

The race was all but over; the drugs scandal was just beginning. Meanwhile, the police were wasting no time. Officers swept into town and detained the six TVM riders remaining in the race, escorting them to hospital for hair, blood and urine samples, then holding them until midnight.

It was heavy-handed, and it was an affront to the entire peloton's self-perceived image, but it was effective. As the sport's authorities continued to bide their time, hoping for a neat and tidy solution to materialize, the police marched in. The response was chaotic. For the first 32 kilometres of the next morning's stage, the peloton crept along the route, refusing to race. Then internal disputes brought it to a halt. Laurent Jalabert, former spokesman for the riders, resigned from the race, led his ONCE team-mates to the team cars and demanded to be taken home. Tour leader Marco Pantani tore off his official race number, and encouraged the rest of the riders to follow suit, meaning that the stage could not

be classified. The race trundled on toward Aix les Bains, with angered spectators hurling verbal abuse at the race organizers. Two more teams – Riso Scotti and Banesto – climbed off *en masse* at the feed station. When they eventually reached the stage finish, two hours late, but with a guarantee from Jean Marie Leblanc that the police would not act in the same manner again, the riders manoeuvred the TVM riders to the front and they crossed the line together, arms aloft. Unity in the peloton had been temporarily restored, but by the end of the evening two more Spanish teams, Vitalicio and Kelme, had also decided to pack their bags.

If anyone hoped the race would finish without any more disasters, they were soon disillusioned. Later that evening police raided hotels again, questioning personnel from ONCE, La Francais Des Jeux and Casino. Rodolfo Massi, the King of the Mountains and Casino's star rider, was detained, and was unable to start the next day's stage. Three days later he was charged with selling banned drugs.

The small matter of a 52-kilometre time trial was all that stood between Marco Pantani and the Giro-Tour double. He had no illusions about winning the stage – it was all but certain that Ullrich would

Above: The TVM team cross the line together at Aix-Les-Bains. Below: Virenque in tears as his tour ends in shame.

take the day's honours. More bad weather meant that pre-riding the course was too dangerous, so the majority of the riders made last-minute checks of the corners and the road surfaces through the electric windows of their team cars. After an afternoon of slipping and sliding on the greasy tarmac the riders came home one by one, with, for a change, everything panning out as expected.

The 1998 Tour de France finally hobbled to Paris, with barely half the riders completing the distance. Marco Pantani was a charismatic winner, just what the fans needed to distract them from the ugly scenes that had punctuated the race.

But it would not be long before he, too, found himself embroiled in doping allegations dating back to 1995. As his athletic powers waned and the investigations intensified, Pantani fell ill with depression, making only sporadic competitive appearances until he went missing in February 2004. He was found dead in a hotel room on Valentine's Day, surrounded by sleeping pills and suspected of having a heart attack brought on by accidental cocaine overuse. Once again, the seediest side of professional cycling was exposed to public scrutiny, and this time at the cost of one of Italy's most popular and talented riders.

Chapter 11: 1999–2005

Armstrong: Too Good to be True

In a seemingly impossible triumph over adversity, Lance Armstrong brought the Tour into the 21st century with a record seven successive victories. His utter dominance brought legions of new fans to the Tour, but his tactics did little to endear him to the French public. And for as long as he was riding, the truth behind his incredible run of form remained stubbornly hidden.

1999

If a brush-with-death experience can change a person's outlook on life, it can certainly change their attitude to racing. Lance Armstrong's well-documented diagnosis and subsequent recovery from cancer is justifiably heralded as one of the greatest sporting comebacks of all time, and his battle with the disease transformed him as a rider. But the signs of a nascent champion were there long before his illness.

FIGHTING THE BIG C

In Oslo, in 1993, Armstrong became the youngest-ever professional World Champion. His style was all that could be expected of a precociously talented 21-year-old American; his self-belief had been nurtured by an intense relationship with his single mother. Following his early brushes with the Tour, he was convinced that it was his race. The death of his friend and team-mate Fabio Casartelli in 1995 – the only time he had completed the Tour in his first four attempts – had sealed his relationship with the French event.

Testicular cancer is one of the most easily cured forms of the disease if caught in its early stages, but when Armstrong was diagnosed he was racked with the illness. He had golf-ball-sized lesions on his brain and tumours in his lungs and abdomen. Complicated surgery and intensive chemotherapy were unavoidable. Even if he were to recover, there was little chance of him ever racing again.

In an act of crass insensitivity and dubious morals his then sponsor, Cofidis, visited him in hospital and, after delivering a bottle of French wine, let Bill Stapleton (Armstrong's agent) know that they wanted to renegotiate terms, as Armstrong would be unable to fulfil his contract to ride for the team in the coming season. An ugly row between Alain Bondue and Bill Stapleton resulted in a compromise, and Armstrong received a moderate sum for the year. But there was a further, more damaging consequence of his deal with Cofidis. The cancer had been present in Armstrong's body before he signed with the French team, so his medical insurance was not valid.

The psychological blow was crippling, and the practical consequences were just as immediate. Having no health insurance meant that Armstrong had no way of paying for treatment. Fortunately for him, Nike came to the rescue. He had been sponsored by the company since his high-school triathlon days, and was contracted to wear Nike cycling shoes and gloves before the

Below: Armstrong proves his newfound health by winning the prologue at Le Puy De Fou, beating Alex Zülle into second place by seven seconds, 1999. Previous page: Armstrong defends the yellow jersey on stage 16, 2000.

discovery of the cancer. With one of the biggest brands in the world on board, others followed suit. Oakley and Giro agreed to continue sponsoring him. Using just a fraction of its corporate might, Oakley persuaded the insurance provider to cover Armstrong, even though his illness was a pre-existing condition.

WHAT DOESN'T KILL YOU...

Recovering from treatment was a long process, made only slightly easier by virtue of the fact that, as a professional sportsman, he was physically very strong. Mentally he was exhausted and, even when he did make a tentative return to racing the following spring, it was no glorious comeback. Poor perform-ances and *abandons* characterized the early part of 1998, but during the latter part of the season Armstrong began to make good progress.

A series of fourth places – overall at the Tour of Spain, and at both the world road race and time trial championships – proved that winning the Tour of Luxembourg in early summer was no fluke. Leaner and lighter, he now had the physique of a three-week tour rider, rather than a powerhouse who could bully his way to a one-day victory. In the run-up to the 1999 Tour, he was tipped with an outside chance for the overall. With his all-American-branded US Postal team, he was hungry to have his revenge on all the people, particularly those of French origin, who had deserted or doubted him.

There was no waiting for revenge to get cold – Armstrong made an impact from the start, winning the prologue ahead of Alex Zülle and former world time-trial champion Abraham Olano. The race organizers could not have asked for a better antidote to the doping stories that had dogged them for 12 months. Who better to lead Jean Marie Leblanc's Tour of Redemption than the cancer survivor?

The race took a turn for the worse only two days later, and in the most bizarre of circumstances. Routed across the Passage du Gois, a

**Above: Armstrong celebrates winning the crucial mountain stage to Sestriere, 1999.
Below: Talking tactics with main man George Hincapie.**

tidal causeway linking the island of Noirmountier to the mainland, the section of *parcours* proved to be more treacherous than a mountain descent. Sea foam glazed the narrow road surface and, as the peloton pushed to get to the front and off the causeway as quickly as possible, the inevitable ensued.

Wheels touched, and there was nowhere to go as half the peloton came crashing and skidding to a halt. Crucially, Armstrong was safely ahead of the crash, while Alex Zülle, Christophe Rinero, Fernando Escartin and Michael Boogerd all lost six minutes.

Others, including Jonathan Vaughters, Armstrong's key mountain helper, spent the rest of the day in an ambulance, being driven back to the team hotel. If the main concern of the organizers was doping and the riders' health, why on earth had the race crossed such a dangerous place?

WINNING FOUNDATIONS

Armstrong created the blueprint for his now-famous Tour preparation in the spring of 1999. He visited the key climbs to familiarize himself with their slopes, and recced the

time-trial course in Metz on two separate occasions. He had spent time in January experimenting in a wind tunnel and adjusting his position minutely in order to be as aerodynamic as possible.

His manager, Johan Bruyneel, knew that the first time trial, coupled with the opening mountain stage, would be a pivotal point in the race. So Armstrong went flat out from the start, posting the fastest times at every intermediate checkpoint, and even catching Abraham Olano after the Spaniard mistimed a bend and was forced to bail out into the safety barrier of hay bales.

Another time-trial rival, Bobby Julich, suffered worse for not knowing every corner of the course. He crashed and was forced to abandon the race, leaving the classification clear for Armstrong, whose diligence paid off; he reclaimed the *maillot jaune* along with the stage win. "It was our intention to intimidate our rivals," stated Bruyneel afterwards.

Part two of the Armstrong assault was scheduled for 24 hours later. It was cold, wet and miserable – conditions that Armstrong revelled in, knowing it would affect him less

wheedled his way into the race at the last minute, dredging up some European Union ruling about his "right to earn his living", and threatening to sue the Societé du Tour if he was excluded from the race.

The organizers backed down. However much they sighed and fussed about it, it was certainly to their advantage – Virenque's enduring popularity was fuelled by his ability to return to the race exactly as he had left it in 1997, rather than as he had exited in 1998.

Having made such an impressive display over two stages, it was now time for Armstrong to sit back and watch for reactions. With a maturity that had been notably absent in his pre-cancer days, he took a measured approach in his defence of the jersey.

The tight-knit Postal team marshalled the peloton through the Massif Central, deterring any would-be attackers from challenging Armstrong's lead. Frankie Andreu, George Hincapie and the other *domestiques* rode as if they had been put on this earth for no other reason than to shelter Armstrong from the wind and to deliver him fresh *bidons* from the following car.

The Texan may not have called on their assistance in the high mountains, when he raced head to head with the select few who could stay with him, but he knew that on the exposed, rolling roads between the Alps and the Pyrenees he needed as much protection as he could get. As ever, this race was an event where teams competed, but only one individual would take the glory.

DIGGING FOR DIRT

Into the Pyrenees and the Postal lackeys continued their work without complaint. Over the first climbs of the stage they held the group in check, and then finally handed the reins over to Armstrong on the climb to Piau-Engaly. The most significant move of the day was that of Fernando Escartin, who rose up into second place after a long attack from 50 kilometres out. Playing to the Spanish supporters that lined the route, the uncomfortable-looking

than most. As he pointedly reminded people after the race, he had won his 1993 world title in Oslo in similar conditions.

Guided by his team manager, Armstrong held back until the final climb to Sestriere and then attacked. He closed the gap to the front riders, Fernando Escartin and Ivan Gotti, in less than a kilometre. And he kept

going. In one six-kilometre effort he elevated himself from the ranks of Tour pretender to potential winner – his two consecutive stage wins illustrating his perfectly balanced talents.

A great day for Armstrong, and a delight for the home fans as their Richard took the climber's jersey. Yet to face charges over his involvement in the Festina affair, Virenque had

Fernando Escartin drives himself on during the climb to Piau-Engaly, 1999.

Kelme rider clung on to his slender lead, moving ahead of Alex Zülle on the general classification and taking his first-ever stage win in eight Tours.

At the time it added a certain frisson: Armstrong looked tired in the final reaches of what was the most difficult stage of the race, amid speculation about the depth of his reserves. But with only one mountain stage to go, the reality was much simpler. The only competition now was the one for second place, a situation that would become the norm over the next three years.

While the riders tried in vain to find a chink in the American's armour, the French Press were more successful. *Le Monde* published a story claiming that Armstrong's urine test after the first road stage had contained traces of cortisone. The substance was allowed only with a prescription, and should have been

Above: Armstrong holds on to the yellow jersey by winning the final time trial at Futuroscope, 1999. Below: Armstrong shares a joke with journalists at a pre-Tour medical but Le Monde later queried his clean bill of health.

declared during the doping control. As Armstrong had not said anything about the drug, *Le Monde* concluded that he was cheating.

Armstrong had used cortisone, but for nothing more than a saddle sore – one of the occupational hazards of professional bike racing. "I didn't realize there was any cortisone in the cream," he told a crowd of breathless journalists.

Even the most suspicious among them had to accept this excuse, sanctioned as it was by the UCI. But for another, less high profile rider, Ludo Dierckxsens, the authorities were prepared to play strictly by the book.

The Belgian had won the stage to St Etienne in a classic 20-kilometre break at the end of the stage, and was taken in for a routine dope control. As part of the procedure, the officials asked him if he had taken any

medication, to which he answered that his GP had given him a cortisone injection for a knee injury sustained during the Tour of Germany earlier in the year.

The drug, which had been administered legitimately, was no longer in his system, and was of no concern to the Tour doctors. But Dierckxsens's sponsors, Lampre, were not happy. The rider had broken the team's stringent rules, by consulting a doctor outside its set-up. He was sacked from the team, and lost his place in the race, even though the Societé du Tour had no issue with him.

After David Etxebarria won the last mountain stage, the star riders bided their time leading up to the final time trial. Armstrong himself may have been sure of victory, but the lower steps on the podium were still undecided. The 57-kilometre

race against the clock at Futuroscope would decide only the minor positions, but that did not mean that Lance Armstrong had finished his virtuoso display.

Winning the final *contre-la-montre*, together with the Metz stage and the prologue, completed a time-trial hat trick – a feat previously achieved by Eddy Merckx, Bernard Hinault and Miguel Indurain. That Alex Zülle was only nine seconds adrift was testament to the Swiss rider's tenacity – his final deficit was 7-37, just over a minute and a half more than the time he had lost on the Passage du Gois on the freakish second road stage. The biggest "what-if" of the race was the one concerning his shocking bad luck on that early stage.

Misfortune had no place in the Armstrong game plan. If onlookers regarded him as an unlikely winner, he did not. As Estonian sprinter Jan Kirsipuu took the yellow jersey in the first week thanks to a clutch of time bonuses, Armstrong had a quiet word: "You're only keeping it warm for the next guy." The benefit of surprise was not going to be his at the next Tour, but even from the start of his 1999 campaign, he regarded it as a luxury he did not need. It had been his race from the moment he won the prologue.

2000

Going for a Tour double means twice the pressure, and this time Armstrong would have to race against two former winners – Jan Ullrich and Marco Pantani – both of whom had been notably absent in the 1999 race.

The German was in woefully bad shape in the lead-up to the race, clearly struggling to maintain his racing weight, and seeming to lack the self-discipline required at the top level of any sporting competition.

Meanwhile Pantani's problems were proving equally difficult to shift – hampered by a series of doping allegations relating to the 1999 Giro d'Italia and other, more distant

Javier Ochoa is chased to victory by the infamous Devil on Stage 10 to Hautacam in 2000.

incidents, the Italian's popularity was starting to falter and wane. Compared to this pair of renegades, Armstrong's fairy tale glistened more brightly than ever. He'd broken from his preparatory races only to return to Austin for the Ride For The Roses – an annual fund-raiser for cancer charities – and was ready to take on anything the Europeans cared to throw at him.

PROVING IT WAS NO FLUKE

The result of the prologue was not as dramatic as at Le Puy de Fou, but signalled the fact that Armstrong – second behind Britain's David Millar – was in top form, and fully intended to stay there for the next three weeks all the way to Paris. For the Tour debutant and now *maillot jaune*, it was an emotional day, but he rose to the occasion. Millar held on to the jersey, as expected, until the team time trial on stage four, and that was despite getting caught up in a crash and being flung into the hay bales on the road-side the previous day.

AT THE PACE OF THE SLOWEST

The return of the team time trial was popular with the fans. The spectacle of 18 legs all working in perfect harmony never fails to impress, although most are secretly hoping that the teamwork will go awry.

A well-drilled ONCE won the stage, with US Postal very nearly coming unstuck as Armstrong dragged them up and over the Pont de Saint-Nazaire into a gale. So used to riding at 100-per-cent effort in a time trial, he found it difficult to step down a gear and ensure that the team held together – a flashback to his early days of uncontrolled aggression. He just about managed to contain himself, and the team finished runners-up on the stage.

There was no individual time trial for Armstrong in the first part of the 2000 Tour, so he skipped straight to climbing mode on stage 10. As at Sestriere, the weather was bad – just how Armstrong liked it. The traditional early breakaway, Javier Ochoa, had been given plenty of leeway to take the stage but, as the main group approached the Hautacam, the yellow jersey was still there for the taking. In a show of typical bravado, Pantani attacked first, then Zülle, but Armstrong dismissed their challenges. The speed at which he left the group was incredible. Accelerating away from them toward Ochoa it was almost as if the two were stationary points. He put four minutes into Ullrich, making him look like an also-ran, while the specialist climbers fared little better.

The stage was a truly memorable one in racing terms, but it took on a new poignancy retrospectively. In the spring of 2001, Javier Ochoa and his twin brother Richard were hit by a car while they were out training. Richard was killed, and Javier remained in a coma for several months. The tragedy touched the whole cycling community and many riders, including Armstrong, continued to offer support to the Spaniard long after he made the first, most dramatic steps to recovery. The peloton has not been able to push the

Neck and neck with Marco Pantani on the harsh inclines of Mont Ventoux, Armstrong eased up to allow the Italian over the line first in the 2000 Tour.

thought of death completely from its collective conscience since 1967.

The mystique of Mont Ventoux means that any time the race passes its summit is special. Its barren slopes leave riders cruelly exposed to the *mistral*, and a stage win there is one of the most prestigious a rider can claim in his *palmarès*. In 2000 the stage was short – just 149 kilometres – but the disputes that resulted from it endured for the rest of the race.

Pantani looked to be in trouble in the early part of the climb, only just making the final selection. Then, after repeatedly losing contact with Armstrong's group and fighting to get back on terms with them, he decided to change tack and made a series of attempts to escape. On his fourth effort he opened a reasonable gap, with only Armstrong able to make it across. No sooner had he reached Pantani's shoulder than he demanded that they press on and leave the others for good. The pair rode together to the top of the climb, and then, as the finish line came in

sight, Armstrong eased up, gifting the stage to Pantani. A magnanimous gesture perhaps, but one that would haunt Armstrong.

It was a premeditated move – one that he said had been in deference to Pantani's reputation. The subtext was clear: Armstrong knew that he was the best, and that he was controlling his own race. By dictating who he would, and would not, allow to win stages, he was further emphasizing his dominance. Pantani was riled by the American's unsubtle gesture, and three days later, with a clear-cut stage win safely under his belt, he spoke up. The two men exchanged words – via the Press – for several days, gradually becoming more personally insulting, until the race exited the mountains, and the Italian finally quit, and flounced back home.

ARMSTRONG FINALLY CRACKS
The final mountain stage, from Courchevel to Morzine, ended on a long descent. In order to win, riders

would need to be physically strong – no small demand after almost three weeks of racing – and completely focused. Armstrong was stressed, by his spat with Pantani, with the Press, and with the race in general. He could not bear feeling out of control. The closer he got to Paris, the harder it was to concentrate. On stage 16 he made a rare mistake.

Riding up the Joux Plane, the fourth and toughest climb of the stage, Armstrong found himself in trouble. He had neglected to eat enough and, surrounded by his rivals, he succumbed to a hunger flat.

Pantani had been provoking him all day and, although it cost him dear when he eventually tired, he took the American with him. Virenque, Ullrich – in second overall, though no real threat – and Roberto Heras led the group away from him, and Armstrong simply did not have the energy to respond.

The darling of the French public could not take back the polka-dot jersey from Santiago Botero, but with descending skills that matched his climbing prowess he drew the sting out of his companions and won the stage, a full two minutes ahead of Armstrong. "That was the worst day I've ever had on a bike," acknowledged the race leader afterward.

Both of the top two riders in the general classification had yet to win a stage in the race. The final time trial was the only opportunity left to them and, with the race passing from Germany back into France, this would be an ideal spot for Ullrich to regain some self-respect after conceding the overall competition.

More than a million spectators gathered along the route, hoping to see their man salvage some glory. But Armstrong had even greater motivation: he needed to silence the critics who were ready to belittle his victory if it came without a stage win.

The last person to have had that honour was, strangely enough, fellow American Greg Lemond. His fondness for the "race of truth", as he called it, was that it showed unequivocally who was the strongest, and setting off two minutes behind

Ullrich he would have a reference for every checkpoint along the way.

At each check he was quickest and, although Ullrich had the incentive of catching Joseba Beloki just at the finish line, he could do nothing to prevent Armstrong from winning.

Mission completed, it was a long but peaceful ride to the capital to meet his wife and their baby son on the podium. His second Tour win had been physically harder than the first, but mentally he had a better idea of what to expect. Armstrong was perfectly comfortable in the yellow jersey, and now he could handle all that came with it. Much as he protested against the title, he had become the new *patron* of the peloton, and his background only served to add more gravitas to the role.

Above: Erik Zabel celebrates a record sixth points' competition win in a row with his son in Paris, 2001. Below: Armstrong gives Ullrich "the look" before heading towards the summit of Alpe d'Huez.

2001

A fortnight before the 2001 Tour started, Lance Armstrong took his team through a dress rehearsal. A difficult, prestigious stage race – including the all-important mountain time trial – the Tour of Switzerland was the perfect warm-up for the Texan's assault on La Grand Boucle. His nearest – some would say his only – rival, Jan Ullrich, decided to spend those vital few weeks in the Pyrenees, tracing the three stages that he believed would play a decisive role in the final outcome of the race. Ullrich

was the fittest he had been since he won the Tour in 1997, but he didn't want to face Armstrong head-on before the prologue in Dunkirk.

PERFECT PREPARATION

US Postal hardly needed to be told what to do in the Swiss Alps. Armstrong predictably won the prologue then eased back to allow the lesser riders to enjoy the tussle for the leader's jersey, while he composed himself for the most important stage of the race.

Rising to the summit of the 1,506-metre Crans Montana, the course of the Swiss race had been fashioned to parallel the one from Grenoble to Chamrousse in the Tour. Race Director Tony Rominger – a former Giro d'Italia winner and runner-up in the Tour – specifically scheduled the mountain climb a number of days before the finish of the race, so that the riders would have time to recover before 7 July. This would be the last time Armstrong would ride at his physical limit before the Grand Départ.

From the moment he rolled down the starting ramp, dozens of stopwatches were charting his progress, not just to see if he was ahead of the riders who had gone before him, but by what margin. Setting off in reverse order of the standings after the previous day's stage, Gilberto Simoni and Wladimir Belli followed Armstrong

up the mountain, but their task was simply one of damage limitation. In that respect, too, it was a preview of what would happen on stage 11 of the Tour. "My last mountain time trial was two years ago," Armstrong said after the stage. "It's a rare discipline, and the main reason I came here today – to practise for the Tour de France."

He wasn't advertising it, but Armstrong had ridden the route of the Tour stage half-a-dozen times over the previous months, learning every curve and change in gradient or camber. His results in Switzerland were not just the finishing touches of his Tour preparation, but an early harvest of the meticulous, Tour-centric training programme that had been in force for six months.

When he did finally get to France, Armstrong found he was not the only one with eyes on the yellow jersey. Festina's Christophe Moreau delighted the home fans as he won the prologue, and the perfect co-operation of the famously friendly Crédit Agricole team saw its sprinter

Stuart O'Grady retain the yellow jersey after the team time trial. On 14 July Laurent Jalabert, this time riding for CSC-Tiscali, repeated his historic Bastille-Day win in 1995. Again he had returned from a terrible accident, but this time it was a domestic, rather than a racing one – he had fallen from a step ladder at home in February and broken several vertebrae. The French public were more than happy.

Then something strange happened. On stage eight, a customary break escaped early on, with 14 men joining forces. The weather was deteriorating from dull through wet to thoroughly miserable and, as the peloton donned rain jackets, the inclination to chase fell. The men at the front had more than just a stage win to motivate them – the quicker they got to Pontarlier, the quicker they could get off their bikes and into the shower.

The gap simply did not close, but grew bigger and bigger. By the time the leaders started to jockey for position it was well over half an hour.

Joy for the French: Laurent Jalabert on his way to Bastille Day victory at Colmar, 2001.

Theoretically, all those not in the break were outside the time limit, and should have been disqualified, but a bending of the rules ensured that no one was sent home. Rabobank's Erik Dekker won the stage, but it was Andrei Kivilev and Francois Simon who benefited most.

Simon would wear the jersey later in the race – three of his older brothers had won Tour stages in previous years, so he was under some pressure to perform – and Kivilev was elevated into a top-five position that he would hold on to all the way to Paris.

The mad breakaway success was the most important flat-stage result of the race, but it was in the mountains that the final classification would be decided. On the first summit finish – Alpe d'Huez – the Tour fell back to its normal pattern, but with added spice. For the first two climbs, Armstrong seemed a little weak, hanging back, not maintaining his usual easy rhythm. Telekom responded by taking over at the front, in the hope of wearing him down. But Armstrong is a man of his time. He knew that the images from the TV motorbike next to him were being viewed by his rivals' *directeurs sportifs* in their team cars, and he was playing a game with them. He wasn't suffering at all – he just wanted them to think that he was. As Bjarne Riis had done before him, he dropped back through the group to assess its strength, and then accelerated forward. As he moved away from Ullrich he looked pointedly over his shoulder, as if to say, "Well, are you coming with me?" and then disappeared from sight over the horizon.

NO UPHILL STRUGGLE

The unlikely time gaps from stage eight meant that Armstrong was not yet in yellow after the first mountain stage, and that he would not be last off in the mountain time trial. The three unfortunates trailing Armstrong to Chamrousse on 18 July were Stuart O'Grady, Kivilev and Simon. The Kazakh was the only one with any climbing pedigree but, marooned 11 minutes behind Simon and nine minutes ahead of Armstrong, he could not hope to take the yellow jersey in a 32-kilometre stage. The American's own prediction was that he would make up three minutes on Kivilev, and five on Simon, moving into third overall.

Not normally one for feigning modesty, Armstrong's little charade for the TV cameras the previous day should have warned everyone that he was learning to be coy. Fairly sprinting up sections of the road while the back-markers trailed in his wake, the time gaps yawned open – six minutes to Kivilev, seven to Simon. Meanwhile Ullrich was relying on the erratic flow of information in his earpiece to keep track of the times Armstrong was clocking at each intermediate checkpoint. Starting six minutes ahead of the defending champion, he lost 60 seconds.

Sometimes labelled the "race of truth" by Armstrong, it proved that he didn't need to see pain in the faces of his rivals in order to beat them. All the anger and frustration that he had so carefully nurtured was funnelled straight out and on to the pedals – the desire to win was still just as deeply felt as it had been when he took his first *maillot jaune*, back in the prologue of the 1999 race at Le Puy de Fou.

The time gap between first and last place on the stage was a staggering 22 minutes – Davide Bramati had lost more than a minute per mile to the stage winner – but the minute that really mattered was the one separating Armstrong and Ullrich.

Armstrong got hold of the yellow jersey after his third stage win, to Lary Soulan, riding to victory past the memorial to his lost team-mate, Fabio Casartelli. The race was finished, and on the next day – the final climbing stage – Ullrich acknowledged his defeat. The

Armstrong completes his 2001 victory by winning the final time trial.

German had come to the Tour in the form of his life, but he was no match for Armstrong. As they crossed the line at Luz-Ardiden side by side, he reached out and grasped the Texan's hand. He was heading for his fourth second place at the Tour, and the memory of his 1997 victory was more distant than ever.

Armstrong had nothing to do now but stay upright for the six long days before the Tour finished. Stuart O'Grady and Erik Zabel were still locked in battle for the green jersey, a competition that remained unresolved until the final sprint on the Champs Elysées, where remarkably the German won a record sixth consecutive points' jersey. And while O'Grady was unlucky, his team-mate Jonathan Vaughters was the greatest victim of the 2001 Tour. Stung on his temple by a wasp in the final week, he suffered an allergic reaction, and his

eye swelled shut. His *directeur sportif*, Roger Legeay, sought medical advice, and Vaughters was given a prescription. Anxious to follow the rules exactly, the team approached the Union Cycliste Internationale (UCI) to get formal permission to use the cream. The sport's governing body refused, as the ointment contained corticosteroid – a banned substance. Vaughters was forced to abandon the race; in its haste to be seen to act, the UCI had applied the letter of the law, but not the spirit of it. In doing so, it denied one man his chance to finish the Tour.

Ullrich's only hope was that he might better Armstrong in the final time trial. The Texan had made it through the race without a murmur of discontent so far – Ullrich hoped that he might show a sign of human frailty on stage 18. But Armstrong had no weaknesses. Winning the final time trial was a matter of pride – it was, in his view, essential that the race leader outperformed the field, to show that he had got there by dint of physical superiority as well as tactical brilliance. He had triumphed in both, and had four stage wins – one in each of the Alps and the Pyrenees, the mountain, and now a flat time trial – to prove it. In 2001, there was nothing that Armstrong could not do.

2002

The 2002 Tour de France started in a familiar fashion, with Armstrong winning the time trial and leading US Postal in a solid team time trial in the opening week. So far so good – the general classification was choking with ONCE riders, and with Igor Gonzalez de Galdeano in the yellow jersey for the first big test, the individual time-trial at Lorient. It was accepted that Armstrong would win the stage but, having being held up behind a crash earlier on in the race, he had a 34-second deficit to make up on the Spaniard if he were to take the jersey, too.

Commentators were talking up the difficulty of his task – speculating that the race was in the balance – although few really believed that

After being led up by team-mate Roberto Heras, Armstrong clinches the stage victory at La Mongie in 2002, ahead of Joseba Beloki.

Armstrong would do anything but win the stage and take the jersey. So when he failed to even match Kelme's Santiago Botero – and could find no explanation for his failure – the race, and the accompanying entourage, was beside itself with excitement. Gonzalez de Galdeano

believed the hype, boasting that the Lance Armstrong of 2002 was not the same man who had won the race for the previous three years, and that he and his Spanish colleagues could take yellow all the way to Paris. Armstrong remained impassive, however, waiting until the first

ULLRICH LOSES CONTROL

ULLRICH LOSES CONTROL

Beloki was way out of contention for the race lead, but was well-positioned to take second place, one better than his two successive thirds in 2000 and 2001. He was taking advantage of Jan Ullrich's absence and, while Beloki was in trouble on the highest slopes of the mountains, the German was in a far worse position without having touched his race bike in months. Injured and unable to start the Tour, Ullrich had struggled to come to terms with a written-off season. He had taken out his frustration, first, by driving his Porsche – while drunk – into a row of bicycles and, then, by taking ecstasy at a nightclub.

Touted as the heir apparent to Miguel Indurain after winning the 1997 Tour when he was just 23, Ullrich had been unable to recapture that form. The emergence of Lance Armstrong as a more complete athlete had sunk him, his fragile psychological balance upset by his invincible rival. In the weeks during which Armstrong constructed his fourth consecutive Tour victory, Ullrich was banned from driving, heavily fined, banned from racing and had his pay suspended by the Telekom team management. While Armstrong was tightening his control on the race, Ullrich was spinning into oblivion.

For any riders in the Tour still looking for glory, stage 14, to the heralded Mont Ventoux, was an ideal opportunity. Eleven riders set off early. Until the final, 19-kilometre climb, the *parcours* was flat and there was little incentive for the bunch to chase. Of the group, Richard Virenque was the clear danger man. He had not shown quite the form of his best years in the Pyrenean stages, but such a gifted climber would certainly drop his breakaway companions on the dusty, exposed road to the summit of the Ventoux if the peloton let them stay away. And that's just what happened. Russian Alexandre Botcharov was the last one to fall away, leaving the Frenchman to ride an agonizing solo to the line. After 200 kilometres of hard racing he crept to the finish, while, behind

mountain stage to La Mongie to make his first move.

He wasn't the only one waiting until the Pyrenees to start his campaign. Laurent Jalabert, who had won the climber's jersey 12 months previously, was about to put in a repeat performance.

And there was an additional incentive – this time he was competing for the polka-dot jersey head to head with the redoubtable Richard Virenque, the five-time winner and long-time favourite with the French public, despite Jaja's more impressive *palmarès*.

So he went early, taking as many points as he possibly could before US Postal started to reel him in. Roberto Heras rode faithfully by Armstrong's side as they neared the top of the final climb and, while ONCE's Joseba Beloki could just about stay in contact with them, it seemed that it was Heras, not Armstrong who was looking the strongest. He controlled the pace until the finish line came in sight, then stepped aside to let Armstrong take the stage win, and with it the yellow jersey.

All hopes that Armstrong would show signs of weakness were quashed the next day as he won the stage without needing Heras to baby-sit him all the way to the line. His team-mate instead took on the role of defender, marking Beloki who tried in vain to make up the distance to the American. Armstrong was unstoppable, and ONCE were silent.

Above: An emotional Richard Virenque wins at Mont Ventoux, 2002. Below: Robbie McEwen lays claim to the points' jersey after crossing the line first on the Champs Elysées.

him, Armstrong fairly motored up the climb. Beloki had made one tiny timid attack, and it was enough to send the race leader into a fierce counter-move which didn't end until he crested the climb. There were some uncharitable comments from the patriotic French crowd, but nothing was going to come between Armstrong and another Tour victory.

Armstrong's one-time conqueror Santiago Botero had suffered badly on the Ventoux, losing 13 minutes on the climb. He made amends on the first Alpine stage, dispensing with Belgium's Mario Aerts and Axel Merckx on the famous road to Les Deux Alpes. No one dared challenge Armstrong now – Beloki was staving off a persistent Raimondas Rumsas

to keep his runner's-up spot, Jalabert was safely in the polka-dot jersey, and Erik Zabel and Robbie McEwen had called a brief truce in the points' competition. Holland's Michael Boogerd took on the hero's mantle, riding solo over the Col de la Madeleine and up to La Plagne, holding off Armstrong as he put the finishing touches to his mountain performance. The only thing left for him to do was to set the record straight at the final time trial.

SILENCING THE DOUBTERS

At just 50 kilometres, the final *contre-la-montre* was a little too short for Armstrong to gain a full minute on next best rider Raimondas Rumsas, who – had the stage been longer

Armstrong glides by the spectacular Beaujolais vineyards on his way to victory in the final time trial of the 2002 Tour.

– could have come perilously close to Beloki's second place. As it was, the top three were unchanged, while a tired Botero did enough to secure fourth overall.

By the time the race reached the Champs Elysées in Paris, Armstrong and the US Postal team had drunk champagne, posed for photos and spent 100 kilometres enjoying themselves, job as well done as ever.

In the green-jersey competition things were a little more serious – McEwen, clearly superior to Zabel, won the stage and took the points' jersey. It was a mildly diverting sideshow to what had been Armstrong's most convincing Tour victory ever. And he had no intention of stopping at four.

2003

"The Drive For Five" – Lance Armstrong's ambition for the 2003 Tour was so carefully managed that it even had its own mission statement. And it was going to be quite a mission. Gilberto Simoni had barely stepped down from the podium of the Giro before announcing his intention of giving Armstrong the fright of his life in the Tour mountain stages, and even Joseba Beloki had raised his head above the parapet. Only Jan Ullrich, beset by sponsorship crises, was modest in the assessment of his chances.

Overriding the competition Armstrong faced from his rivals was a worse set of domestic and political problems. The second Iraq war had cooled relations between the Texan and the French public, despite his attempts to distance himself from George W Bush. On top of this, he and his wife Kristen had formally separated, and he had spent most of the season in Europe without her and their children. He came to the centenary Tour with more than just the weight of expectation on his shoulders.

Armstrong's failure to make a detailed inspection of the prologue course, and his subsequent seven-second loss to Bradley McGee over

the 6.5 kilometres, produced much speculation as to whether he was fully focused on the race in hand. Similar questions were asked of Britain's David Millar, who had missed out on wearing the yellow jersey by 0.08 seconds after his chain slipped off his front mech. Fastest through the half-way checkpoint, Millar's mechanical failure was caused by his decision – against his mechanic's advice – to ride without a derailleur. He knew he would not need to use the smaller chain-ring on the flat course, and insisted on going without the extra few grammes of weight. But when his chain bounced, there was nothing to hold it in place; it was the kind of avoidable mistake that would simply never happen to Lance Armstrong.

Frenchman Damian Nazon took the *maillot jaune* thanks to some canny riding for the intermediate sprints on the first three road stages, but he was back in his Jean Delatour strip by the end of the team time trial. US Postal won the stage – a significant coup against ONCE and Ullrich's newly formed Bianchi squad – but it was the Colombian Victor Hugo Pena who took the yellow jersey, having finished a single second

Above: A hundred years to the day since the first-ever Tour set off from the Cafe au Réveil Matin, the peloton passes by once more.
Below: Despite a broken collar bone, Tyler Hamilton receives orders from Bjarne Riis on his way to a win in Bayonne after his remarkable lone breakaway.

ahead of Armstrong in the prologue. It created an interesting dynamic: the defending champion and team leader taking turns on the front to protect his *domestique's* lead in the overall race. It was not a situation that would last. Pena got to spend his birthday in yellow, a day at the centre of attention, before resuming his normal role as workhorse for Armstrong. Besides, there was someone else hogging the attention in week one – Alessandro Petacchi took an incredible four stage wins in five sprint finishes. The Italian knew his weaknesses as well as his strengths; 24 hours after taking his fourth win, the Tour made its first foray into the Alps, and he climbed off, knowing he had done more than enough to please his sponsors.

The stage was the longest of the race, at 230.5 kilometres. Ending on the descent into Morzine, the contenders for the overall title used the stage as a warm-up for the following day's ride to Alpe d'Huez.

When Richard Virenque rode away on the Col de Portes, Armstrong did not flicker. He wanted to save his energy, and that of his team-mates, to control the group that he was with. Virenque duly took both the yellow and polka-dot jerseys, and Armstrong

remained in second place.

According to the Armstrong masterplan, the first summit finish should have been where he laid the peloton low with an attack that would ride him into yellow. But something told the four-time winner to hold back. He did not trust himself to be able to catch Iban Mayo as he accelerated away; he was suddenly cautious, all attention on his overall rivals, unwilling to gamble for stage wins.

To try and win the Tour at less than 100 per cent was a calculated risk, but it was one he had been forced to take. Even when Tour of Switzerland winner Alexandre Vinokourov launched a counter-move, Armstrong sat tight. He would take the jersey, and, for the moment at least, that was enough.

ARMSTRONG GOES OFF-ROAD

While Vinokourov was establishing himself as a credible rival to the Texan, his erstwhile shadow, Joseba Beloki, was determined to assert his own challenge. Mocked for his timidity in previous years, the Basque rider had decided that a change of tack was the only way he could win the race and the hearts of the public and was riding with a new-found aggression. But as he led Armstrong down the final 20 kilometres of the stage to Gap, he was robbed of his chance. The roads were so hot that his back tyre stuck to the tarmac and, as the rubber was ripped from the rim, he was catapulted across the road.

All that Armstrong could do to avoid crashing into him was to make an abortive escape into a field. Beloki broke his leg, his wrist and his elbow; Armstrong broke nothing more than his rhythm, and bounced across the furrows to rejoin the race. Luck was on the side of the yellow jersey.

High temperatures were affecting the riders' comfort more than usual; Andre Kivilev had been killed during the Paris-Nice race in March – he crashed and fractured his skull – and the UCI made helmets compulsory for all professional races. The only

exception was that riders could remove them at the foot of the final climb of a stage with a summit finish.

Armstrong had forged his previous Tour wins on the coldest, most miserable mountain ascents: Sestriere in 1999, Hautacam in 2000, and the heat proved his undoing in the first long time trial. In 47 kilometres he lost 96 seconds to Ullrich, and, he claimed, more than six kilograms of body weight through dehydration. It was Ullrich's first Tour stage win since 1998, the year before Armstrong came back to the race. With both the German and Vinokourov now within a minute of him, Armstrong was suddenly vulnerable.

Another seven seconds lost to Ullrich in the first Pyrenean stage – and the 12 that Ullrich gained for taking second on the stage – confirmed what Armstrong's detractors had hoped: the American was not as strong, either mentally or physically, as he had been in previous years. The stage to Luz

Above: Armstrong is forced off the road as he avoids crashing into Joseba Beloki on the run in to Gap. Below: Jan Ullrich calls for help from his team car after his fall during the rain-soaked final time trial.

Ardiden, the final summit finish of the race, would decide the winner of the centenary Tour.

SUNSHINE AFTER THE RAIN

Finally the weather turned in Armstrong's favour. Mist dropped down on to the Tourmalet and, when Ullrich attacked him, he remained unmoved. With 30 kilometres still to ride, he kept tight in the saddle and maintained his tempo, never allowing his rival more than 100 metres of leeway. They regrouped for the final climb.

In the final time trial, it was the rain, rather than the riders, which dominated. Ullrich could have made up a handful of seconds on the stage, but slid off into the barriers and saw his faint hopes of victory dashed. Armstrong rode cautiously, leaving Britain's David Millar to win the day, while plaudits went to Tyler Hamilton, who had ridden with a fractured collar bone since a crash on stage one and still time-trialled himself into fourth place overall.

It was a dishevelled peloton that made it to Paris for the centenary celebrations and, as Armstrong joined Eddy Merckx, Bernard Hinault and Miguel Indurain to pose for the cameras in the group of five-time winners, it was with a sense of joy tinged with no little relief that the race was finally over. He had won his toughest Tour yet. Although it had certainly not been his intention, he had shown just a little human frailty, and in doing so had finally inspired a little warmth in the hearts of the French fans.

Above: Armstrong tangles unintentionally with a spectator and Iban Mayo on the ascent of the Tourmalet.
Right: Armstrong is close to exhaustion after winning the Pyrenean mountain stage to Luz Ardiden.

It was Basque hero Iban Mayo who made the decisive attack, pulling away with only Armstrong and Ullrich on his wheel. As the trio accelerated, Armstrong rounded a corner too tightly, brushing up against the crowds and catching his brakehood on a spectator's bag. Before he had hit the ground Mayo was sprawled out next to him, with Ullrich just dodging across the road to stay upright.

In an instant both riders were back on their bikes. Perhaps remembering his own fall in the 2001 race, Ullrich soft-pedalled until Armstrong regained his composure. But this was no time for pleasantries; no sooner had the American reached his rival than he attacked. Ullrich was momentarily caught out. He was not even riding tempo when Armstrong tore past him, and he was too tired to get out of the saddle and chase. Riding on pure fury, Armstrong crested the climb with a 40-second lead, taking his first stage win of the Tour and finally asserting his rights over the race.

2004

Having won the Tour five times, Lance Armstrong had little reason to change his strategy for a record sixth attempt. Results at other, lesser events meant nothing to him. He remained unruffled by a below-par performance in the Dauphine Libère in June; after winning the 2002 and 2003 editions of the race he finished only fourth overall, and looked almost human as he slumped to fifth in the Mont Ventoux time trial behind climbing ace and eventual overall winner Iban Mayo. But, despite all the speculation that he was not at his best, Armstrong was building up to the Tour according to his own schedule. While Mayo was propelled to the top of the list of potential rivals, old foe Jan Ullrich was more circumspect about his alleged lack of form. "Believe me, he's a lot better than he's letting on," he said. "That's Lance's style, to try and fool his rivals."

The German was right. With rock-star girlfriend Sheryl Crowe in tow, and the Discovery Channel committed to take over team sponsorship from US Postal at the end of the season, Armstrong's status and media exposure in America was at its peak in July. He did not disappoint, finishing second in the prologue to specialist Fabian Cancellara, more than 15 seconds clear of his main competitors. On a 6.1-kilometre course, it was a huge margin.

With Cancellara's Fasso Bortolo team busy protecting the yellow jersey, the Postal riders were fully occupied keeping Armstrong safe. They steered him clear of a first day crash that took Tyler Hamilton down, and kept him out of trouble over the cobbled roads as the race snaked its way out of Belgium. The pavé cost Mayo his dreams of a podium: he crashed on the first section of cobbles and was simply too light and too inexperienced to get back to the main group. He eventually trailed in almost four minutes behind the group containing all the other main

**Above: Richard Virenque who went on to win King of the Mountains for a record seventh time.
Below: Emotion spills over as Armstrong crosses the line first on stage 15 at Villars-de-Lans, just ahead of Ivan Basso.**

contenders. Four days into the Tour and already Armstrong was looking like a winner.

Perhaps fearful of US Postal's collective strength, Tour organizers ruled that the times in the team time trial would not count directly towards the overall classification. So when Armstrong's team trounced the opposition, they received a modest time bonus over their rivals, rather than the one to seven minutes that they had beaten them by.

Despite having sprayed champagne over one another to wash away the rain and road dirt, the Postal riders had no intention of defending the yellow jersey which Armstrong acquired in the team time trial. Instead, they dispensed with it within 24 hours. French national champion Thomas Voeckler got in a five-man break with Australian Stuart O'Grady, and finishing almost ten minutes ahead of the main bunch on stage five, they took the overall lead and the

stage win respectively. The next day O'Grady took the green jersey from compatriot Robbie McEwen.

With the key mountain stages, including the Alpe d'Huez time trial, packed into the final week, the middle section of the Tour was played out at 70kph between the fiercely competitive sprinters. McEwen and O'Grady were joined by Norwegian powerhouse Thor Hushovd and German stalwart Erik Zabel in their battle, but with so many other riders still vying for a slice of action, crashes were frequent, and sometimes serious. Immediately under the one-kilometre-to-go flag on stage six, Rene Haslebacher's handlebars broke, causing a mass pile-up. As the Austrian lay writhing on the ground with several broken ribs, a broken nose and damaged kidneys, an irate McEwen – himself covered in scrapes and bruises – stormed over and subjected him to a verbal assault that matched the physical one. Even when he learned

that the crash was called by a mechanical failure rather than human error McEwen, who had never taken pains to cultivate friends in the peloton, was unrepentant. Still angry, he managed to channel his aggression into his sprinting for the next phase of the race. Back in green, he took the final flat stage – cruelly usurping longtime breakaways Filippo Simeoni and Inigo Landaluze less than 100 metres from the finish – before the mountains and then sat back to watch the fireworks.

The first climbing stage fell on Bastille Day, and it was no surprise to see Richard Virenque attack with 200 kilometres, and nine categorized climbs, ahead of him. He took the stage, and enough points to set him well on his way to a record seventh King of the Mountains title.

Above: Hincapie (middle) congratulates his team leader after a faultless performance in the team time trial puts Armstrong in yellow.
Right: The courageous Voeckler reaches the Plateau de Beille with just 22 seconds in hand over Armstrong.

Armstrong kicked at the finish to sneak a handful of seconds over Hamilton and Ullrich, and send out a small but significant warning shot. It was not until the ride to La Mongie on stage 12 that he made his presence truly felt and, when he did, the rider closest to him was not Ullrich or Mayo, but Ivan Basso.

On the first summit finish of the race he did not contest the sprint with the young Italian; his major rivals were scattered down the mountainside, grovelling to limit their losses, and he had assumed the role of race leader, if not the jersey. Voeckler lost nearly half his advantage over Armstrong during the 198-kilometre stage, and his role now was to keep the *maillot jaune* warm until the American asked for it back.

Stage 13 saw the race pivot in Armstrong's favour. The only surprise for the Texan was how easy it was to dismiss Ullrich and Mayo again. At one point in the stage Mayo actually climbed off his bike, only to be coerced into remounting by his *directeur sportif* and carrying on again. He finished the day's ride at 38 minutes, in the same group as sprinters such as Thor Hushovd and Stefano Zanini. Hamilton abandoned, bruised from his earlier fall and distraught that his dog, Tugboat, which had near-cult status among cycling fans, had died. Armstrong had no such sentimental weaknesses, and even Basso, the only rider who could stay with him as he took his first stage win of 2004, admitted he was racing for second place.

Voeckler got a huge cheer as he crossed the line behind Armstrong. He had clung onto the back of the group as the pace became harder to bear, burying himself on the final climb to the Plateau du Beille. He held on to the jersey by just 22 seconds, and would wear it as far as the Alps.

When they got there, Armstrong executed a repeat performance, dropping all but Basso on the final climb at Villars-de-Lans, and then easily outsprinting him for the stage

win. This time he took the jersey, and the right to ride last in the Alpe d'Huez time trial.

More than a million fans lined the 15.5-kilometre course on stage 16. On each of the 21 hairpins, Armstrong and his rivals were led by police motorbikes parting the sea of spectators. While most of the crowd was supportive, Armstrong was spat at as he chased down and overtook Basso, who had started the ride two minutes before him, and won the stage in 39 minutes and 41 seconds, just a second outside Marco Pantani's record for the climb. He absorbed the spitting from the French spectators, and the abusive graffitti on the road, as fuel for his legs. Like his detractors, Armstrong knew that, barring accident, the Tour was his.

There were no accidents. Armstrong won the next day's stage to La Grand Bornand and the final time trial before the race arrived in Paris, where Ullrich's team-mate Andreas Klöden rode into second place overall ahead of Basso. But there were incidents. Filippo Simeoni, a rider whose athletic prowess was no threat to the yellow

Above: Armstrong gets full protection from his team-mates on the descent of the Col de la Madeleine during stage 17. Below: He celebrates the record-breaking sixth consecutive win in Paris with an army of American fans.

jersey, was Armstrong's most hated opponent on the Tour. Simeoni was suing the Texan for libel after he called him a liar when he cited the Tour winner in his witness statements in the ongoing trial of Michele Ferrari, the doctor at the heart of Italy's biggest doping investigation and sometime advisor to Armstrong.

When Simeoni got into a breakaway group on stage 18, the yellow jersey rode out from the shelter of his team-mates, and personally chased him down. Armstrong told him unequivocally that, unless he sat up and allowed himself to be caught, he would order the might of US Postal to bring back the entire group, and spoil the chances of the others who had broken away. Simeoni had no choice but to give up any hope of a stage win. The bullying was so blatant that all but the most dedicated of Armstrong's fans were appalled, but it proved one thing: Armstrong's desire not only to win but also to control the Tour absolutely was in no way diminished with a record sixth victory.

2005

In April 2005, Lance Armstrong made the announcement that many had anticipated: he would climb off his bike for good at the end of the Tour. Armstrong cited his three children – rapidly growing up in Texas while he pedalled across Europe – as the main factor in his decision.

With six Tours already to his name, he was now aiming to do what none of the Tour greats – Anquetil, Merckx, Hinault or Indurain – had been able to do: to win his final race, and walk away with the yellow jersey still wrapped round his shoulders.

It took less than 20 minutes of riding for Armstrong to prove that his desire to win was undimmed. In the Tour's opening 19-kilometre time trial he caught and passed Jan Ullrich, who had started a minute before him – and took second place on the stage behind compatriot David Zabriskie. Armstrong's performance was mesmerizing; he rode fluidly, unfazed when his foot slipped out of his pedal momentarily, and overtook Ullrich as if the German was out for a leisurely Sunday ride.

With the first psychological blow landing squarely on target, the Discovery Channel squad turned its attention to the team time trial scheduled for day four. All they had to do was keep Armstrong out of trouble while Tom Boonen took successive wins on the first two road stages – and with the likes of Robbie McEwen letting his desperation for a stage win get the better of him, it was no mean feat. The Australian found himself shoulder to shoulder with compatriot Stuart O'Grady as he hurtled to the finish line on stage three: unable to find a gap to get through, McEwen used his head – literally – to barge O'Grady out of his way. While Armstrong was ushered back to his hotel, McEwen was relegated to last place on the stage.

SKIDDING INTO TROUBLE

The Discovery Channel team were going head to head with Team CSC – who were defending Zabriskie's jersey – and with only two seconds separating the Americans there was no margin for error.

CSC was the last team off, and at the first two checkpoints was six seconds up on Armstrong's men. But now they were entering the hardest part of the course. The CSC train hurtled around the road into Blois just two seconds up on Discovery, but as Zabriskie clung to the wheel of his team-mate he took a corner too fast, and skidded across the road. There was no hesitation from the team; he was left to ride the lonely two kilometres to the finish with his Tour dream – like his skinsuit – hanging in shreds. Discovery won the stage by two seconds, and Armstrong was back in yellow.

The Texan avoided the biggest crash of the race on stage six, but in his efforts to stay out of trouble he conceded seven seconds to Alexandre Vinokourov, who also snatched a time bonus for second place on the stage behind Lorenzo Bernucci.

While the American was disgruntled at the stage result, Tom Boonen and Robbie McEwen were exasperated: the pair were locked in battle for the green jersey, with the Belgian winning stages two and three, and McEwen getting even with victory on days five and seven. The competition for the green jersey provided plenty of entertainment as the overall contenders looked forward to stage eight, and the mountains.

As a precursor to the Alpine stages, the peloton tackled the hills of the Vosges. According to the usual Armstrong formula, the first mountain stage is the day to set the tone – the winning one, of course – for the rest of the race.

Above: Lance Armstrong starts to overhaul Jan Ullrich during the stage 1 time trial. Below: Armstrong applies steely concentration to the task of winning the hilly St Etienne time trial to seal his 2005 Tour win.

But when Vinokourov attacked repeatedly on the Col de la Schlucht, the biggest climb of the day, the Texan found himself isolated from his team-mates and so he was obliged to do the chasing himself. He succeded in keeping the group together, and, crucially, ensured that Jan Ullrich could not make any gains, but meant that Telecom could make its strength in numbers count.

Andreas Klöden, who had finished as runner-up in the 2004 Tour, slipped away in the final kilometres to gain half a minute in the overall classification. Although it wasn't exactly a decisive move from the German squad, it did beg a question: was Armstrong strong enough to win the race without his team-mates putting on their usual performance?

TRIUMPH OF THE WORKHORSE

Whatever *directeur sportif* Johan Bruyneel said to the Discovery team that evening, it certainly worked. The chastised *domestiques* rode superbly for Armstrong the next day, protecting him while Michael Rasmussen stayed away all day to take the stage and consolidate his King of the Mountains lead. The Texan relinquished the *maillot jaune* to CSC workhorse Jens Voigt, but it was clear that he would give it up only temporarily, and in a manner of his choosing.

Reaching the Alps, Armstrong strengthened his resolve to re-establish his dominance. He began the final climb to Courchevel with six team-mates, and systematically dropped every one of his major rivals in the final 10 kilometres of the climb. Ullrich at least tried one brief

Above: Rasmussen's disastrous final time trial culminated with the indignity of being caught by Armstrong for six minutes.
Below: The shape of things to come? Hincapie takes his first Tour stage at the Pla d'Adet.

attack, but by the end of the stage he had lost a further two minutes in the general classification. Spain's Alejandro Valverde took the stage, Armstrong crossed the line next to him to reclaim the jersey, and Rasmussen finished third. Once again, the Texan appeared invincible.

IN A CLASS OF HIS OWN

The next day he was happy to let Vinokourov ride away to a stage victory over the Madeleine and the Galibier; the Kazakh was out of contention for the yellow jersey, and Armstrong would not risk wasting any of his or his team's energies for a stage win with the Pyrenees still to come. Less happy was Jens Voigt – 24 hours after being relieved of the *maillot jaune*, he was out of the race, excluded by the race organizers, after

finishing more than 40 minutes behind Vinokourov and so missing the time cut for the stage.

On the first Pyrenean stage Armstrong whittled down the lead group, finally dropping Ullrich in the last two kilometres, and outsprinting Ivan Basso at the summit of Ax-3-Domaines, but was a frustrating second place behind Georg Totschnig, who had been away for 200 kilometres.

The final high mountain stage, 15, offered a glimpse of what a post-Armstrong Tour might be like: his most loyal *domestique*, George Hincapie, slotted into the early break, and led all the way to the Plat d'Adet to take his first-ever Tour stage win. His tactics were pure Armstrong, and his team leader congratulated him generously on his victory.

Now the Texan was left with one final chance to take a stage win, at the final time trial in St Etienne. A

Above: Armstrong glances back at Ivan Basso and Jan Ullrich during the Ax-3-Domaines stage. Below: Alexandre Vinokourov wins the final stage in Paris. Opposite: Lance signals his seventh win.

seventh consecutive title was within his reach, but Armstrong did not want to go down in history as the first person since Greg Lemond to win the Tour without taking a stage.

Over 55.5 technical, hilly kilometres Armstrong rode as if the race was still in the balance, rather than all but secure in his hands. The single-minded focus which had seen

him catch Ullrich for a minute 19 days earlier brought him the stage win he craved; though the German raised his game to take second on the stage and move into third overall, he was outclassed once more.

While Armstrong savoured his final laps of the Champs Elysees, Alex Vinokorouv had one last tilt at Tour glory, punctuating the closing kilometres with attacks. Persistence paid off – he broke away with Brad McGee in the final straight, and snatched his second stage of the race. The time bonus he accrued pushed him up to fifth overall, but it was, of course, Armstrong who topped the podium once again in Paris.

In winning again, Armstrong put himself beyond reach in the pantheon of Tour greats. He had won more Tours than any rider in history, and had achieved that rarest of sporting feats: he had quit while he was ahead.

Tour Legends
Richard Virenque

"I've tried to win with style."

Virenque, 1997

Left: Richard Virenque has even the great Lance Armstrong (behind right) trailing in the mountains. Right: Virenque set a new Tour record by winning the maillot pois on seven occasions and he claimed stage wins on some of the most famous climbs of all, Ventoux, Luz Ardiden and Courchevel. He also enjoyed two podium finishes, in 1996 and 1997.

RICHARD VIRENQUE (FRA)
b 19/11/69 Casablanca, Morocco

12 PARTICIPATIONS
7 STAGE WINS

1992 25TH OVERALLL

1993 19TH OVERALL

1994 FIFTH OVERALL
KING OF THE MOUNTAINS
ONE STAGE WIN: stage 12, Lourdes-Hautacam–
Luz Ardiden

1995 NINTH OVERALL
KING OF THE MOUNTAINS
ONE STAGE WIN: stage 15, Saint-Girons–Cauterets

1996 THIRD OVERALL
KING OF THE MOUNTAINS

1997 SECOND OVERALL
KING OF THE MOUNTAINS
ONE STAGE WIN: stage 14, Bourg d'Oisans–
Courchevel

1998 DID NOT FINISH

1999 EIGHTH OVERALL
KING OF THE MOUNTAINS

2000 SIX OVERALL
ONE STAGE WIN: stage 16,
Courchevel–Morzine

2002 16TH OVERALL
ONE STAGE WIN: stage 14, Lodeve–Mont Ventoux

2003 16TH OVERALL
KING OF THE MOUNTAINS
ONE STAGE WIN: stage 7, Lyon–Morzine-Avoriaz

2004 15TH OVERALL
ONE STAGE WIN: stage 10, Limoges–Saint Flour

Tour Legends
Lance Armstrong

"This is a hard Tour and hard work wins it. Vive le Tour."

Lance Armstrong on winning his seventh Tour

Left: Armstrong holds the Texan Lone Star flag on the podium in Paris, 2001. In 2012, he was stripped of all race results from 1998 onwards, including his seven Tour titles, for doping. Right: Armstrong wins stage 17 at Le Grand Bornand in 2004, just ahead of his main rivals for the _maillot jaune_, Andreas Klöden (out of shot), Ivan Basso and Jan Ullrich.

LANCE ARMSTRONG (USA)
b. 18/9/71 Plano, Texas

13 PARTICIPATIONS
SEVEN VICTORIES
24 STAGE WINS

1993 DID NOT FINISH
ONE STAGE WIN: stage 8, Châlons sur Marne–Verdun

1994 DID NOT FINISH

1995 36TH OVERALL
ONE STAGE WIN: stage 18, Montpon Ménestérol–Limoges

1996 DID NOT FINISH

1999 FIRST OVERALL*
FOUR STAGE WINS: prologue, Le Puy du Fou; stage 8, Metz (time trial); stage 9, Le Grand Bornand–Sestriere; stage 19, Futuroscope (time trial)

2000 FIRST OVERALL*
ONE STAGE WIN: stage 19, Fribourg en Brisgau–Mulhouse (time trial)

2001 FIRST OVERALL*
FOUR STAGE WINS: stage 10, Aix les Bains–L'Alpe d'Huez; stage 11, Grenoble–Chamrousse (time trial); stage 13, Foix–Saint-Lary Soulan; stage 18, Montluçon–Saint Amand Montrond (time trial)

2002 FIRST OVERALL*
FOUR STAGE WINS: prologue, Luxembourg; stage 11, Pau–La Mongie; stage 12, Lannemezan–Plateau de Beille; stage 19, Régnié Durette–Mâcon (time trial)

2003 FIRST OVERALL*
ONE STAGE WIN: stage 15, Bagnères-de-Bigorre–Luz-Ardiden

2004 FIRST OVERALL*
SIX STAGE WINS: stage 4, Cambrai–Arras (team time trial); stage 13, Lannemezan–Plateau de Beille; stage 15, Valréas–Villard-de-Lans; stage 16, Bourg d'Oisans–L'Alpe d'Huez (time trial); stage 17, Bourg d'Oisans–Le Grand Bornand; stage 18, Besançon–Besançon (time trial)

2005 FIRST OVERALL*
TWO STAGE WINS: stage four, Tours–Blois (team time trial); stage 20, St Etienne–St Etienne (time trial)

AFTER COMEBACK: 2009 THIRD OVERALL

2010 23RD OVERALL

* Stripped of all seven titles in 2012, for doping offences.

Chapter 12: 2006–2012

Searching For a New Champion

After seven straight victories, Lance Armstrong climbed off his bike as the Tour's most successful rider. But the lure of the *maillot jaune* was too much and he came out of retirement, riding his final Tour in 2010. Finally, the peloton emerged from his shadow, with Britain's Bradley Wiggins heading up a new generation of riders. But before 2012 was out, Armstrong was back in the headlines, sensationally exposed as a dope cheat.

2006

Three months after Lance Armstrong had claimed his seventh straight Tour victory, the relief that he had finally left the race open to fresh talent was palpable. Announcing the 2006 route, the event organizers made reference to the end of a "long, long chapter in the history of the Tour de France". In August, French newspaper *L'Equipe* had claimed Armstrong used EPO to win the 1999 Tour – and although nothing was proved, the Tour bosses preferred to distance themselves from the American, safe in the knowledge he would not be returning to their race.

Armstrong would continue to fight doping allegations for months after his retirement – even threatening at one point to get back on his bike at ride the Tour, only half-jokingly telling *The American Statesman* that it would be the best way of upsetting the French.

By the time the 2006 race rolled round, Armstrong was not the only one having to defend himself in the press. Two podium regulars, Jan Ullrich and Ivan Basso, were unceremoniously pulled from their respective teams before the prologue when their names were linked with *Operation Puerto*, a doping enquiry in Spain, and Kazakh hope Alexandre Vinokourov found himself without a ride after five of his Team Astana team-mates suffered the same fate.

In total 56 riders were implicated in the investigation, along with 144 other sportsmen and women. What could the Tour do? As they had in 1998, the organizers sent the jettisoned competitors packing, and looked to a depleted field to deliver some pure, racing excitement to an increasingly cynical public.

Above: Norway's Thor Hushovd loses the jersey after a high-speed crash on stage two.
Below: McEwen frustrates Boonen (in yellow) in another hard-fought sprint finish.
Previous spread: London's Tower Bridge provided a dramatic backdrop for the start of stage one of the 2007 Tour.

It was a Norwegian, Thor Hushovd, who took the first yellow jersey of the race, beating Armstrong's former team-mate George Hincapie by less than a second in the 7.1-kilometre prologue. Fourteen seconds further back, Britain's David Millar rode competitively for the first time since completing a two-year ban for using EPO. By the end of the three-week race, it would be clear that the lesson Millar had learned the hard way was still going unheeded by some of his fellow professionals.

An collision with a fan waving a giant plastic hand (a sponsor's freebie) saw Hushovd lose the jersey – and an impressive spray of blood – in the run-up to the stage finish on day two of the race. Hincapie became only the fourth American to wear the *maillot jaune*, as sprinter Robbie McEwen took on all-comers, winning three of the first six road stages.

By the time the peloton arrived in Saint Gregoire for the first individual time trial, world champion

Tom Boonen had been consistent enough to wriggle his way into the yellow jersey, but McEwen was looking more than comfortable in its green counterpart.

The time trial, as always, reshuffled the general classification to bring the real contenders to the surface. Specialist Serguei Gonchar revived Team T-Mobile's race, taking the stage, and the jersey, while Floyd Landis came second. The American was a minute off the race lead, but with Andreas Klöden another 45 seconds back – and with plenty of T-Mobile team-mates ready to help him – the race to the Pyrenees was still wide open.

The first mountain stage ended with a long descent to Pau, making it ideally suited for a long breakaway. Spain's Juan Miguel Mercado and Frenchman Cyril Dessel duly obliged, escaping over the Col du Soudet. Dessel worked hard to make the gap big enough to put him in yellow; Mercado took the stage. Meanwhile

the big guns sheltered in the bunch, more than seven minutes back: they knew that the next day's ride across the mountains and into Spain would be the most decisive yet.

Stage 11 was brutal, with an hors category and four first category climbs, including the ascent to the finish at the Pla de Beret. Initially, T-Mobile controlled the pace, but the team's effort was ill-judged; Michael Rasmussen sparked a show of strength from Rabobank as the final climb loomed close, whittling down the lead group and providing a spring board for his team leader Denis Menchov to attack.

Menchov's move, six kilometres from the line, forced the final selection. Only Landis, Carlos Sastre, Cadel Evans and Levi Leipheimer could stay with him. There was temporary cohesion as the five men established their lead, then an explosion of attacks as the gradient eased. Leipheimer went, then Menchov and Landis countered. The

Above: Frenchman Cedric Vasseur leads the peloton through the rain on stage five, keeping the break in check for his team leader and jersey-holder Tom Boonen. Right: Yaroslav Popovych (left) works with Oscar Friere to make a winning move on stage 12 to Carcassonne.

Russian went again, and Landis, knowing the jersey was his, let Leipheimer pass him for second on the stage.

The next day there was a stage victory for a member of the Armstrong-less Discovery Channel team. But it wasn't down to one of Johan Bruyneel's clinically executed assaults, it was from some astute riding from Yaroslav Popovych, the 2005 white jersey winner. Then, as the race descended from the mountains, Landis slipped out of yellow in a way that the seven-time champion would never have allowed.

A 230-kilometre transition stage provided rich pickings for gutsy Jens Voigt. He led a five-man escape to win the stage, half an hour ahead of Landis, and his companion Oscar Pereiro took the jersey. The next day Pierrick Federigo won the stage despite being hit on the head by Rik Verbrugghe's bike in a freakish crash. The Frenchman stayed upright, while the Belgian was left with a broken leg: real drama, but nothing that changed the overall standings.

Landis reclaimed yellow on L'Alpe d'Huez with a show of tenacity, grinding out fifth place on the stage while Pereiro and Menchov limited their losses. It was a solid

ride, but Landis paid the real cost the next day. Stunned by the American's failure to respond to Menchov's initial attack on the final climb to the finish at La Toussuire, Sastre followed suit.

Landis barely lifted his eyes from the tarmac. The exhaustion, which he had so carefully concealed over the previous three climbs, was exposed for all his rivals to see. It was not just the Spaniard who pounced; another eight riders accelerated mercilessly, leaving Landis to grovel his way to the summit. He lost ten minutes in as many kilometres, and with them, the jersey.

MIRACULOUS RECOVERY

A day later, Landis proved he could succeed as spectacularly as he could fail, attacking on the first climb of the day. His performance was as unexpected as it was epic – his rivals' certainty that he would crack turned out to be wishful thinking as Landis won the stage and moved to within 30 seconds of the race lead.

Of the four remaining stages, the only one that mattered was the time trial. Pereiro put up a spirited defence, but lost two minutes to Landis over the 57 kilometres. For the eighth successive year, an American rode

Above: Landis loses the maillot jaune in excruciating fashion on stage 16 of the race.
Below: Fans and well-wishers campaign for Pereiro to be instated as the winner of the 2006 Tour de France.

into Paris wearing yellow at the end of the Tour.

For four days, Landis was hailed as a hero. Then the race organisers announced that an unnamed rider had failed doping control and, within 24 hours, Landis had pulled out of a post-Tour criterium, forfeiting around €60,000 in appearance fees. The rumour mill

flew into overdrive and, within 48 hours, he had been outed by his team as having tested positive for testosterone on the day of his 120-kilometre, race-winning move.

In a sport that was constantly bracing itself against doping scandals, Landis's failed A sample was a body blow. The closest the Tour had come to a winner testing positive was when Pedro Delgado failed a dope control while in yellow in 1988. Landis first claimed the test was faulty; second, that the result was caused by drinking too much Jack Daniel's after the disastrous stage 16; and, finally, that he had a naturally high testosterone/epitestosterone ratio. But the B sample confirmed the result, and revealed exogenous – a synthetic, not naturally-produced – testosterone in Landis's system.

Landis pursued his case through every legal machination he could, and even published a book explaining how he had produced ax false positive result, but to no avail. He was stripped of his Tour title, banned from racing, and Oscar Pereiro was retrospectively named the race winner; a result which would always be marked with an asterisk, and another sorry footnote.

2007

The doping cloud hanging over Floyd Landis at the end of the 2006 was still evident as the 2007 race began in London. Landis had been stripped of his win, with the yellow jersey being passed to second-placed Oscar Periero. The American was still embroiled in a legal battle when the tour crossed the Channel for the first time since 1994.

With the Olympics five years away, London mayor Ken Livingstone was determined to show that the capital could host a world-famous sporting event, and do it well. The prologue was a huge success, with about one million people gathering in Hyde Park to see the British time-

Above: Bradley Wiggins passes Buckingham Palace during the 2007 Tour prologue.
Below: Switzerland's Fabio Cancellara adds a win on stage three to his prologue victory.

trial specialist Bradley Wiggins come fourth, missing out on the *maillot jaune* by 23 seconds to Fabian Cancellara.

The Swiss rider snatched a second win on stage three in Compiegne, but lost on Bastille Day, stage seven, when the young German rider Linus Gerdemann took the jersey having been in a breakaway for most of the day. They might have been denied a home winner, but at least the organisers knew that Gerdemann was an outspoken critic of doping, who wanted to prove you could still win clean.

The peloton went into the mountains for stage eight, and Michael Rasmussen – a climber who had twice won the King of the Mountains competition – was quick to attack. He made his move on the Cormet de Roselend, passing the early breakaways on the 20-kilometre climb, gathering his strength on the descent before attacking again on the

Montée de Hauteville. Only two riders – Antonio Colom and David Arroyo – could match his pace. The Dane led the trio over the summit while behind him Australia's Michael Rogers – tipped as an outside favourite before the start – abandoned the race after crashing. The final ascent, to Tignes, saw Rasmussen go clear, riding solo uphill for more than 10 kilometres to become King of the Mountains and take the yellow jersey.

After a rest day, the riders faced a gruelling start to stage nine. Setting off from the base of the Col d'Iseran, they had to ride over the Telegraphe and the Galibier to reach Briançon. The three mountains were enough to end Alexandre Vinokourov's hopes in the overall classification, but left several riders, including Cadel Evans, Alberto Contador and Alejandro Valverde within three and a half minutes of Rasmussen. But then, 10 days into the race, the inevitable happened. News of a positive dope test from the German Patrick Sinkewitz of T-Mobile, during an out-of-competition test in June, led to the German state broadcasters ARD and ZDF refusing to cover the rest of the race.

While Vinokourov restored some pride with a win in the time trial at stage 13, Rasmussen shocked both commentators and his rivals by maintaining his grip on the jersey, holding onto a minute lead over Cadel Evans. The Dane did not let up, escaping with Contador on the final climb during stage 14 to the Plateau de Beille. The Spaniard won the stage, and moved to second place overall.

By the time the peloton emerged from the Pyrenees, both Vinokourov and Rasmussen had taken another stage, and both had been banished from the Tour in disgrace. First, the Astana team withdrew when press reports revealed that Vinokourov had had an illegal blood transfusion after his time-trial win on stage 13, leaving organisers with little hope that there would be space in the sports pages for the final mountain

Above: Michael Rasmussen's brilliant climbing brought him victory on the Col d'Aubisque, but he left the tour in disgrace. Below: Alexandre Vinokourov's joy at winning stage 13 was short-lived. Days later his Astana team pulled out of the race.

stage of the race. But when Rasmussen rode away from his nearest rival, Contador, on the slopes of the Col d'Aubisque, the organisers got more than they'd hoped for.

The Dane held a press conference on the rest day after his stage win, and admitted he had not been as meticulous as he should have been in informing the sport's governing body – the UCI – where he was during the off-season, making him miss the out-of-competition dope tests. But despite his insistence that he had been careless, rather than calculating, in failing to make his whereabouts known, Rasmussen received some boos amongst the cheers when he won his second stage. He stepped onto the podium as stage winner and *maillot jaune* but, before the end of the evening, his past had really caught up with him.

A stony-faced Theo de Rooy, manager of the Rabobank team, issued a brief statement: Rasmussen had been withdrawn from the race and sacked from the team for wrongly reporting his whereabouts to the UCI and so violating its rules. After days of rumours, the move was no surprise. And any illusions that this might finally be the year when the Tour shook off its dirty-race reputation were absolutely shattered when the Italian, Christophe Moreni, was taken away by the gendarmes for failing a dope test for testosterone. His entire Cofidis team pulled out, leaving only 142 riders in the peloton.

Floyd Landis's annulled win had meant that the 2007 Tour began without a rider wearing the number one shirt and now, at the 17th stage, it began without a rider in yellow, although Contador was awarded the jersey at the end of the stage.

Australia's Cadel Evans did what he could to return the world's attention to the racing on stage 18, clawing back three seconds from Contador. He went into the 55-kilometre time trial with a deficit of one minute and fifty seconds, but his rival had more than just a time advantage. Contador rode the race against the watch with seven-time winner Lance Armstrong in the Discovery team car behind him. Some of the Texan's magic brushed onto the Spaniard, and he finished off the stage with a 23-second advantage over Evans. It was Contador's first overall victory, but the eighth for directeur sportif Johan

Isle of Man rider Mark Cavendish sprints to victory in the longest stage of the 2008 Tour, a 232km ride from Cholet to Châteauroux.

Bruyneel. In some respects, the more things changed, the more they stayed the same.

2008

Alberto Contador's faith in Johan Bruyneel was so great that when the *directeur sportif* took up a new post with the Astana team, Contador went with him. But the change of management was not enough for the Tour's organisers. Fed up with the team's doping problems, not least Alexandre Vinokourov's dismissal from the previous year's race, they refused to invite Astana to the 2008 race, leaving Contador unable to defend his title. Bruyneel protested, but it was to no avail. The 95th

Tour started without an outright favourite.

For the first time since 1967, there was no opening prologue at the Tour. Instead, the first day took the riders 197 kilometres over the undulating roads of Brest, where the Spanish national champion Alejandro Valverde took the stage win and the first *maillot jaune*. It passed briefly onto the shoulders of Frenchman Romain Feillu on stage three, before stage four's time trial allowed the main contenders to test themselves for the first time. Stefan Schumacher won the 29.5-kilometre stage and got his hands on the yellow jersey, but all eyes were on third-placed Cadel Evans, who was ahead of several key rivals – Valverde, Andy

**Right: Stefan
Schumacher loses the
maillot jaune on stage
six. Three months
later he would be
named as one of the
riders who had tested
positive for the latest
form of EPO.**

greatest threat came from the Schleck brothers and Carlos Sastre, all riding for CSC-Saxo Bank. With just two kilometres to go the Austrian Bernard Kohl made his first move, momentarily leaving behind everyone but Denis Menchov. The group came back together, but the CSC riders could sense their chance. First Andy Schleck and then Sastre attacked, going clear with Menchov and Kohl. Evans was eventually overtaken by Frank Schleck and Christian Vande Velde in the last few hundred metres.

The peloton took its second rest day with fans on tenterhooks – just eight seconds separated Franck Schleck, Kohl and Evans, with the next three riders within a minute of Schleck's *maillot jaune*. In fact CSC had not only two riders with a genuine chance of winning the race, but also Andy Schleck, a brilliant climber. The three made their strength count on the most prestigious stage of the race, to Alpe dHuez. They set the pace over the Col de la Croix de Fer, reeling in the early breakaway group to within catching distance by the start of the day's final ascent.

As the first of the 21 hairpin bends came into view, Sastre attacked. Menchov went with him, and Evans began to chase. Sensing the Australian's presence, Sastre eased up and then, as the rest of the group

Schleck and Damiano Cunego – by about a minute.

The British sprinter Mark Cavendish got his first Tour success at the fifth stage, before the race headed into the mountains. A tangle between Schumacher and Kim Kirchen in the final kilometre of the second-category Super-Besse left the wearer of the yellow jersey on the tarmac, and Italy's Riccardo Ricco rode away to win the stage. Kirchen got up quickly and snatched the jersey by six seconds from Cadel Evans.

There was a distinct feeling of deja vu at stage nine as Ricco triumphed at Bagneres de Bigorre, but it was not until two days later that a genuine contender took the jersey. Australia's Cadel Evans – wrapped in bandages from a crash on the previous stage – inched just one second ahead of Frank Schleck on the ride to Hautacam, with the stage going to Leonard Piepoli.

But his victory was soon overshadowed by what the race organisers had been dreading: news of a positive dope test. The double stage winner Ricco had failed an EPO test and the organisers threw him out of the Tour. His Saunier Duval team-mates went with him.

By the time the race reached the Alps, Cavendish had increased his tally to four wins, while Evans was still holding onto his precious one-second lead. Stage 15 – which included the ominous-sounding Colle de Morte – proved his undoing. All the contenders for the general classification reached the bottom of the final climb together, oblivious of the four riders contesting the stage ahead of them. Evans knew that the

**Below: Double stage
winner Ricardo Ricco
was expelled from the
2008 Tour for a
positive dope test.**

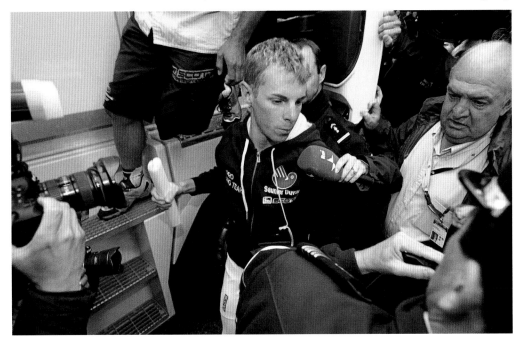

came back at them, attacked again. This time he made it count, leapfrogging Jerome Pineau, the last remaining rider from the earlier breakaway. But as Sastre rode away to win the stage, Evans was left with two of his team-mates. Brothers Frank and Andy Schleck worked brilliantly together, forcing Evans to accelerate whenever anyone got close. Evans battled valiantly, but perhaps the most impressive ride was from Frank Schleck who did not hesitate to sacrifice his yellow jersey to help Sastre.

The last race against the clock was over 53 kilometres – almost twice the distance of stage four. In theory, Evans should have got the better of Sastre, whose advantage over the Australian was just 94 seconds. The Spaniard had the *maillot jaune* on his shoulders, and was determined to show that he was wearing it because of his ability and not because of the strength of his team. As the last man off, he went

flat out from the start, losing less than 10 seconds to Evans by the 36-kilometre time check. In the final five kilometres he confirmed his position as CSC's strongest rider, passing team-mate Frank Schleck who had started three minutes ahead of him. Evans finished runner-up for the second year, while Sastre became the third Spaniard to win the Tour in a row. CSC's efforts were rewarded with the team award, and the best young rider prize for Andy Schleck.

Two months later, an unthinkable rumour surfaced – Lance Armstrong was coming back to the 2009 Tour, "to raise awareness of the burden of cancer". He said he wanted to win, and win clean, to prove his previous seven victories were untarnished. As organisers ASO digested the news, they were hit by a double doping whammy – 2008 stage winners Leonardo Piepoli and Stefan Schumacher had tested postive for the latest version of EPO. By the end of the year, two names had been

struck off the 2008 roll call and Armstrong had been reunited with Johan Bruyneel at team Astana. The question now was if he would make it to the 2009 Grand Départ in Monaco.

Carlos Sastre's success on l'Alpe d'Huez was only the second stage win of his career, but it was the foundation for his overall victory.

2009

Sixteen years after riding his first Tour, its most successful ever participant, Lance Armstrong, returned to the race. And it wasn't just the Texan who was back. His biggest rival, and now Astana team-mate, Alberto Contador, joined him at the *Grand Départ* in Monaco.

The course had the makings of a classic, with a summit finish on Mont Ventoux on the penultimate day. But first there was the matter of the opening 15-kilometre time trial; it was won by specialist Fabian Cancellara, while Contador struck the first blow in what became the Astana leadership battle, finishing third to Armstrong's 10th.

British sprinter Mark Cavendish wasted no time beginning his campaign for the green jersey, winning the first road stage. He won again on stage three, while behind him the psychological warfare between Armstrong and Contador moved into the open. Armstrong made it into the front group when the peloton split, leaving Contador obliged to soft pedal, unable to race for fear of being branded a poor team player. Armstrong leapfrogged the Spaniard in the overall standings, boldly claiming the position of team leader.

Both men put aside their differences for the team time trial on stage four. Astana's winning margin over Cancellara's Saxo Bank squad was 40 seconds, which put Armstrong on

the same time overall as the Swiss rider. Cancellara held onto the yellow jersey only by virtue of the fraction of a second he gained in the opening time trial.

The truce at Astana lasted less than 72 hours. On the race's first mountain stage, Contador imitated Armstrong's signature move, attacking on the final climb. He reached the summit at Arcalis in Andorra with a 21-second lead, asserting his authority over their shared *domestiques,* and pulling out a two-second advantage in the general classification.

The race moved towards the Alps with Cavendish and Thor Hushovd tussling for the green jersey. The Manxman regained the lead in the sprint competition by winning stage 11, only to lose it again two days later. The nadir of their battle came on stage 14, when Hushovd lodged an official complaint that Cavendish had pushed him into the barriers at Besancon – an offence which saw the British rider relegated to last place on the stage.

But the exchanges between the sprinters were a mere diversion that kept fans occupied until stage 15 and the climb to Verbiers, a new ascent in the Tour. With a rest day the day after, no-one would be holding back on the final nine-kilometre ascent to the line. A group containing all the favourites – including Britain's Bradley Wiggins – began the climb together. With a little under six kilo-

Above: Contador's attack on stage seven to Arcalis confirms that he, rather than Armstrong, is the strongest rider in team Astana.
Left: Britain's Bradley Wiggins (centre) mixes with the peloton's finest on stage 15 to Verbiers.

metres to go, Contador attacked with such a devastating acceleration that only Andy Schleck made any meaningful attempt to go with him.

Without his ear-piece in, Contador was unaware of what was happening in his wake. Schleck was marooned ahead of the other podium contenders, while Wiggins proved himself worthy of the company he was keeping, attacking the group and refusing to be dropped when he was brought back. And Armstrong? He dug deep, finishing ninth and moving up into second overall. Contador had the *maillot jaune*, but with another summit finish and a time trial still to ride, the American was far from conceding the race.

During the next stage, Contador waited to see who would challenge him. Obeying cycling etiquette, Armstrong did not attack his team-mate, leaving it to Andy Schleck, and then his brother Frank, to test the Spaniard. Their double-pronged

attack whittled down the group but did nothing to phase Contador, who responded immediately. In fact, they succeeded in dropping Armstrong, while Wiggins continued to ride the Tour of his life, moving into third overall by the end of the day.

CONTADOR ATTACKS

The Schleck brothers joined forces again on stage 17, but even together they could not shake off the *maillot jaune*. They dropped everyone but Contador and his team-mate Andreas Klöden on the penultimate of five climbs, leaving Wiggins and Armstrong to keep each other company. Then, once the foursome had built up a decent gap, Contador dropped any pretence of working for the overall benefit of Astana, attacking and dropping Klöden, and leaving just the Schlecks with him at the head of the race. From that point on, Contador sat on, knowing his lead, and his superior time-trialling, meant that he could afford to let the

Luxembourgers do the work. Andy Schleck allowed brother Frank to take the stage win, and the pair moved into second and third overall. Had Contador adopted different tactics, Astana could have filled the top three, with him, Armstrong and Klöden, but by now they were riding not so much as a team, but as a group of men who happened to be wearing the same sponsors' logos.

If Armstrong could not be sure of grabbing the headlines for his third-place ride against the watch in Annecy on stage 18, he garned plenty of column inches with the announcement that he would be creating a new team for 2010 complete with a US backer, RadioShack. And he would be taking team manager Johan Bruyneel with him. Contador, meanwhile, let his legs do the talking, winning the time trial ahead of Fabian Cancellara.

A brief interlude from the overall competition allowed Mark Cavendish to take another sprint victory on

**Above: Even working together on stage 17, Frank (in front) and Andy Schleck cannot drop Contador.
Right: Contador wins the final time trial ahead of specialist Fabian Cancellara, his second stage victory of the 2009 Tour.**

stage 19, leaving the small matter of Mont Ventoux to contend with. Victory at the summit of the legendary mountain was one of the few gaps in Armstrong's *palmarès*. He had gifted a stage win here to the late Marco Pantani in 2000, a gift which the Italian accepted although he later accused Armstrong of being patronising. Should he find himself at the front of the race in 2009, the American would not make the same gesture again.

Unfortunately for Armstrong, he never got the chance to vie for the stage win. Spain's Juan Manual Garate broke away early on and crossed the line first, while Contador shadowed Andy Schleck less than a minute behind. The top four – with Wiggins holding on to his fourth position, the equal best finish by a Briton at the Tour – remained unchanged as the peloton boarded the TGV to Montereau-Fault-Yonne for the final ride to Paris.

There was more British success on the Champs Elysées, with a sixth stage win for Cavendish. Several metres behind him, Contador rolled across the line in the yellow jersey. Armstrong had made it onto the podium, but this time, he had to settle for third place.

Above: Britain's Mark Cavendish wins by such a margin on the Champs Elysées that even his lead-out man, Mark Renshaw, has time to celebrate.
Left: Armstrong (right) stands on the 2009 podium, but only third behind overall winner Contador (centre) and Andy Schleck, who also won the white jersey for the best rider under 26.

2010

The 2010 Tour was billed, in the US at least, as a final showdown between Alberto Contador and Lance Armstrong, before the latter retired for good. But for those with more European sensibilities, Andy Schleck and Dennis Menchov were considered the main threat to Contador's crown.

The 97th race began much like the 96th, with time-trial specialist Fabian Cancellara winning the opening prologue. But this time Armstrong bettered Contador, with five seconds' advantage.

Ahead of a series of calamatous crashes, Alessandro Petacchi claimed the first road stage, signalling his intent to contest the green jersey with Mark Cavendish and Thor Hushovd. There were more crashes the next day, involving both Schleck

and Armstrong. Schleck's Saxo Bank team-mate Cancellara organised a go-slow to protest against the treacherous conditions, a move which cost him his *maillot jaune*, but allowed Schleck to rejoin the bunch. The stage and the jersey went to breakaway Sylvan Chavanel.

There was no let-up for Tour medics as the peloton crossed the cobbles of the Arenberg Forest on stage three. The biggest victim of the *pavé* was Andy Schleck's brother Frank, who ended his Tour lying in the gutter with a broken collar bone.

As Schleck senior was lifted into an ambulance, his brother was being towed across the cobbles by Cancellara in a move which broke the race apart. Armstrong was dropped, and Contador was left clinging on, reaching the line a few seconds behind the leaders.

Above: Insult is added to injury on stage three as Armstrong – who had crashed the previous day – is dropped, then punctures, on the brutal cobbles.
Right: Sylvan Chavanel completes a heroic stage win at Station de Rousses, claiming the yellow jersey just three months after fracturing his skull in a crash.

Cancellara reclaimed the jersey, and Hushovd, who had ridden cannily to stay out of trouble, took the stage.

The next three stages were flat, one going to Petacchi, and two to Cavendish. On stage seven, the favourites bided their time, allowing a familiar face – Chavanel – to make two visits to the Station des Rousses podium, once as a stage winner then as overall race leader. Not bad for a man who had fractured his skull in the Liège-Bastogne-Liège classic only three months earlier.

There was now only stage eight to ride – the first big mountain stage to the Alpine ski station at Avoriaz – before the first rest day. Chavanel was not expected to retain the *maillot jaune* but the question now was who would take it from him.

At 40 kilometres to go, all the contenders were together. But not all had had an easy ride to get there, notably Armstrong. After multiple crashes he had only just rejoined the group as the climb of the Col de la Ramaz started.

Inevitably, Chavanel was dropped. But then came the biggest shock of the race so far: Armstrong, unable to hide how much he was suffering, slipped backwards, and straight off the back. His RadioShack team-mates rallied round, but the truth was painfully exposed. Armstrong simply couldn't keep up.

The Texan was game enough to try and chase back on the descent, but on the final climb the gap widened. His chance of winning an eighth Tour, or even getting on the podium, was over.

With just a kilometre to ride, Schleck attacked, taking Olympic champion Samuel Sanchez with him. Schleck jumped again at the line, taking his first ever stage win. Behind him, Cadel Evans rode himself into yellow, with Contador moving into third place.

Any skepticism about the route for stage nine, with the Col de la Madeleine 30 kilometres from the line, was forgotten as the simmering tension in the bunch erupted as soon as the climb began. Both Schleck's and Contador's *domestiques* churned their pedals, shaking off rider after rider until they claimed the scalp they wanted: Evans, who was left to claw his way up with the also-rans.

The group thinned until only Contador and Schleck remained. They sized each other up, and decided for now, at least, there was more to gained working together than competing. They might not be able to catch the breakaways, but they had removed all doubt that there were any more than two contenders for the 2010 Tour title.

The green jersey contest took precedence as the peloton rode across

southern France, with high drama on stage 11. Cavendish took his third win, only to see his key lead-out man, Mark Renshaw, thrown out of the race for repeatedly head-butting Julian Dean in an effort to deliver Cavendish to the line.

While HTC-Columbia vowed to appeal the decision, the race rumbled on. Contador snatched a handful of seconds back from Schleck on the short, sharp climb to the Mende aerodrome on stage 12, leaving them 31 seconds apart. It was not until stage 15 that they started to do battle again.

Ascending the final *col* of the Port de Balès, Saxo Bank set the pace, setting Schleck up to attack with three kilometres to climb. He momentarily distanced himself from the group, but flicking through his gears, derailed his chain. As he fumbled with his levers, Contador rode straight past. Schleck was left in an undignified hunch, trying to get the chain back on as roadside fans bellowed in his ears. He crossed the line 39 seconds behind Contador, and stormed to his team bus.

Schleck had two reasons to be so angry. First, that he had made such an error in continuing to pedal as he changed gear, and second, that Contador had attacked while he struggled with a mechanical problem. At first, the Spaniard feigned

Below left: Andy Schleck jumps across the line ahead of Samuel Sanchez to take his first ever Tour stage win at the Avoriaz ski station. Below right: Cadel Evans, who had been in the *maillot jaune* for just 24 hours, loses the the race lead, and hope of a place on the podium, after finishing more than eight minutes down on stage nine.

Left: Andy Schleck's mechanical failure almost turns to farce on stage 15, when, having dropped his chain, he is unable to put it back on, and needs a spare bike and a push to rejoin the race.

innocence, claiming he had not realised what had happened. But race footage showed he had a clear view of the incident, and 24 hours later he issued an apology.

Amends were not made until stage 17, when the race made its second ascent of the Tourmalet in as many stages. Again, the pair found themselves alone on the final climb. With Contador's advantage just eight seconds, Schleck knew he must attack, to take back the jersey before the final time trial. But he simply could not shake Contador, who showed no inclination to take a turn on the front. Mindful of his previous breach of race etiquette, Contador did not contest the sprint, allowing Schleck to take a second prestigious stage win.

The Tour came full circle on stage 19, with Cancellara winning the time trial, and Contador finishing ahead of Schleck. His final overall winning margin was only 39 seconds – exactly equal to Schleck's time loss on stage 15.

CAVENDISH DENIED GREEN

Mark Cavendish repeated his 2009 achievement of winning the final stage on the Champs Elysées. But again, he was denied the green jersey, this time by Alessandro Petacchi. Fans were left to mull over Cavendish's 15th Tour stage win, Schleck's slipped chain, and the fourth closest finish in Tour history.

Below: Schleck and Contador go head to head on stage 17 to the summit of the Tourmalet. Contador rode defensively, securing his yellow jersey, while Schleck took the stage.

2011

Defending champion Alberto Contador lined up at the start of the 2011 race hoping to join the elite group of seven riders to have won the Giro d'Italia and the Tour in the same year. But for many, it was an unresolved doping question, not his victory in the Italian race, that was at the forefront of their minds. Contador, who tested positive for clenbuterol at the 2010 Tour, claimed he had ingested the substance unwittingly in contaminated meat. He was banned by his native Spanish Federation, had the ban lifted and, by July, was still waiting for the conclusion of an appeal started by the UCI against the lifting of the ban.

The ongoing controversy surrounding Contador meant that his presence in the race caused unease in some quarters, and when he was denied victory on stage four on the Mur de Bretagne in a photo finish, not all cycling fans were disappointed. The win was given to Australia's Cadel Evans who, by virtue of his second place on the opening stage and second place in the team time trial, was only a single second behind Thor Hushovd in the overall standings.

British riders – and their international comrades on Team

Above: Team Garmin work flat out to put Thor Hushovd in yellow.
Below: Alberto Contador celebrates at the end of stage four, but the photo-finish victory belongs to Cadel Evans (right).

Sky – made headlines throughout the first week of the race. Mark Cavendish won stages five and seven, with Edvald Boasson Hagen securing Team Sky's first-ever Tour stage win on stage six. Less fortunate was his team leader Bradley Wiggins. The triple Olympic champion was one of three riders who didn't make it to

Chateauroux, crashing out with a fractured collarbone in a pile-up 38 kilometres from the finish.

Thor Hushovd, still in yellow by one second, held onto the *maillot jaune* over the hills of the Massif Central on stage eight, despite Evans sprinting for third place.

Stage nine was more eventful than could have been predicted by its hilly profile, but it was drama created, rather than just captured, by the TV cameras. In a crash-ridden stage, Juan Antonio Flecha and Johnny Hoogerland were shunted off the road by a French TV car and catapulted into a field, with the Dutchman tangling badly with a barbed-wire fence. Despite the crash, Hoogerland continued and, combined with his efforts in the day's breakaway, finished the day with both the King of the Mountains jersey and 33 stitches.

The sprinters were back in action again on stages 10 and 11, with Cavendish finishing second to Andrei Griepel, then winning the stage into Lavaur to claim the green sprinters' jersey. Then, at last, the race reached the Pyrenees: Contador,

erstwhile *maillot jaune* Thor Hushovd took full advantage of the gradient to win his first road stage of the 2011 race.

Voeckler's dogged defence of the yellow jersey continued on stage 14, delighting French fans and sending ripples through the peloton as it rode out its final day in the Pyrenees. Only the Schlecks tried to attack and without success. Could Voeckler's supporters dare to hope he might be able to hold on to yellow through the Alps and on to Paris?

Mark Cavendish took another text-book sprint victory on stage 15 and Hushovd repeated his efforts from stage 13 with a commanding win after a long downhill run-in to Gap. But behind him, the overall contenders decided not to wait until the high Alps to recommence battle.

On the day's only categorised climb, the Col de Manse, 11 kilometres from the finish, Contador launched a surprising attack. Strongman Fabian Cancellara hauled himself to the front of the group bringing his team-mates Andy and Frank Schleck – and Cadel Evans – back to the Spaniard.

Contador attacked again, and this time Andy Schleck and Thomas Voeckler chased him down. Then

Above: Bradley Wiggins' dream of winning the Tour is ended by a broken collar bone after a crash on stage seven. Right: Juan Antonio Flecha (left) and Jonny Hoogerland (in the barbed wire fence) after being hit by a French TV car. Miraculously, both recovered to complete the stage.

Evans and the Schleck brothers had their first chance to relieve Thomas Voeckler of the yellow jersey he had been wearing since stage nine. But the French *rouleur* would not be shaken off; Olympic road-race champion Samuel Sanchez took the stage win and the polka-dot jersey at Luz Ardiden, while Frank Schleck escaped from his rivals with 2.5 kilometres to go, cutting 20 seconds off his deficit by the summit.

Stage 13 was short – just over 150 kilometres – with a 40-kilometre downhill finish into Lourdes, creating an ideal opportunity for a breakaway. Sure enough, a 10-man group went clear early on, splintering on the Aubisque. World champion and

Contador went on the attack again on stage 17 and again was tamed by Evans, this time with the Schlecks. Voeckler was still clinging to the *maillot jaune*, now by just under 80 seconds.

After two consecutive downhill finishes, Andy Schleck knew stage 18 would play to his strengths, finishing at the summit of the Galibier. At 2,645m, it was the Tour's highest-ever stage finish (though the mountain itself had been a regular feature in the race since 1911, the first time Tour riders had tackled the high Alps). The Luxembourger attacked on the Izoard, and didn't glance back. Instead, he left his rivals looking at one another as he rode alone for a mammoth 60 kilometres to his first stage victory of the 2011 race. He had not won many fans by grumbling about the previous days' slippery descents but after two hours riding alone, race followers were delighted to have him back in the frame as a genuine GC contender.

While Schleck junior soared to the Galibier, Evans found no-one to help him in the chase. The Australian limited his losses, and as Voeckler heroically stuck with him to hold onto the jersey by just 15 seconds, Contador imploded, losing four minutes in the last 2.5 kilometres of the climb.

THE LEAD CHANGES HANDS

Voeckler finally conceded the yellow jersey to Andy Schleck on stage 19 to Alpe d'Huez. It was a short day's riding at just 109.5 kilometres, but was enough to finally banish Voeckler from the top three. Contador made another early move and while he could not find the strength to put him within reach of a podium finish, he salvaged a little pride by finishing ahead of the Schleck brothers and Evans on the stage.

As is so often the case, the final result of the 2011 Tour came down to the individual time trial. Before the stage began, it seemed that Andy Schleck's 57-second advantage over Evans could give the Luxembourger a real – albeit slender

Above: Andy Schleck powers away on stage 18, riding alone for two hours to claim victory on the summit of the famous Galibier.
Left: Alberto Contador tries to stay in touch with the race leaders on stage 18 but gets dropped and loses almost four minutes.

he went again, and this time neither of the Schlecks, nor their team-mates, had any answer. But Evans and Samuel Sanchez did, latching onto his rear wheel when he tried to shake them off and then working with him to reach the summit.

As Hushovd sized up the remaining breakaways before launching his stage-winning effort, the trio behind him were descending at an astonishing pace. On the same roads that had ended Joseba Beloki's Tour in 2003 – and seen Lance Armstrong's legendary cross-country diversion to avoid him – Evans attacked. Across the rain-soaked tarmac, the former mountain bike champion unleashed the kind of aggression he had not shown since stage four, dropping both Spaniards as he plummeted towards Gap. His reward was a handful of seconds and a psychological boost that put him firmly at the top of the list of favourites.

– chance of holding the jersey. But as the Australian powered away from the starting ramp, it was soon clear that he was going to win the Tour, and do it with some style. He finished second on the stage to time trial specialist Tony Martin.

Many of the faces on the podium in Paris were familiar. Cavendish had won the final stage for the third consecutive year and took the green jersey for the first time. On the GC podium, Cadel Evans, wrapped in his national flag, was proud to be Australia's first Tour winner. Andy Schleck finished overall runner-up for the third year in succession and was joined by his brother Frank, who took third place. It was the first time in Tour history that siblings had made it into the top three in the same year. Andy Schleck might shake off his nearly-man mantle in 2012 and even set up a brotherly one-two.

**Right: If it's Paris, it must be Cavendish. The British sprinter claims his fifth stage win of the race – and his first *maillot vert* – on the Champs Elysées.
Below: An emotional moment as Cadel Evans (centre) is crowned 2011 Tour winner. Andy Schleck (left) was second and brother Frank (right) was third.**

2012

Six months after the end of the 2011 race, Andy Schleck's name appeared on the Tour's role of honour in the most joyless way possible – Alberto Contador's appeal against his doping ban failed and he was stripped of his 2010 win by the Court of Arbitration for Sport. After Floyd Landis in 2007, it was the second time in five editions of the race that a doped winner had been held to account, and, for clean riders in the peloton, a welcome sign that those who cheat would be caught.

Schleck hoped to win the race the bona fide way – by riding the course in the quickest time – but a crash at the Dauphiné Libéré in June resulted in a broken pelvis just weeks before the Grand Départ. Traditionally, victory at the Dauphiné marks out a rider as a favourite for the Tour, and this year's winner looked to be in imperious form even before Schleck's accident. His name? Bradley Wiggins.

The Londoner's 2012 *palmarès* already included overall victories at Paris-Nice and the Tour of Romandie. After a below-par performance in 2010, and his crash in 2011, he, and his team-mates, were determined to do everything right. World champion and sprint specialist Mark Cavendish acknowledged he would not get the support he was used to in his hunt for stage wins – he knew Team Sky were solely focused on getting Wiggins into the yellow jersey.

The race began as perfectly as it could for Wiggins, with second place behind Fabian Cancellara in the opening prologue. He kept out of trouble on the first road stage as Tour debutant Peter Sagan won, and

Left: In with the new: 22-year-old Peter Sagan opens his Tour de France career with a convincing victory on stage one.
Below: German sprinter Andrei Griepel steered clear of a crash on stage four to take his first stage win of the 2012 race.

again as Mark Cavendish took the sprint for stage two, even without the benefit of a lead-out train.

Things did not go so smoothly on stage three, with crashes waylaying the unfortunate, including Wiggins' *domestique*, Kanstantin Siutsou, who had to abandon. Up front, Sagan proved his previous stage victory was no fluke, taking his second win in three days. And he did it again on stage six, racing ahead of the crashes and punctures on the road to Metz, taking a commanding hold of the points competition as the first week of the race ended.

TOP SPOT COMES EARLY

In a perfect world, Wiggins would have kept just shy of the race lead right up to the final time trial on the penultimate day of the Tour, forcing other teams to defend the jersey before he swiped it from under their noses, just before reaching Paris. But when the peloton reached the first mountain-top finish of the race, on stage seven, the combined strength of Team Sky landed him in yellow ahead of schedule.

The final climb was not long – just six kilometres – but it was steep. The pace set by Richie Porte, Michael Rogers and Edvald Boasson Hagen lay the foundations for Wiggins and his lieutenant Chris Froome, leaving them with only a handful of riders for company as they tackled the ascent. Froome, who had lost 1 minute 25 seconds following a puncture on stage one, powered up the climb with Wiggins on his wheel. The Kenyan-born rider – who had ridden so strongly with the Londoner at the Tour of Spain 10 months previously – then somehow found the strength to counter Cadel Evan's attack in the final 500m to win the stage. Wiggins was in yellow, and suddenly Team Sky's stated aim – to have a British winner of the Tour within five years – didn't seem so far-fetched.

A hilly day on stage eight saw Wiggins develop a taste for defending the jersey, while the youngest man in the peloton, Thibaut Pinot, took France's first stage win of the race.

Above: World champion Mark Cavendish sacrifices his legs – and chances of the green jersey – to act as water-carrier for Bradley Wiggins on stage seven.
Right: The youngest man in the race, France's Thibaut Pinot, rides solo to victory on stage eight.

Then came the first long time trial of the Tour. With almost mechanical brilliance, Wiggins put almost a minute into the mighty Fabian Cancellara, winning the stage with Froome in second place. Sky now had riders in first and third overall, with Cadel Evans sandwiched awkwardly between them.

Stage 10 saw another popular win from a Frenchman, this time the irrepressible Thomas Voeckler, who characteristically made no effort to hide how much he was suffering as he rode, or how ecstatic he was to cross the line first.

A poker face might not be necessary for riders bidding for glory on individual stages, but for those contesting the overall competition, being able to hide pain and anxiety is a vital psychological ploy. And when it came to the final climb on stage 11, defending champion Cadel Evans could not hide his suffering. Yet again, Froome set the pace on behalf of Wiggins, and proved to be too strong not just for Evans, but for the yellow jersey wearer himself. With three kilometres to go, and the Australian nowhere in sight, Froome just kept pushing, only to he reined in by the voice in his earpiece from the team car. He eased up and ushered Wiggins safely to the line. There was no doubting the team's plan, or Froome's loyalty, but the question now being asked was whether Team Sky were actually defending their strongest rider.

The next morning's *Guardian* newspaper carried a column by Bradley Wiggins. In it he talked not about team tactics, but about doping. About how much he loved the sport, and how proud he was to ride clean. It earned him as much

Left: An exhausted but elated Thomas Voeckler is mobbed by the media after winning stage 10, the race's first day in the high Alps.
Below: Defending champion Cadel Evans has to be paced by team-mate and leading young rider Tejay Van Garderen on stage 12.

Stage 16 was a brutal way to restart the race, with the first *hors catégorie* climb coming after barely 50 kilometres. While the ever-eager Voeckler won the stage from an early break, the overall contenders were shepherded by the Team Sky *domestiques* over the Col d'Aubisque, the Tourmalet and onto the lower slopes of the Aspin. But as Nibali and his team-mate Ivan Basso took on their share of the pace-making, Cadel Evans was found wanting. Tellingly, his team manager did not order Evans's teammate, Tejay Van Garderen, to drop back and pace the Australian; Van Garderen was in the white jersey for the best young rider, and if Evans was not going to challenge for yellow, the white jersey was worth hanging onto.

So the defending champion was left to grind his way over the summit in the wake the leaders, and, showing that his heart was willing, even if his legs were not, he rejoined the group on the approach to the Peyresourde. But he did not last long. The climb and the intense heat sapped what strength he had left. Evans lost

respect as his performances on the bike had done. And only hours later, his compatriot David Millar, a strong anti-doping campaigner since coming back from a two-year ban in 2006, proved that he, too, could win clean. He did it by out-sprinting a small breakaway group on July 13, the 45th anniversary of Tom Simpson's death on Mont Ventoux.

Three days of racing and long transfers across southern France brought the peloton to a rest day in Pau, with neither Wiggins, Froome, or third-placed Vincenzo Nibali showing any signs of weakness. But Evans' misery was compounded by an incident which defied belief. He punctured three times on stage 14, along with a dozen or more others, after riding over carpet tacks which had been maliciously strewn across the road. As race leader, Wiggins neutralized the peloton, showing a sensitivity to Tour etiquette which further endeared him to the watching French public.

Above: Bradley Wiggins digs deep to hold Chris Froome's wheel on stage 11, as Cadel Evans struggles to stay with them. Right: Despite his past, Britain's David Millar proves you can now win clean, outsprinting his breakaway companions on stage 12.

almost five minutes to Wiggins on the stage, and Nibali could do nothing to prise the two British riders apart. With only one mountain stage to go, Wiggins could almost dare to feel comfortable in the *maillot jaune*.

Mindful of the adage that the Tour cannot be won but can be lost in a single day, Wiggins and Froome slipped into defensive mode as expected on the final climb of stage 17, knowing that the one survivor of the early break, Alejandro Valverde, was no threat to the jersey. They still dropped everybody and just two kilometres from the line, Froome came through to take another turn on the front, and, seemingly more focused on the chance of catching Valverde for the stage win, rather than protecting the *maillot jaune*, found he had also dropped his team leader. Realizing what he had done, Froome deliberately slowed, leading Wiggins home safely. The Londoner said afterwards that he had, after almost three long weeks of racing, and literally years of working towards winning the Tour, allowed his mind to wander. He paid homage to Froome's dedication, saying that he hoped to repay it one day. It was another team-mate who felt the benefit of Wiggins' *domestique* services on stage 18, as he played a key part in leading out Mark Cavendish for another sprint win.

WIGGINS WRAPS IT UP

The final time trial left no doubt that the strongest man had won the race. Wiggins beat Froome into second place by over a minute, a result that reinforced their positions at the top of the general classification. And just to emphasize that this Tour was one for the Brits, Cavendish took an incredible fourth consecutive victory in Paris, again with Wiggins in the lead-out. There were Union Jacks up and down the Champs-Elysées, and jubilant fans from both sides of the Channel delighted in cheering home Britain's first-ever Tour winner, Bradley Wiggins.

As the exhilaration of the Tour began to die away, the furore

Right: Christopher Froome and Bradley Wiggins refuse to panic as Vincenzo Nibali attacks on stage 16. The Italian failed to distance the British pair.
Below: Wiggins confirms his rightful place in the yellow jersey by winning the final time trial of the 2012 Tour.

surrounding its most successful rider, Lance Armstrong, reached a crescendo. The Texan had batted away accusations of doping time and again, despite a growing number of former teammates – Tyler Hamilton, Floyd Landis, Jonathan Vaughters and George Hincapie among them – admitting to using drugs. The US Anti-Doping Agency had begun an investigation into Armstrong going back to 1996, amassing reams of circumstantial evidence, and had

persuaded a series of former riders and team staff to testify against him.

Armstrong tried, and failed, to dismiss the case a "witch hunt", and went to court to try and stop the USADA pursuing him. Fighting the case would mean bringing every shred of evidence into public view, a prospect which provoked the most unlikely response from the American: he gave up. The USADA promptly handed him a lifetime ban, and stripped him of his seven Tour wins.

Above: The *maillot jaune* leads out the rainbow jersey – Wiggins goes some way to repaying Mark Cavendish's sacrifice by helping the Manxman to stage victory on the Champs-Elysées.

Two weeks later the UCI, accused of being in thrall to Armstrong, announced its support for the decision. Armstrong also lost his long-term sponsors, including Nike, and stepped down from the board of his Livestrong cancer charity. Throughout, Armstrong made no public comment about the revelations, apart from the quiet removal of his Tour wins from his Twitter biography. Cycling's biggest star had been brought down.

Tour Legends
Alberto Contador

"Why not just give the jersey to Contador tomorrow and say, 'here you are – instead of racing to Paris we'll go on holidays?'"

Former Tour winner Stephen Roche on Contador's rivals failure to challenge him in the 2009 race

Left: Contador on the Tour in 2009, which he won. But he was stripped of his 2010 win following a positive dope test. Right: Contador, in the colours of the US Discovery Channel team, rides to his first overall Tour victory in Paris in 2007.

ALBERTO CONTADOR (SPA)
b. 6/12/82 Madrid, Spain

FIVE PARTICIPATIONS
THREE VICTORIES
THREE STAGE WINS

2005 31ST OVERALL

2007 FIRST OVERALL
ONE STAGE WIN: stage 14,
Mazamet–Plateau de Beille

2009 FIRST OVERALL
TWO STAGE WINS: Stage 15,
Pontarlier–Verbier; stage 18 Annecy
(time trial)

2010 FIRST OVERALL*

2011 5TH OVERALL

* Later stripped of the title following a
positive dope test.

Tour Legends

Cadel Evans

"Champagne does taste a wee bit better after you have crossed the line on the Champs in yellow." Evans in 2011

Right: Cadel Evans enjoys a glass of bubbly on the way to Paris on the last stage of the 2011 Tour.
Opposite: The green jersey at last for Mark Cavendish in 2011. He capped a brilliant year by winning the world championship three months later.

CADEL EVANS (AUS)
b. 14/02/77, Katherine, Northern Territory, Australia

EIGHT PARTICIPATIONS
ONE VICTORY
ONE STAGE WIN

2005 EIGHTH OVERALL

2006 FOURTH OVERALL

2007 SECOND OVERALL

2008 SECOND OVERALL

2009 30TH OVERALL

2010 26TH OVERALL

2011 FIRST OVERALL
ONE STAGE WIN: Stage 4, Lorient–Mur de Bretagne

2012 SEVENTH OVERALL

Tour Legends
Mark Cavendish

"I need to get to the line first and that's all I think about."

Cavendish in 2011

MARK CAVENDISH (GBR)
b. 21/05/85, Isle of Man

SIX PARTICIPATIONS
23 STAGE WINS

2007 DID NOT FINISH

2008 DID NOT FINISH
FOUR STAGE WINS: Stage 5, Cholet–
Chateauroux; Stage 8, Figeac–Toulouse;
Stage 12, Lavelanet–Narbonne; Stage
13, Narbonne–Nimes.

2009 131ST OVERALL
SIX STAGE WINS: Stage 2, Monaco–
Brignoles; Stage 3, Marseille–La
Grande-Motte; Stage 10, Limoges–
Issoudun; Stage 11, Vatan–Saint-
Fargeau; Stage 19, Bourgoin-Jallieu–
Aubenas; Stage 21, Montereau-Fault-
Yonne–Paris Champs-Elysées.

2010 154TH OVERALL
FIVE STAGE WINS: Stage 5, Epernay–
Montargis; Stage 6, Montargis–
Gueugnon; Stage 11, Sisteron–Bourg-
les-Valence; Stage 18, Salies-de-Bearn–
Bordeaux; Stage 20, Longjumeau–Paris
Champs-Elysées.

2011 130TH OVERALL
WINNER POINTS COMPETITION
FIVE STAGE WINS: Stage 5, Carhaix–
Cap-Frechel; Stage 7, Le Mans–
Chateauroux; Stage 11, Blayes-les-Mines–
Lavaur; Stage 15, Limoux–Montpellier;
Stage 21, Creteil–Paris Champs-Elysées.

2012 142ND OVERALL
THREE STAGE WINS: Stage 2, Vise–
Tournal; Stage 18, Blagnac–Brive-la-
Gaillarde, Stage 20, Rambouillet–Paris
Champs-Elysées

Tour Legends

Bradley Wiggins

"I really feel this could be my year... I feel poised, hopefully, to make history."

Wiggins before the 2012 Tour

Left: Wiggins looking relaxed before the start of the 2012 Tour in Liège, Belgium, the country of his birth.
Right: After crashing out of the Tour in 2011, Wiggins protects the yellow jersey on stage 12 of the 2012 race.

BRADLEY WIGGINS (GBR)
b. 28/4/80 Ghent, Belgium

SIX PARTICIPATIONS
ONE VICTORY
TWO STAGE WINS

2006 124TH OVERALL

2007 DID NOT FINISH

2009 FOURTH OVERALL

2010 24TH

2011 DID NOT FINISH

2012 FIRST OVERALL
TWO STAGE WINS: Stage 9, Arc et Senans–Bescanon (time trial); Stage 19, Bonneval–Chartres (time trial)

Chapter 13

A Matter of Record

Anyone who wins a jersey at the Tour, or finishes in the top three overall, is sure to make the headlines – the race was founded by a newspaper editor, after all. But more than that, success at La Grand Boucle earns riders a place in a sporting history, going all the way back to 1903.

HOW THE TOUR HAS EVOLVED...

The first riders set off from Paris in 1903. Between 1905 and 1912, the winner was decided on a points system, with the lowest scorer taking first place. In 1913, the Tour returned to a timed format. The *maillot jaune* given to the overall race leader first appeared in 1919. The King of the Mountains competition (KoM) began in 1933 but the polka-dot jersey now worn by the KoM leader was only introduced in 1975. The green jersey for the points competition (Pts), decided by placings during each day's racing, has been a permanent fixture since 1953. No races were held 1915–1918 or 1940–1946 due to the two world wars.

THE JERSEYS

Overall Winner – worn since 1919

Points Winner (PTS) – worn since 1953

King of the Mountains Winner (KoM) – worn since 1975

Le Tour 1903 (2428km)
July 1–July 21, Paris–Paris

1. Maurice Garin (FRA) 94HRS-33MINS-14SECS
2. Lucien Pothier (FRA) +2-49-45
3. Fernand Augereau (FRA) +4-29-38

Le Tour 1904 (2420km)
July 2–July 24, Paris–Paris

1. Henri Cornet (FRA) 96-05-55
2. Jean-Baptiste Dortignacq (FRA) +2-16-14
3. Alois Catteau (FRA) +8-07-20

Le Tour 1905 (2994km)
July 9–July 30, Paris–Paris

1. Louis Trousselier (FRA) 35 PTS
2. Hippolyte Aucouturier (FRA) 61 PTS
3. Jean-Baptiste Dortignacq (FRA) 64 PTS

Le Tour 1906 (4545km)
July 4–July 29, Paris–Paris

1. René Pottier (FRA) 31 PTS
2. Georges Passerieu (FRA) 45 PTS
3. Louis Trousselier (FRA) 59 PTS

Le Tour 1907 (4488km)
July 8–August 4, Paris–Paris

1. Lucien Petit-Breton (FRA) 47 PTS
2. Gustave Garrigou (FRA) 66 PTS
3. Emile Georget (FRA) 74 PTS

Le Tour 1908 (4488km)
July 13–August 9, Paris–Paris

1. Lucien Petit-Breton (FRA) 36 PTS
2. François Faber (LUX) 68 PTS
3. Georges Passerieu (FRA) 75 PTS

Le Tour 1909 (4497km)
July 5–August 1, Paris–Paris

1. François Faber (LUX) 37 PTS
2. Gustave Garrigou (FRA) 57 PTS
3. Jean Alavoine (FRA) 66 PTS

Previous page: Eddy Merckx celebrates his 1969 Tour win from the bonnet of a car. Merckx's list of *palmarès* is second to none. Below: Winner Lucien Petit-Breton, known as "The Little Argentine", poses alongside third-placed finisher Emile Georget at the end of the 1907 Tour.

Le Tour 1910 (4737km)
July 3–July 31, Paris–Paris

1. Octave Lapize (FRA) 63 PTS
2. François Faber (LUX) 67 PTS
3. Gustave Garrigou (FRA) 86 PTS

Le Tour 1911 (5344km)
July 2–July 30, Paris–Paris

1. Gustave Garrigou (FRA) 43 PTS
2. Paul Duboc (FRA) 63 PTS
3. Emile Georget (FRA) 84 PTS

Le Tour 1912 (5289km)
June 30–July 28, Paris–Paris

1. Odile Defraye (BEL) 49 PTS
2. Eugène Christophe (FRA) 108 PTS
3. Gustave Garrigou (FRA) 140 PTS

Le Tour 1913 (5287km)
June 29–July 27, Paris–Paris

1. Philippe Thys (BEL) 197-54-00
2. Gustave Garrigou (FRA) +8-37
3. Marcel Buysse (BEL) +3-30-55

Le Tour 1914 (5380km)
June 28–July 26, Paris–Paris

1. Philippe Thys (BEL) 200-28-49
2. Henri Pelissier (FRA) +1-40
3. Jean Alavoine (FRA) +36-53

THE FIRST WORLD WAR YEARS

Philippe Thys (left) won his second victory in a row for Peugeot in 1914 but it was to be the last Tour de France for four years as the First World War broke out and columns of troops and military convoys criss-crossed the roads where the Tour once passed. Eerily, within hours of the starter's pistol being fired in Paris on 28 June 1914, the Archduke Ferdinand was shot dead in Sarajevo, an event which eventually led to war between the Great Powers. During the fighting, three former winners of the Tour were killed: François Faber perished in the Foreign Legion, "Tatave" Lapize was shot down in a plane and Lucien Petit-Breton, "The Little Argentine", died in a car crash behind the front lines. When the competition returned in 1919, many cyclists were in a poor state of fitness – only ten finished – but, to spur them on, organizer Henri Degrange introduced the maillot jaune (the same colour as his newspaper) for the first time. A new era had begun.

Le Tour 1919 (5560km)
June 29–July 27, Paris–Paris

1. Firmin Lambot (BEL) — 231-07-15
2. Jean Alavoine (FRA) — +1-43-54
3. Eugène Christophe (FRA) — +2-16-31

Le Tour 1920 (5503km)
June 27–July 28, Paris–Paris

1. Philippe Thys (BEL) — 228-36-13
2. Hector Heusghem (BEL) — +57-21
3. Firmin Lambot (BEL) — +1-39-35

Le Tour 1921 (5485km)
June 26–July 24, Paris–Paris

1. Léon Scieur (BEL) — 221-50-00
2. Hector Heusghem (BEL) — +18-36
3. Honoré Barthélemy (FRA) — +2-01-00

Le Tour 1922 (5375km)
June 25–July 23, Paris–Paris

1. Firmin Lambot (BEL) — 222-08-06
2. Jean Alavoine (FRA) — +41-15
3. Félix Sellier (FRA) — +42-02

Le Tour 1923 (5386km)
June 24–July 22, Paris–Paris

1. Henri Pelissier (FRA) — 222-15-30
2. Ottavio Bottechia (ITA) — +30-41
3. Romain Bellenger (FRA) — +1-04-43

Le Tour 1924 (5425km)
June 22–July 20, Paris–Paris

1. Ottavio Bottechia (ITA) — 226-18-21
2. Nicolas Frantz (LUX) — +35-36
3. Lucien Buysse (BEL) — +1-32-13

Le Tour 1925 (5440km)
June 21–July 19, Paris–Paris

1. Ottavio Bottechia (ITA) — 219-10-18
2. Lucien Buysse (BEL) — +54-20
3. Bartolomeo Aymo (ITA) — +56-17

Le Tour 1926 (5745km)
June 20–July 18, Paris–Paris

1. Lucien Buysse (BEL) — 238-44-25
2. Nicolas Frantz (LUX) — +1-22-25
3. Bartolomeo Aymo (ITA) — +1-22-51

Le Tour 1927 (5340km)
June 19–July 27, Paris–Paris

1. Nicolas Frantz (LUX) — 198-16-42
2. Maurice Dewaele (BEL) — +1-48-21
3. Julien Vervaecke (BEL) — +2-25-06

Le Tour 1928 (5476km)
June 17–July 15, Paris–Paris

1. Nicolas Frantz (LUX) — 192-48-58
2. André Leducq (FRA) — +50-07
3. Maurice Dewaele (BEL) — +56-16

Le Tour 1929 (5257km)
June 30–July 28, Paris–Paris

1. Maurice Dewaele (BEL) — 186-39-16
2. Giuseppe Pancera (ITA) — +44-23
3. Joseph Demuysère (BEL) — +57-10

Le Tour 1930 (4822km)
July 2–July 27, Paris–Paris

1. André Leducq (FRA) — 172-12-16
2. Learco Guerra (ITA) — +14-13
3. Antonin Magne (FRA) — +16-03

Two-times winner Nicolas Frantz poses for the camera during stage 12 in 1927.

Sylvère Maes on stage 13 in Monaco in 1939.

Le Tour 1931 (5091km)
June 30–July 26,
Paris–Paris

1. Antonin Magne (FRA)   177-10-03

2. Joseph Demuysère (BEL)   +12-56

3. Antonio Pesenti (ITA)   +22-51

Le Tour 1932 (4479km)
July 6–July 31,
Paris–Paris

1. André Leducq (FRA)   154-11-49

2. Kurt Stoepel (GER)   +24-01

3. Francesco Camusso (ITA)   +26-21

Le Tour 1933 (4395km)
June 27–July 23,
Paris–Paris

1. Georges Speicher (FRA)   147-51-37

2. Learco Guerra (ITA)   +4-01

3. Giuseppe Martano (ITA)   +5-08

KoM: Vicente Trueba (SPA)   126 PTS

Le Tour 1934 (4470km)
July 3–July 29,
Paris–Paris

1. Antonin Magne (FRA)   147-13-58

2. Giuseppe Martano (ITA)   +27-31

3. Roger Lapébie (FRA)   +52-15

KoM: René Vietto (FRA)   111 PTS

Le Tour 1935 (4338km)
July 4–July 28,
Paris–Paris

1. Romain Maes (BEL)   141-32-00

2. Ambrogio Morelli (ITA)   +17-52

3. Félicien Vervaecke (BEL)   +24-06

KoM: Félicien Vervaecke (BEL)   118 PTS

Le Tour 1936 (4418km)
July 7–August 2, Paris–Paris

1. Sylvère Maes (BEL)   142-47-32

2. Antonin Magne (FRA)   +26-55

3. Félicien Vervaecke (BEL)   +27-53

KoM: Julian Berrendero (SPA)   132 PTS

Le Tour 1937 (4415km)
June 30–July 25, Paris–Paris

1. Roger Lapébie (FRA)   138-58-31

2. Mario Vicini (ITA)   +7-17

3. Leo Amberg (SWI)   +26-13

KoM: Félicien Vervaecke (BEL)   114 PTS

Le Tour 1938 (4687km)
July 5–July 31, Paris–Paris

1. Gino Bartali (ITA)   148-29-12

2. Félicien Vervaecke (BEL)   +18-27

3. Victor Cosson (FRA)   +29-26

KoM: Gino Bartali (ITA)   108 PTS

Le Tour 1939 (4224km)
July 10–July 30, Paris–Paris

1. Sylvère Maes (BEL)   132-03-17

2. René Vietto (FRA)   +30-38

3. Lucien Vlaemynck (BEL)   +32-08

KoM: Sylvère Maes (BEL)   85 PTS

Le Tour 1947 (4640km)
June 25–July 20, Paris–Paris

1. Jean Robic (FRA)   148-11-25

2. Ed Fachleitner (FRA)   +3-58

3. Pierre Brambilla (ITA)   +10-07

KoM: Pierre Brambilla (ITA)   98 PTS

Le Tour 1948 (4922km)
June 30–July 25, Paris–Paris

1. Gino Bartali (ITA)   147-10-36

2. Brik Schotte (BEL)   +26-16

3. Guy Lapébie (FRA)   +28-48

KoM: Gino Bartali (ITA)   62 PTS

Le Tour 1949 (4808km)
June 30–July 24, Paris–Paris

1. Fausto Coppi (ITA)   149-40-49

2. Gino Bartali (ITA)   +10-55

3. Jacques Marinelli (FRA)   +25-13

KoM: Fausto Coppi (ITA)   81 PTS

Le Tour 1950 (4773km)
July 13–August 7, Paris–Paris

1. Ferdi Kubler (SWI)   145-36-56

2. Constant "Stan" Ockers (BEL)   +9-30

3. Louison Bobet (FRA)   +22-19

KoM: Louison Bobet (FRA)   58 PTS

Le Tour 1951 (4690km)
July 4–July 29, Paris–Paris

1. Hugo Koblet (SWI)   142-20-14

2. Raphaël Geminiani (FRA)   +22-00

3. Lucien Lazarides (FRA)   +24-16

KoM: Raphaël Geminiani (FRA)   66 PTS

Le Tour 1952 (4898km)
June 25–July 19, Brest–Paris

1. Fausto Coppi (ITA)   151-57-20

2. Constant "Stan" Ockers (BEL)   +28-27

3. Bernardo Ruiz (SPA)   +34-38

KoM: Fausto Coppi (ITA)   92 PTS

Le Tour 1953 (4476km)
July 3–July 26, Strasbourg–Paris

1. Louison Bobet (FRA)   129-23-25

2. Jean Malléjac (FRA)   +14-18

3. Giancarlo Astrua (ITA)   +15-01s

PTS: Fritz Schaer (SWI)   271 PTS

KoM: Jésus Lorono (SPA)   54 PTS

Swiss rider Hugo Koblet strengthens his grip on the yellow jersey on stage 20 in 1951.

Le Tour 1954 (4656km)
July 8–August 1, Amsterdam–Paris

1. Louison Bobet (FRA)   140-06-05

2. Ferdi Kubler (SWI)   +15-49

3. Fritz Schaer (SWI)   +21-46

PTS: Ferdi Kubler (SWI)   215 PTS

KoM: Federico Bahamontès (SPA)   95 PTS

Le Tour 1955 (4495km)
July 7–July 30, Le Havre–Paris

1. Louison Bobet (FRA)   130-29-26

2. Jean Brankart (BEL)   +4-53

3. Charly Gaul (LUX)   +11-30

PTS: Constant "Stan" Ockers (BEL)   322 PTS

KoM: Charly Gaul (LUX)   84 PTS

Le Tour 1956 (4498km)
July 5–July 28, Reims–Paris

1. Roger Walkowiak (FRA)   124-01-16

2. Gilbert Bauvin (FRA)   +1-25

3. Jan Adriaenssens (BEL)   +3-44

PTS: Constant "Stan" Ockers (BEL)   280 PTS

KoM: Charly Gaul (LUX)   71 PTS

Le Tour 1957 (4665km)
27 June–July 20, Nantes–Paris

1. Jacques Anquetil (FRA)   135-44-42

2. Marc Janssens (BEL)   +14-56

3. Adolf Christian (AUT)   +17-20

PTS: Jean Forestier (FRA)   301 PTS

KoM: Gastone Nencini (ITA)   44 PTS

Le Tour 1958 (4319km)
June 26–July 19, Brussels–Paris

1. Charly Gaul (LUX)   116-59-05

2. Vito Favero (ITA)   +3-10

3. Raphaël Geminiani (FRA)   +3-41

PTS: Jean Graczyk (FRA)   347 PTS

KoM: Federico Bahamontès (SPA)   79 PTS

Le Tour 1959 (4391km)
June 25–July 18, Mulhouse–Paris

1. Federico Bahamontès (SPA)   123-46-45

2. Henri Anglade (FRA)   +4-01

3. Jacques Anquetil (FRA)   +5-05

PTS: André Darrigade (FRA)   613 PTS

KoM: Federico Bahamontès (SPA)   73 PTS

Le Tour 1960 (4173km)
June 26–July 17, Lille–Paris

1. Gastone Nencini (ITA)   112-08-42

2. Graziano Battistini (ITA)   +5-02

3. Jan Adriaenssens (BEL)   +10-24

PTS: Jean Graczyk (FRA)   74 PTS

KoM: Imerio Massignan (ITA)   56 PTS

Le Tour 1961 (4397km)
June 25–July 16, Rouen–Paris

1. Jacques Anquetil (FRA)   122-01-33

2. Guido Carlesi (ITA)   +12-14

3. Charly Gaul (LUX)   +12-16

PTS: André Darrigade (FRA)   174 PTS

KoM: Imerio Massignan (ITA)   56 PTS

Le Tour 1962 (4274km)
June 24–July 15,
Nancy–Paris

1. Jacques Anquetil (FRA) — 114-31-54

2. Jef Planckaert (BEL) — +4-59

3. Raymond Poulidor (FRA) — +10-24

PTS: Rudi Altig (GER) — 173 PTS

KoM: Federico Bahamontès (SPA) — 137 PTS

Le Tour 1963 (4137km)
June 23–July 14,
Nogent, Paris–Paris

1. Jacques Anquetil (FRA) — 113-30-05

2. Fedrico Bahamontès (SPA) — +3-35

3. José Perez-Frances (SPA) — +10-14

PTS: Rik Van Looy (BEL) — 275 PTS

KoM: Federico Bahamontès (SPA) — 147 PTS

Le Tour 1964 (4504km)
June 22–July 12,
Rennes–Paris

1. Jacques Anquetil (FRA) — 127-09-44

2. Raymond Poulidor (FRA) — +55SECS

3. Federico Bahamontès (SPA) — +4-44

PTS: Jan Janssen (HOL) — 208 PTS

KoM: Federico Bahamontès (SPA) — 173 PTS

Le Tour 1965 (4177km)
June 22–July 14,
Cologne–Paris

1. Felice Gimondi (ITA) — 116-42-06

2. Raymond Poulidor (FRA) — +2-40

3. Gianni Motta (ITA) — +9-18

PTS: Jan Janssen (HOL) — 144 PTS

KoM: Julio Jiminez (SPA) — 133 PTS

Le Tour 1966 (4322km)
June 21–July 14,
Nancy–Paris

1. Lucien Aimar (FRA) — 117-34-21

2. Jan Janssen (HOL) — +1-07

3. Raymond Poulidor (FRA) — +2-02

PTS: Willy Planckaert (BEL) — 211 PTS

KoM: Julio Jimenez (SPA) — 123 PTS

Le Tour 1967 (4758km)
June 29–July 23,
Angers–Paris

1. Roger Pingeon (FRA) — 136-53-50

2. Julio Jiminez (SPA) — +3-40

3. Franco Balmamion (ITA) — +7-23

PTS: Jan Janssen (HOL) — 154 PTS

KoM: Julio Jiminez (SPA) — 122 PTS

Le Tour 1968 (4492km)
June 27–July 21,
Vittel–Paris

1. Jan Janssen (HOL) — 133-49-32

2. Herman Van Springel (BEL) — +38 SECS

3. Ferdinand Bracke (BEL) — +3-03

PTS: Franco Bitossi (ITA) — 241 PTS

KoM: Aurelio Gonzales (SPA) — 98 PTS

Roger Pingeon acknowledges the crowd on the podium in Paris, 1967.

Le Tour 1969 (4117km)
June 28–July 20,
Roubaix–Paris

1. Eddy Merckx (BEL) — 116-16-02

2. Roger Pingeon (FRA) — +17-54

3. Raymond Poulidor (FRA) — +22-13

PTS: Eddy Merckx (BEL) — 244 PTS

KoM: Eddy Merckx (BEL) — 155 PTS

Le Tour 1970 (4254km)
June 27–July 19,
Limoges–Paris

1. Eddy Merckx (BEL) — 119-31-49

2. Joop Zoetemelk (HOL) — +12-41

3. Gösta Pettersson (SWE) — +15-54

PTS: Walter Godefroot (BEL) — 212 PTS

KoM: Eddy Merckx (BEL) — 128 PTS

Le Tour 1971 (3608km)
June 26–July 18,
Mulhouse–Paris

1. Eddy Merckx (BEL) — 96-45-14

2. Joop Zoetemelk (HOL) — +9-51

3. Lucien Van Impe (BEL) — +11-06

PTS: Eddy Merckx (BEL) — 202 PTS

KoM: Lucien Van Impe (BEL) — 228 PTS

Le Tour 1972 (3846km)
July 1–July 23,
Angers–Paris

1. Eddy Merckx (BEL) — 108-17-18

2. Felice Gimondi (ITA) — +10-41

3. Raymond Poulidor (FRA) — +11-34

PTS: Eddy Merckx (BEL) — 196 PTS

KoM: Lucien Van Impe (BEL) — 229 PTS

Le Tour 1973 (4090km)
June 30–July 22,
La Hay, Scheveningen–Paris

1. Luis Ocana (SPA) 122-25-34

2. Bernard Thévenet (FRA) +15-49

3. José Manuel Fuente (SPA) +17-15

PTS: Herman Van Springel (BEL) 187 PTS

KoM: Pedro Torrès (SPA) 225 PTS

Le Tour 1974 (4098km)
June 27–July 21,
Brest–Paris

1. Eddy Merckx (BEL) 116-16-58

2. Raymond Poulidor (FRA) +8-04

3. Vicente Lopez-Carril (SPA) +8-09

PTS: Patrick Sercu (BEL) 283 PTS

KoM: Domingo Perurena (SPA) 161 PTS

Le Tour 1975 (3999km)
June 26–July 20,
Charleroi–Paris

1. Bernard Thévenet (FRA) 114-35-31

2. Eddy Merckx (BEL) +2-47

3. Lucien Van Impe (BEL) +5-01

PTS: Rik Van Linden (BEL) 342 PTS

KoM: Lucien Van Impe (BEL) 285 PTS

Le Tour 1976 (4016km)
June 24–July 18,
Saint-Jean-de-Monts–Paris

1. Lucien Van Impe (BEL) 116-22-23

2. Joop Zoetemelk (HOL) +4-14

3. Raymond Poulidor (FRA) +12-08

PTS: Freddy Maertens (BEL) 293 PTS

KoM: Giancarlo Bellini (ITA) 170 PTS

Le Tour 1977 (4092km)
June 20–July 24,
Fleurance–Paris

1. Bernard Thévenet (FRA) 115-38-30

2. Hennie Kuiper (HOL) +48SEC

3. Lucien Van Impe (BEL) +3-32

PTS: Jacques Esclassan (FRA) 236 PTS

KoM: Lucien Van Impe (BEL) 244 PTS

Le Tour 1978 (3914km)
June 29–July 23,
Leiden–Paris

1. Bernard Hinault (FRA) 108-18-00

2. Joop Zoetemelk (HOL) +3-56

3. Joaqim Agostinho (POR) +6-54

PTS: Freddy Maertens (BEL) 242 PTS

KoM: Mariano Martinez (SPA) 187 PTS

Le Tour 1979 (3720km)
June 27–July 22,
Fleurance–Paris

1. Bernard Hinault (FRA) 103-6-50

2. Joop Zoetemelk (HOL) +3-07

3. Joaquim Agostinho (POR) +26-53

PTS: Bernard Hinault (FRA) 253 PTS

KoM: Giovanni Battaglin (ITA) 239 PTS

Le Tour 1980 (3946km)
June 26–July 21,
Frankfurt–Paris

1. Joop Zoetemelk (HOL) 109-19-14

2. Hennie Kuiper (HOL) +6-55

3. Raymond Martin (FRA) +7-56

PTS: Rudy Pevenage (BEL) 194 PTS

KoM: Raymond Martin (FRA) 210 PTS

Lucien Van Impe, first-ever winner of the polka-dot jersey in 1975, dons the yellow one after winning at St-Lary Soulan on stage 14 in 1976.

Le Tour 1981 (3757km)
June 25–July 19,
Nice–Paris

1. Bernard Hinault (FRA) 96-19-38

2. Lucien Van Impe (BEL) +14-34

3. Robert Alban (FRA) +17-04

PTS: Freddy Maertens (BEL) 393 PTS

KoM: Lucien Van Impe (BEL) 277 PTS

Le Tour 1982 (3512km)
July 2–July 25,
Basle–Paris

1. Bernard Hinault (FRA) 92-08-46

2. Joop Zoetemelk (HOL) +6-21

3. Johan Vandevelde (HOL) +8-59

PTS: Sean Kelly (IRE) 429 PTS

KoM: Bernard Vallet (FRA) 273 PTS

Le Tour 1983 (3962km)
July 1–July 24,
Fontenay-sous-Bois–Paris

1. Laurent Fignon (FRA) 105-07-52

2. Angel Arroyo (SPA) +4-04

3. Peter Winnen (HOL) +4-09

PTS: Sean Kelly (IRE) 330 PTS

KoM: Lucien Van Impe (BEL) 272 PTS

Le Tour 1984 (4021km)
June 29–July 22,
Montreuil-sous-Bois–Paris

1. Laurent Fignon (FRA) 112-03-40

2. Bernard Hinault (FRA) +10-32

3. Greg Lemond (USA) +11-46

PTS: Frank Hoste (BEL) 322 PTS

KoM: Robert Millar (GBR) 284 PTS

Le Tour 1985 (4127km)
June 28–July 21,
Plumelec–Paris

1. Bernard Hinault (FRA)	🎽	113-24-23
2. Greg Lemond (USA)		+1-42
3. Stephen Roche (IRE)		+4-29
PTS: Sean Kelly (IRE)	🎽	434 PTS
KoM: Luis "Lucho" Herrera (COL)	🎽	440 PTS

Le Tour 1986 (4083km)
July 4–July 27,
Boulogne-Billancourt–Paris

1. Greg Lemond (USA)	🎽	110-35-19
2. Bernard Hinault (FRA)		+3-10
3. Urs Zimmermann (SWI)		+10-54
PTS: Eric Vanderaerden (BEL)	🎽	277 PTS
KoM: Bernard Hinault (FRA)	🎽	351 PTS

Le Tour 1987 (4231km)
July 1–July 26,
West Berlin–Paris

1. Stephen Roche (IRE)	🎽	115-27-42
2. Pedro Delgado (SPA)		+40SEC
3. Jean-François Bernard (FRA)		+2-13
PTS: Jean-Paul Van Poppel (HOL)	🎽	263 PTS
KoM: Luis "Lucho" Herrera (COL)	🎽	452 PTS

Le Tour 1988 (3282km)
July 4–July 24,
La Baule–Paris

1. Pedro Delgado (SPA)	🎽	84-27-53
2. Steve Rooks (HOL)		+7-13
3. Fabio Parra (COL)		+9-58
PTS: Eddy Planckaert (BEL)	🎽	278 PTS
KoM: Steve Rooks (HOL)	🎽	326 PTS

Le Tour 1989 (3285km)
July 1–July 23,
Luxembourg–Paris

1. Greg Lemond (USA)	🎽	87-38-35
2. Laurent Fignon (FRA)		+8SEC
3. Pedro Delgado (SPA)		+3-34
PTS: Sean Kelly (IRE)	🎽	277 PTS
KoM: Gert Theunisse (HOL)	🎽	441 PTS

Le Tour 1990 (3449km)
June 30–July 22,
Futuroscope–Paris

1. Greg Lemond (USA)	🎽	90-43-20
2. Claudio Chiappucci (ITA)		+2-16
3. Erik Breukink (HOL)		+2-29
PTS: Olaf Ludwig (GER)	🎽	256 PTS
KoM: Thierry Claveyrolat (FRA)	🎽	321 PTS

Le Tour 1991 (3914km)
July 6–July 28,
Lyon–Paris

1. Miguel Indurain (SPA)	🎽	101-01-20
2. Gianni Bugno (ITA)		+3-36
3. Claudio Chiappucci (ITA)		+5-56
PTS: Djamolidine Abdoujaparov (UZB)	🎽	316 PTS
KoM: Claudio Chiappucci (ITA)	🎽	312 PTS

Le Tour 1992 (3983km)
July 4–July 26,
San Sébastian–Paris

1. Miguel Indurain (SPA)	🎽	100-49-30
2. Claudio Chiappucci (ITA)		+4-35
3. Gianni Bugno (ITA)		+10-49
PTS: Laurent Jalabert (FRA)	🎽	293 PTS
KoM: Claudio Chiappucci (ITA)	🎽	410 PTS

Le Tour 1993 (3714km)
July 3–July 25,
Le Puy de Fou–Paris

1. Miguel Indurain (SPA)	🎽	95-57-09
2. Tony Rominger (SWI)		+4-59
3. Zenon Jaskula (POL)		+5-48
PTS: Djamolidine Abdoujaparov (UZB)	🎽	298 PTS
KoM: Tony Rominger (SWI)	🎽	449 PTS

Le Tour 1994 (3978km)
July 2–July 24,
Lille–Paris

1. Miguel Indurain (SPA)	🎽	103-38-38
2. Piotr Ugrumov (LAT)		+5-39
3. Marco Pantani (ITA)		+7-19
PTS: Djamolidine Abdoujaparov (UZB)	🎽	322 PTS
KoM: Richard Virenque (FRA)	🎽	392 PTS

Le Tour 1995 (3653km)
July 1–July 23,
Saint Brieuc–Paris

1. Miguel Indurain (SPA)	🎽	92-44-59
2. Alex Zülle (SWI)		+4-35
3. Bjarne Riis (DEN)		+6-47
PTS: Laurent Jalabert (FRA)	🎽	333 PTS
KoM: Richard Virenque (FRA)	🎽	438 PTS

Le Tour 1996 (3907km)
June 29–July 21,
's-Hertogenbosch–Paris

1. Bjarne Riis (DEN)	🎽	95-57-16
2. Jan Ullrich (GER)		+1-41
3. Richard Virenque (FRA)		+4-37
PTS: Erik Zabel (GER)	🎽	335 PTS
KoM: Richard Virenque (FRA)	🎽	383 PTS

Jan Ullrich leads out team-mate and race leader Bjarne Riis on stage 10 in 1996.

Le Tour 1997 (3950km)
July 5–July 27,
Rouen–Paris

1. Jan Ullrich (GER) 100-30-35

2. Richard Virenque (FRA) +9-09

3. Marco Pantani (ITA) +14-03

PTS: Erik Zabel (GER) 320 PTS

KoM: Richard Virenque (FRA) 579 PTS

Le Tour 1998 (3875km)
July 11–August 2,
Dublin–Paris

1. Marco Pantani (ITA) 92-49-46

2. Jan Ullrich (GER) +3-21

3. Bobby Julich (USA) +4-08

PTS: Erik Zabel (GER) 327 PTS

KoM: Christophe Rinero (FRA) 200 PTS

Le Tour 1999* (3686km)
July 3–July 25,
Le Puy de Fou–Paris

1. Lance Armstrong (USA) 91-32-16

2. Alex Zülle (SWI) +7-37

3. Fernardo Escartin (SPA) +10-26

PTS: Erik Zabel (GER) 323 PTS

KoM: Richard Virenque (FRA) 279 PTS

Le Tour 2000* (3630km)
July 1–July 23,
Futuroscope–Paris

1. Lance Armstrong (USA) 92-33-08

2. Jan Ullrich (GER) +6-02

3. Joseba Beloki (SPA) +10-04

PTS: Erik Zabel (GER) 321 PTS

KoM: Santiago Botero (COL) 347 PTS

Le Tour 2001* (3446km)
July 7–July 29,
Dunkirk–Paris

1. Lance Armstrong (USA) 86-17-28

2. Jan Ullrich (GER) +6-44

3. Joseba Beloki (SPA) +9-05

PTS: Erik Zabel (GER) 252 PTS

KoM: Laurent Jalabert (FRA) 258 PTS

Le Tour 2002* (3282km)
July 7–July 29,
Luxembourg–Paris

1. Lance Armstrong (USA) 82-05-12

2. Joseba Beloki (SPA) +07-17

3. Raimondas Rumsas (LIT) +08-17

PTS: Robbie McEwen (AUS) 280 PTS

KoM: Laurent Jalabert (FRA) 262 PTS

Le Tour 2003* (3350km)
July 5–July 27,
Paris–Paris

1. Lance Armstrong (USA) 83-41-12

2. Jan Ullrich (GER) +01-01

3. Alexandre Vinokourov (KAZ) +04-14

PTS: Baden Cooke (AUS) 216 PTS

KoM: Richard Virenque (FRA) 324 PTS

Le Tour 2004* (3390km)
July 3–July 25,
Liege–Paris

1. Lance Armstrong (USA) 83-36-02

2. Andreas Kloden (GER) +06-19

3. Ivan Basso (ITA) +06-40

PTS: Robbie McEwen (AUS) 272 PTS

KoM: Richard Virenque (FRA) 226 PTS

Le Tour 2005* (3607km)
July 2–24,
Fromentine–Paris

1. Lance Armstrong (USA) 86-15-02

2. Ivan Basso (ITA) +4-40

3. Jan Ullrich (GER) +6-21

PTS: Thor Hushovd (NOR) 194 PTS

KoM: Michael Rasmussen (DEN) 185 PTS

Le Tour 2006** (3657km)
July 1–July 23,
Strasbourg–Paris

1. Floyd Landis (USA) 89-38-39

2. Oscar Pereiro (SPA) +57SEC

3. Andreas Klöden (GER) +1-29

PTS: Robbie McEwen (AUS) 288 PTS

KoM: Michael Rasmussen (DEN) 166 PTS

Le Tour 2007 (3547km)
July 7–July 29,
London–Paris

1. Alberto Contador (SPA) 91-00-26

2. Cadel Evans (AUS) +23

3. Levi Leipheimer (USA) +31

PTS: Tom Boonen (BEL) 256 PTS

KoM: Mauricio Soler (COL) 206 PTS

Le Tour 2008 (3554km)
July 5–July 27,
Brest–Paris

1. Carlos Sastre (SPA) 87-52-52

2. Cadel Evans (AUS) +58

3. Bernard Kohl (AUT) +1-13

PTS: Oscar Freire (SPA) 270 PTS

KoM: Bernard Kohl (AUT) 128 PTS

* In 2012, Lance Armstrong was stripped of all seven of his victories, for a range of doping offences. The UCI decided not to re-allocate his titles.

** Following a positive dope test during the 2006 Tour, Floyd Landis was stripped of his victory and Oscar Pereiro was named as the winner. Andreas Klöden was promoted to second place and third was Carlos Sastre of Spain at +3-13.

Carlos Sastre acknowledges the crowd as he completes the time-trial performance of his life to seal victory in the 2008 Tour.

Le Tour 2009 (3459.5km)
July 4–July 26,
Monaco–Paris

1. Alberto Contador (SPA)		81-46-17
2. Andy Schleck (LUX)		+04-11
3. Lance Armstrong (USA)		+05-24
PTS: Thor Hushovd (NOR)		260 PTS
KoM: Franco Pellizotti (ITA)		210 PTS

Le Tour 2010*** (3642km)
July 3–July 25,
Rotterdam–Paris

1. Alberto Contador (SPA)		91-58-48
2. Andy Schleck (LUX)		+39
3. Denis Menchov (RUS)		+02-01
PTS: Alessandro Petacchi (ITA)		243 PTS
KoM: Anthony Charteau (FRA)		143 PTS

*** Following a positive dope test
during the 2010 Tour, Alberto Contador
was stripped of his victory and Andy
Schleck was named as the winner.
Denis Menchov was promoted to second
place, and third was Samuel Sanchez
of Spain at +3-01.

Le Tour 2011 (3430km)
July 2–July 24,
Passage du Gois La Barre-de-Monts–
Paris

1 Cadel Evans (AUS)		86-12-22
2 Andy Schleck (LUX)		+1-34
3 Frank Schleck (LUX)		+2-30
PTS: Mark Cavendish (GBR)		334PTS
KoM: Samuel Sanchez (SPA)		108PTS

Le Tour 2012 (3497km)
June 30-July 22,
Liège–Paris

1 Bradley Wiggins (GBR)		87-34-47
2 Chris Froome (GBR)		+3-21
3 Vincenzo Nibali (ITA)		+6-19
PTS: Peter Sagan (SLO)		421PTS
KoM: Thomas Voeckler (FRA)		135PTS

**Below: Swiss rider
Rolf Graf hitches
a ride on the
broomwagon, ending
his participation in
the 1957 Tour.**

Glossary

Le Tour still mainly uses the mother tongue for its terminology. Here is a selection of the most frequently encountered words and phrases.

BIDON water bottle

BONIFICATION time bonus

COL a climb, which is classified as fourth, third, second, first category, depending on the height gained, the gradient, the length of the climb and how far through the stage it features. *Hors-categorie* climbs are literally "beyond classification" and include Alpe d'Huez and Galibier

COMBINE COMPETITION a competition to determine the best all-round rider by combining position on general classification with scores in the points' classification

COMMISSAIRE race official

CONTRE-LA-MONTRE a time trial, where each rider, or team, competes separately, setting off at timed intervals rather than head to head

COUREURS GROUPÉS sponsored riders

COUREURS ISOLÉS self-sufficient individual riders

DIRECTEUR SPORTIF team manager, responsible for day-to-day running of the team, and dictating race tactics on the road

ÉTAPE stage

FLAMME ROUGE the final-kilometre marker, a red flag

HOT-SPOT SPRINT a point partway through a stage where points and small time bonuses are awarded for the first three riders

KING OF THE MOUNTAINS King of the Mountains points are awarded on a sliding scale on each category of climb, and the leading rider wears the polka-dot jersey

LANTERNE ROUGE "red light", the last-placed rider in the general classification

MAILLOT BLANC white jersey, worn by the best-placed rider aged 25 or under

MAILLOT JAUNE yellow jersey, worn by the overall leader of the race

MAILLOT POIS polka-dot jersey, worn by the rider who leads the King of the Mountains competition

MAILLOT VERT green jersey, worn by the points competition leader

MUSETTE feed bag

NEUTRAL ZONE the area between the *départ fictif* and the *départ réel*, where riders' speed is controlled by the leading car

PARCOURS the route

PAVÉ cobbled roads, mostly found in northeast France and Flanders

PELOTON the group of riders, or the main group if the race has broken up

POINÇONNÉES unsponsored riders of the 1900s who were obliged to use identical bikes. The machines were *poinçonnée*, or stamped, so that at the finish of the race it could be proved that they were the same models that the riders had started with

POINTS' COMPETITION points are awarded after each stage, with a maximum of 35 for first place. The scoring is weighted in favour of the flat stages, and the *maillot vert* is contested by the sprinters

PRIME a point along the route where there is a subsidiary prize – either for a hotspot sprint, a King of the Mountains point or a cash prize

RANDONÉE a leisure ride, which may be timed, but is not a race

RAVITAILLEMENT feed zone

ROULEUR a rider who is strongest on long, rolling or flat stages, particularly in windy conditions, and who often excels at long breakaways

SOIGNEUR staff member responsible for preparing the team's food and drink during the stage, ensuring all kit is clean, and for massaging riders

TIFOSI Italian fans

TIME LIMIT all riders must finish within a percentage of the stage winner's time to be allowed to continue racing

TOURISTE-ROUTIER the name given to riders not competing in the professional ranks of the 1930s

UCI Union Cycliste Internationale, the International Cycling Union, based in Switzerland

VOITURE BALAI the broom wagon, which picks up any rider who abandons the race or falls too far behind on a stage

Below: Laurent Fignon swigs from his bidon, 1989. Right: Rolf Graf of Switzerland ends up as a passenger in the *voiture balai* during the 1957 Tour.

Index